PRESENTED TO

_____

FROM

_____

OCCASION

_____

DATE

_____

A COUPLES

I Will

DEVOTIONAL

---

365 DAILY PROMISES
FOR YOUR MARRIAGE

JIMMY & KAREN EVANS

XO
PUBLISHING

I Will: 365 Daily Promises for Your Marriage
Copyright © 2023 by Jimmy and Karen Evans

ISBN: 978-1-960870-06-3 Paperback
ISBN: 978-1-960870-08-7 eBook

XO Publishing is a leading creator of relationship-based resources. We focus primarily on marriage-related content for churches, small group curriculum, and people looking for timeless truths about relationships and overall marital health. For more information on other resources from XO Publishing, visit XOMarriage.com.

XO Marriage®, an imprint of XO Publishing
1021 Grace Lane
Southlake, TX 76092

Every effort is made to provide accurate URLs at the time of printing for external or third-party Internet websites. Neither the authors nor the publisher assume any responsibility for changes or errors made after publication.

Printed in the United States of America

23 24 25 26 27—5 4 3 2 1

The Authors

JIMMY & KAREN EVANS founded MarriageToday (now called XO Marriage) in 1994 to help couples thrive in strong and fulfilling marriages. Together, they hosted *MarriageToday with Jimmy and Karen*, a television show and ministry designed to bring hope and healing to hurting couples. Jimmy has written more than 50 books, including *Marriage on the Rock, The Four Laws of Love, 21 Day Inner Healing Journey*, and *Tipping Point*. Karen is the author of *From Pain to Paradise*, and she and Jimmy are the coauthors of *Fighting for the Soul of Your Child* and *Vision Retreat*. Jimmy and Karen have been married for 50 years and have two married children and five grandchildren.

To the many couples who have found healing
through XO Marriage and then went on to tell other couples
how to find hope by doing marriage God's way.

Introduction

"I will."

If you are married, then you said those words at your wedding ceremony, or you may have said the other traditional words—*"I do."* If you are getting married soon, then you will give one of those two responses to the wedding officiant. The person conducting the wedding will ask you to make certain promises, and then they will wait for you to respond by saying either "I will" or "I do." Those responses are part of your vows—you are making promises for how you will live with your spouse in the future, even until one of you dies. *Remember, these are promises.*

Marriage is a sacred covenant between a man and a woman, established by God from the very beginning of creation and sealed with vows (promises) that are meant to be taken seriously. Marriage vows are promises made *to each other* and *to God*. They are not simply words spoken during a ceremony but are a life-long commitment to love, honor, and cherish one another. The importance of marriage vows cannot be overstated, because they set the foundation and tone for a strong and lasting marriage.

Yes, God created marriage, but He also created people *to be married*. Sadly, our culture has devalued marriage, and many people view it as a temporary arrangement that can be dissolved easily. In fact, many people today do not take marriage vows seriously at all. Some people become focused on themselves and their own desires, which makes it difficult for them to keep their promises, so they simply decide not to keep them. We live in a throwaway culture where things are easily discarded, and relationships are often treated the same way. Some people may not fully understand the gravity of the promises they are making, or they may not be emotionally mature enough to keep them. Even worse, a number of people go into marriage with no intention of keeping their vows.

However, it is important to remember that your marriage vows are not just promises made to your spouse, but as we said, they are also promises made to God. As the Author of marriage, God established it as a lifelong commitment between a man and a woman. The Bible is clear that marriage is a covenant that is not to be broken. In Matthew 19:6, Jesus says, "So then, they are no longer two but one flesh. Therefore what God has joined together, let not man separate" (NKJV).

So, as a couple, you must reaffirm and recommit to your marriage promises every day. We have had to do that in our own marriage, and that is why we wrote this book. As you go through it, you can recommit to your vows by praying together and asking for God's guidance and strength to keep them. You can make a conscious effort to show love, respect, and kindness to each other. You can make time for each other and prioritize your relationship above all other commitments. We believe *your marriage has a 100 percent chance of success* if you do it God's way.

As you read and pray about each day's devotion, it's important to remember that no one is perfect. We are all still learning and growing, both as believers and as spouses. This book is designed to help you make intentional choices every day that will bless and grow your marriage. It is not meant to be used as a weapon against yourself or your spouse for past mistakes or future failures. Your marriage will see great days, good days, and even some bad days, but in every day, you can choose to keep your eyes focused on Jesus as you declare, "This *is* the day the Lord has made" and decide, "We will rejoice and be glad in it" (Psalm 118:24 NKJV).

Reading this devotional together means you are carving a dedicated time out of the day for each other and for God. The days are numbered 1 through 365, with "Day 1" simply meaning the day you begin. In other words, you don't have to wait until January 1 to start using this devotional. Some days are written to the husband and some to the wife, while others are for both spouses. Read all of them as a couple because they will help both of you understand and affirm God's design for marriage. These are not long devotions; they should take you less than five minutes. But they will also help you set aside a time each day to say once again what you did on your wedding day: *"I will."* We encourage you to read through this devotional every year because we believe God will speak to you and your spouse in a fresh way each time you do.

At XO Marriage, we provide resources to strengthen your marriage. These include special marriage conferences and events; mediation to help marriages get back on track; and hundreds of written, video, and audio resources. For more information, visit our website at xomarriage.com or check out the list of marriage and family resources we have compiled on the next page. We are here to offer support and encouragement to help you keep the promises you made to your spouse and to God. By keeping your vows, you can experience the joy, fulfillment, and blessing that God intends for you as a couple. We are praying for you to have everything God wants for your marriage.

Jimmy & Karen Evans

Other Marriage and Family Resources

from Jimmy and Karen Evans

Marriage on the Rock 25th Anniversary Edition
Marriage on the Rock Couple's Workbook
Marriage on the Rock Discussion Guide
The Four Laws of Love
The Four Laws of Love Discussion Guide
Lifelong Love Affair
Fighting for the Soul of Your Child
Our Secret Paradise
7 Secrets of Successful Families
Blending Families
Blending Families Workbook
From Pain to Paradise
One Devotional
Strengths Based Marriage
The Keys to Sexual Fulfillment in Marriage
The Right One
Finding the Right One Workbook
The Stress-Free Marriage
Vision Retreat Guidebook

I WILL build my marriage on the Rock.

*When the storms of life hit, the Rock is the
most peaceful place on earth.*

Truly he is my rock and my salvation;
  he is my fortress, I will not be shaken (Psalm 62:6 NIV).

When laying the foundation of your marriage, you have two choices—building on the shifting sand of the world or the firm Rock that is Jesus Christ. It's tempting to opt for the sand because it's comfortable and conforms to your desires. But Jesus doesn't conform to anyone; rather, He calls you to conform to Him. If you choose to build your life on the Rock, Jesus offers two promises: you will face persecution from the world, and in the midst of these trials, you will experience total security in Him. Yes, you will face storms, but your family will survive, your marriage will endure, and every aspect of your life will be blessed. Trust in the Rock, Jesus Christ, and find peace and security in His unchanging love and unwavering strength.

Dear Father, I choose to build my marriage on the Rock. Holy Spirit, keep my eyes and heart focused on Jesus in the midst of life's distractions. In Jesus' name, Amen.

What does building your marriage on the Rock look like in your everyday life?

Day 2

I WILL obey God's Law of Priority.

*If we give marriage any other priority than
what God has done, it will not work.*

That is why a man leaves his father and mother ... (Genesis 2:24 NIV).

Marriage holds a unique place in God's design for relationships. The Law of Priority requires that your relationship with your spouse must be first among all your human relationships and second only to your relationship with God. If anything besides God comes before your marriage, it's like playing with fire—nothing good can come of it. Now, the greatest threat to your relationship with your spouse usually isn't from negative things; rather, it is from positive things that are out of priority. It is not wrong to love your children, your career, and your hobbies, but your spouse must come first in both your affection and attention. Marriage is meant to be special and beautiful, and it stays that way when you keep your priorities in the correct order.

Dear Father, I believe Your design for marriage is perfect. Holy Spirit, help me to obey the Law of Priority as I put You first and my spouse second, above everyone else. In Jesus' name, Amen.

What changes do you need to make in order to uphold the Law of Priority?

I WILL follow God's Law of Pursuit.

*You must work every day so your marriage
can be rewarding and healthy.*

And shall cleave to his wife ... (Genesis 2:24 NKJV).

Many people enter marriage with the belief that finding the right person means love will always come easily and effortlessly. They are surprised and often disappointed to discover that each and every day requires work to keep their marriage strong and fulfilling. Think of it like your muscles—regular exercise makes them strong and attractive, but inactivity leads to weakness. If you let your relationship go idle, then it becomes harder to muster the effort needed to revive it. Don't lose heart, though. It doesn't matter how distant you feel from love today. By actively working to love your spouse and meet their needs (even if they are not doing so in return), your feelings can resurrect. The joy you lost forever can return. Even better, when both spouses commit to this daily work, the results can be life changing.

Dear Father, You can bring life to any situation, including mine. Holy Spirit, I release any unforgiveness I've been holding in my heart, and I choose to love my spouse with my whole heart. In Jesus' name, Amen.

What are some ways you can actively demonstrate love to your spouse?

Day 4

I WILL uphold God's Law of Partnership.

*Marriage is a lifelong bond only surpassed by
our eternal union with our Creator.*

And they shall become one flesh (Genesis 2:24 NKJV).

God's design for marriage calls for total sharing and commitment. This life-long union requires us to lay down our entire lives for our spouse. In this sacred bond, the words "mine" and "yours" must be replaced with a new vocabulary: "ours." The beauty of giving everything to your marriage is the complete sharing it brings. You both belong to each other entirely, leaving no doors closed and no parts of life segregated. Anything not willingly surrendered to the other person creates a legitimate cause for jealousy. True intimacy in marriage isn't built solely on passionate moments or deep conversations. It flourishes when two lives are so interwoven that the boundaries between them blur. It's a beautiful merging where you can't discern where one life ends and the other begins.

Dear Father, thank You for my wonderful spouse. I am so grateful to be their partner for life. Holy Spirit, help me to lay down any selfishness or fear in my heart so I can truly be one with my spouse. In Jesus' name, Amen.

What excites you the most about being partners for life with your spouse?

I WILL honor God's Law of Purity.

*In any relationship, sin is the single greatest hindrance
to our ability to relate openly to each other.*

And the man and his wife were both naked and were not ashamed
(Genesis 2:25 ESV).

Adam and Eve's relationship in the Garden of Eden was marked by complete and utter transparency. They shared their entire selves with each other and God in an atmosphere of profound intimacy and openness. This is a perfect picture of God's vision for marriage. The greatest obstacle to this kind of openness is sin, and this is where the principle of purity comes into play. Both spouses must carefully consider everything they allow into their lives. Each person's thoughts, words, and actions impact the other, and "private sin" does not exist. Thankfully, when we confess our sins to God, He forgives us through Jesus' sacrifice on the cross. We don't need to bear the burden of our sins, but sincere confession is essential for restoring our relationship with God and with our spouse.

Dear Father, I understand that I must live in purity in order to receive Your best for my life. Holy Spirit, please convict me of any sin I've allowed to fester and give me courage to repent to both You and my spouse. In Jesus' name, Amen.

What do you need to confess to the Lord and to your spouse in order to walk in freedom?

Day 6

I WILL stand strong for marriage.

Satan hates marriage because marriage reflects God's love.

Put on the whole armor of God, that you may be able to stand against the wiles of the devil (Ephesians 6:11 NKJV).

The biblical definition of marriage—one man and one woman for life—is facing unprecedented attack. Many people are redefining marriage or opting to just live together, and those who do marry often find themselves disappointed, disillusioned, and divorced. Why is this happening? Satan despises marriage because it mirrors God's love, so he will employ every tactic to stop couples from experiencing the marriage of their dreams. But here's the encouraging news: God has equipped you with everything necessary to overcome Satan. You can pick up the sword of the Spirit (the Word of God) and the shield of faith to stop the enemy's "fiery darts" from reaching you. Always remember that "He who is in you is greater than he who is in the world" (1 John 4:4).

Dear Father, I refuse to allow the enemy's schemes to tear down my marriage. Holy Spirit, I ask You to bless not only my marriage but also every marriage in my community, state, and nation. In Jesus' name, Amen.

How does God's Word give you the power to stand against Satan's attacks on your marriage?

I WILL keep our marriage safe by honoring God's laws.

When God's laws are honored, marriage is the safest relationship on the earth, and the love we need is promoted and protected within it.

"If you love me, obey my commandments" (John 14:15).

God designed everything with order and perfection, never intending to harm us. Marriage is no exception, as God created it to bring blessings and fulfillment to our lives. It is the primary human relationship and gives us an opportunity to experience the deepest level of love. However, to enjoy the full benefits of marriage, we must honor and understand God's love. Sadly, some people fear marriage because of the pain and heartache they associate with bad marriages. It is important to remember that while marriage may have its challenges, it is a God-given gift that brings immense joy and fulfillment to our lives. By following God's laws, you can build a strong and healthy marriage that will honor Him and bless you in countless ways.

Dear Father, I want to obey in every area of my life, especially in my marriage. Holy Spirit, convict me when I stray from God's plan for me and my marriage. In Jesus' name, Amen.

Throughout the day, ask the Holy Spirit to show you how to follow God's laws in your life and marriage.

Day 8

I WILL "leave" my parents and "cleave" to my spouse.

As children growing up under the authority of our parents, we are taught to obey them, and rightly so. But when we leave home and get married, we no longer live under their authority.

This explains why a man leaves his father and mother and is joined to his wife ... (Genesis 2:24).

Prioritize your spouse and protect your marriage by leaving and cleaving. Leaving doesn't mean disrespecting or cutting off your parents, but it gives your spouse their deserved priority. If a parent won't let go or remains emotionally enmeshed with you, or even tries to control or manipulate you or become adversarial toward your spouse, it can be a problem. However, the issue isn't with your parent, but with *you*, because you didn't "leave." You are no longer under your parents' authority, but under God's. Chart your own course with godly counsel. You still honor your parents, but they don't have authority over you anymore.

Dear Father, teach me to honor my parents without being under their authority. Holy Spirit, help me to have any difficult but necessary conversations. In Jesus' name, Amen.

Has your relationship with your parents caused a rift with your spouse? Set a time to discuss how you will set things right.

I WILL honor my marriage as a sacred covenant.

A covenant is far more binding and intimate than a promise or a contract.

This mystery is profound, and I am saying that it refers to Christ and the church (Ephesians 5:32 ESV).

In the Garden of Eden, God unveiled His vision for marriage as a covenantal bond. The term "covenant" carries immense weight. In the Old Testament, "covenant" translates to "to cut." Envision two individuals making a deep pact by literally "cutting covenant"—splitting an animal and placing the halves on either side of a path. Now, imagine them walking side by side between those halves, vowing not only to abide by the oath's terms but also accepting a dire consequence if they betray it. Thus God bound them together with more than mere human promises but in a sacred covenant. His vision for your marriage is to be one rooted in covenant.

Dear Father, forgive me for the times that I have thought of our marriage as an arrangement of convenience. Help me to remember that it is a sacred covenant with each other and with You. Help me to remember that You are in this relationship with us to help us. In Jesus' name, Amen.

How does the idea of a covenant differ from the way marriage is often represented in popular media?

Day 10

I WILL work daily to keep romance alive.

A couple who prioritizes romance as a daily feature in their relationship will never wake up and find themselves emotionally rusted out.

Nevertheless I have *this* against you, that you have left your first love (Revelation 2:4 NKJV).

To understand the danger of losing your first love in marriage, it's essential to understand the laws of physics that govern matter in the universe. All matter exists in three forms: dynamic, static, or entropic. Think of a flower: if it's growing, it's dynamic; if it's not growing, it's static; and if it's dying, it's entropic. When a relationship stops growing or loses its focus and passion, it will grow worse over time until it dies. Prioritizing romance in your marriage keeps your relationship dynamic and your passion alive. It's like a rustproof solution for your marriage, ensuring it never gets emotionally rusted out. By prioritizing daily romance, you'll keep your marriage "shining like new" and dynamic for a lifetime.

Dear Father, help me to remind my spouse daily of my love. Holy Spirit, keep love fresh and new in my heart. In Jesus' name, Amen.

What are you doing today to romance your spouse? It doesn't have to be a big gesture, but don't fall into the habit of doing nothing.

I WILL do the work that is necessary to build true intimacy.

If you believe that intimacy is automatic when you are married to the right person, you are set up for disappointment and possible failure.

Now may the God of peace himself sanctify you completely, and may your whole spirit and soul and body be kept blameless at the coming of our Lord Jesus Christ (1 Thessalonians 5:23 ESV).

Many people believe that if they marry their perfect soulmate, then they will have guaranteed happiness. However, you will have to work at your marriage for it to be fulfilling and intimate. No couple has inherent advantages when it comes to achieving true intimacy or happiness. Success is not just chemistry, attractiveness, wealth, or anything else. If you believe that intimacy is automatic when you marry the right person, then you are setting yourself up for disappointment. Intimacy is not solely based on feelings; it requires intentional actions. You have to work on love, respect, and selflessness.

Dear Father, I am committed to working toward true intimacy with my spouse. Holy Spirit, give us the strength to do the work it takes to have complete unity and intimacy. In Jesus' name, Amen.

Have you ever thought intimacy would come automatically once you married? When was the first time you realized your expectation might need to be adjusted?

Day 12

I WILL not (as a husband) dominate my wife.

A servant's heart is the most important quality in leadership.

"But among you it will be different. Whoever wants to be a leader among you must be your servant" (Matthew 20:26).

One of your wife's deepest needs in marriage is for you to be a leader and take initiative. However, leadership does not mean dominance. Your wife wants you to be a loving initiator while treating her as an equal. She wants her voice to be heard and her input to be valued equally. As a husband, you have choices to make regarding your leadership style. You can choose pride or humility, to lead from the front or support from behind, to seek wisdom from God's Word or rely on others' advice. A dominant approach, driven by fleshly thinking, leads to resentment and rebellion from those under your authority. Instead, God desires men to be loving leaders, using servant authority rather than relying on domination.

Dear Father, You sent Your Son to show us how to be servants. Holy Spirit, teach me to serve my spouse with humility and understanding. In Jesus' name, Amen.

Is domination a temptation for you? How do you think God can help you in this area?

I WILL keep my focus on the vison God gives us for our marriage.

Vision brings discipline and focus.

When people do not accept divine guidance, they run wild.
But whoever obeys the law is joyful (Proverbs 29:18).

Do you ever feel bored or distracted when you lack a clear purpose in your endeavors? Without a shared vision with your spouse, division and its problems can arise. However, having a vision brings discipline and focus. When working together toward something great, you don't want to mess things up. A positive goal restrains impure desires and gives purpose to your energies. Some people live with negative motivations like the fear of divorce, repeating their parents' mistakes, or committing adultery. However, these desires don't necessarily lead to positive behavior. Vision, on the other hand, is about positivity and forward thinking. It focuses on the future and urges you to restrain negative desires as you collaborate with your spouse to achieve your dreams.

Dear Father, help me to keep focused on the vision You have given us. Holy Spirit, keep me from distraction. We want to have a common vision. Keep us in unity. In Jesus' name, Amen.

Why do you think it is so easy to become distracted from God's vision for you marriage? What can help you stay on track?

Day 14

I WILL only maintain friendships with those who respect the boundaries of my marriage.

One of the most important ways we communicate love to our spouses is by what we are willing to give up for them.

A perverse person stirs up conflict,
and a gossip separates close friends (Proverbs 16:28 NIV).

Protect your marriage from unhealthy relationships with certain friends. A friend who disrespects your marriage boundaries or has ungodly behaviors can harm your relationship. A "good friend" who is bad for your marriage isn't a true friend. While some problematic friendships can be mended, others require ending the relationship. Showing love for your spouse is crucial, and sacrificing certain friendships is one way to do it. Prioritizing your spouse over friendships shows your spouse they are the most important. Be mindful of who you surround yourself with and ensure your relationships don't negatively impact your marriage. Protecting your marriage from negative influences is crucial for a healthy and lasting relationship.

Dear Father, lead me as I seek out friends who will lift up You, me, and my marriage. Holy Spirit, give me wisdom and courage as I interact with my friends. In Jesus' name, Amen.

Are either of you trying to maintain relationships you know are harmful to your marriage? Have an honest conversation with each other. How will you address those unhealthy friendships?

I WILL find my identity in Jesus.

Knowing Jesus is everything, and we as believers must first and foremost find our identity in Him.

But to all who believed him and accepted him, he gave the right to become children of God (John 1:12).

In this busy world that constantly tries to tell you who and what you should be, it's important to understand your true identity as a beloved child of God. In Christ, you find your worth, purpose, and significance. By spending time in God's Word, you learn about His character and the depth of His love, and He empowers you to navigate life's challenges with confidence and hope. No longer do you seek validation from others—your worth is secure in Him. Make time for God daily, allowing His truth to shape your identity. Let your identity in Jesus be your foundation, and let His love define you. Through Him, you can live a transformed life for His glory.

Dear Father, I am so grateful to belong to You. Holy Spirit, remind me that above all else, my identity is a beloved child of God. In Jesus's name, Amen.

What happens when you find your identity in other people or things? What happens when you find your identity in God?

Day 16

I WILL hand down a healthy example of marriage to the future generations.

The devil desires to destroy us and to perpetuate that damage to our children and grandchildren.

Behold, children *are* a heritage from the LORD,
The fruit of the womb *is* a reward (Psalm 127:3 NKJV).

Righteousness doesn't happen by chance. We live in a sinful world, with an enemy seeking to harm us daily. To achieve a positive outcome, you must make deliberate choices. Living righteously brings blessings to you and future generations. Parents often overlook the impact of their unrighteousness on their descendants. Divorce is an example of a negative generational effect. Research shows its lasting harm, affecting children and parents, and perpetuating failure. The devil aims to destroy and continue this cycle. He counts on parents cooperating, making it easier to harm their children. Understand the consequences of your actions, good or bad, and make choices that positively impact future generations. Avoid a self-centered mindset that prioritizes immediate desires, an attitude that is prevalent in our nation today.

Dear Father, I want to leave a good and godly heritage for future generations. Holy Spirit, keep me from self-centered thinking as I seek to follow Your direction. In Jesus' name, Amen.

What kinds of messages have you heard from today's culture about divorce? How are these messages the same as or different from God's design?

I WILL be a patient communicator.

If you are too busy to talk, then you have to find another area of your life to sacrifice rather than sacrificing your marriage.

My dear brothers and sisters, take note of this: Everyone should be quick to listen, slow to speak and slow to become angry (James 1:19 NIV).

Effective communication is vital for a healthy marriage, and it cannot be substituted or rushed. Sacrificing communication is not an option, and you must prioritize your relationship over other areas of your life. Neglecting communication violates the Law of Priority and ignores your spouse's needs. Developing communication skills involves active listening, empathy, and understanding. Listening to your partner's perspective, seeking to understand their emotions, and validating them are all crucial. Busyness can hinder communication, but carving out time for regular conversations and prioritizing marriage over other obligations is so important. If you neglect communication, it can cause disconnection and other marital problems.

Dear Father, I want communication with my spouse to have high priority. Holy Spirit, keep busyness from taking me away from what is most important. In Jesus' name, Amen.

Pay close attention when your spouse speaks today. Work to keep your mind from wandering. Watch for the temptation to speak when you should be listening.

Day 18

I WILL avoid "keeping score" as I serve my spouse.

Serving each other is a commitment that must transcend our emotions or circumstances.

Love keeps no score of wrongs (1 Corinthians 13:5 NEB).

When facing hard times in your marriage, it's tempting to start keeping score. A tit-for-tat attitude creates a self-protecting punishment and reward program, which is the opposite of the grace of Jesus. In difficult times, each of you must act above pain and offenses, responding with grace and treating your spouse better than they deserve. This ethic is important in redeeming difficult and destructive situations, and in marriage, it's as important as your work ethic. Responding with selflessness instead of selfishness is a scriptural principle that can defeat negative attitudes. Therefore, serving each other must be a commitment that transcends emotions or circumstances, and a good work ethic toward your marriage is needed to make it strong.

Dear Father, I don't want to become a "scorekeeper" in my marriage. Holy Spirit, convict me when I try to respond to a negative attitude with a negative attitude. Help me to respond with the mind of Christ. In Jesus' name, Amen.

Have you ever fallen into a pattern of scorekeeping in any relationship? If so, what were the results?

I WILL accept and celebrate my spouse's differences.

Men and women are different by God's design.
One of the surest ways to fail is to try to change an
unchangeable. Our differences are unchangeable.

But among the Lord's people, women are not independent of men, and men are not independent of women (1 Corinthians 11:11).

God created you and your spouse differently as a man and a woman, and it's crucial to understand and accept this truth. Failing to appreciate these differences can harm your marriage. Embracing differences in thoughts and behaviors is essential. Marriage compatibility is based on shared faith, values, character, and life goals, not on sameness. Women require security, honest communication, nonsexual affection, and leadership, while men need honor, sex, friendship, and domestic support. Effective communication requires both of you to accept and celebrate your differences. Rejecting or merely tolerating differences can damage the unity and teamwork your marriage requires. Celebrate uniqueness instead of forcing sameness. It will foster deep trust, healing of wounds, and intimacy.

Dear Father, I believe You created men and women to have different needs. Holy Spirit, help me to accept and celebrate the differences I have with my spouse. In Jesus' name, Amen.

Ask your spouse how their needs as a man/woman are different from yours. Ask your spouse to remind you when you are overlooking their deepest needs.

Day 20

I WILL work hard to keep my marriage strong.

In many ways, marriage is like the muscles in our bodies. When we exercise them regularly, our bodies become strong and attractive.

And may the Lord make your love for one another and for all people grow and overflow, just as our love for you overflows (1 Thessalonians 3:12).

If you feel your marriage needs a boost, know that positive change is possible. Work hard to love and meet the needs of your spouse, even if they're not doing the same for you. Commit to working hard every day, and the results will be incredible. Don't let your marriage slip into apathy. Decide that your spouse is the right person for you and commit to keeping them happy and fulfilled. Even if your emotions come and go, working on your marriage will ensure permanent, healthy feelings for each other. Don't allow your marriage to emotionally drift. If you've lost that spark, God can restore the passion in your marriage. With His help, you can create a fulfilling and satisfying relationship with your spouse.

Dear Father, give me strength to work hard on my marriage. Holy Spirit, give me willpower when my own will is weak. In Jesus' name, Amen.

What are you doing today to work hard on your marriage?

I WILL refuse to allow fear and anxiety to control my marriage.

Fear isn't our emotion; it is the devil's. And it isn't a condition—it is a choice.

For God has not given us a spirit of fear, but of power and of love and of a sound mind (2 Timothy 1:7 NKJV).

Have you ever considered that many controlling people are actually motivated by fear and insecurity? They try to control their surroundings to prevent their fears from becoming reality. Often, these individuals grew up in homes of turbulence and pain, and control becomes their coping mechanism. However, allowing fear to dictate your actions can lead to disastrous results. If you have suffered damage from your past, the devil may use it to access your scars and manipulate you. Confront and reject him and his control. Treat fear as an external entity, and command it to leave you. Don't let your marriage be ruled by fear. Responding with faith can make your dreams come true, while responding to fear only makes your fears a reality.

Dear Father, I stand with You now against fear and anxiety. Holy Spirit, give me the strength to resist the devil's voice. In Jesus' name, Amen.

When was a time that you were negatively influenced by fear and anxiety? How did you overcome those feelings?

Day 22

I WILL allow God to heal my heart.

To be able to give and receive love the way God intended, the wounds in your heart have to be healed. And the only medicine powerful enough to heal them is a revelation of God's love.

He heals the brokenhearted
 and binds up their wounds (Psalm 147:3 NIV).

Every person experiences heartache at some point in life. It's very common to try to find fulfillment, satisfaction, and love in earthly pursuits. However, no human relationship or worldly experience can ever fill the void within you. Only God's love is capable of satisfying your deepest longings. As you immerse yourself in God's Word and keep your heart turned toward His light, His love gradually brings about change within you. Your wounds will be healed, and you will experience God's true, unconditional love. Do not be discouraged by the time it takes. Trust in God's perfect timing. Your life will be transformed, and your spouse will witness the remarkable changes that His love brings forth.

Dear Father, I believe You love me and can heal even my deepest wounds. Holy Spirit, give me faith and patience to trust the divine transformation process. In Jesus' name, Amen.

What wounds would you like God to heal? Will you allow Him to transform your heart?

I WILL (as a wife) resist the desire to be controlling in my marriage.

Since the Garden of Eden, women have had a natural, sinful tendency to try to control the men in their lives.

To the woman he said,
"I will surely multiply your pain in childbearing;
   in pain you shall bring forth children.
Your desire shall be contrary to your husband,
   but he shall rule over you" (Genesis 3:16 ESV).

As a wife, you must understand your instinct to control your husband. It's important to acknowledge your sin nature without normalizing, justifying, or minimizing it. Trying to control your spouse, whether you are a man or a woman, is sinful. If you come from a family where generations of controlling women have been the norm, then it's crucial to reject that role model entirely, repent, and turn to God for healing and help.. While you may love your family, your loyalty to God and His plan for your life and marriage must be higher. God values humility and is always ready to assist you when you admit your weaknesses and seek His strength.

Dear Father, my loyalty is to You above anything and everyone else. Holy Spirit, convict me when my humility begins to morph into control. In Jesus' name, Amen.

How can you learn to recognize when you are being controlling?

Day 24

I WILL consult and include my spouse in the decisions that affect our family.

We were created by God in marriage to be loving equals and to share life together as one.

Don't look out only for your own interests, but take an interest in others, too (Philippians 2:4).

If you have a strong personality, you must humble yourself and commit to treating your spouse as a complete equal. Give them as much stake in the marriage as you have. Solicit your spouse's advice without intimidation, pressure, or manipulation. Use your personality to encourage them and boost their confidence. You'll be amazed at what will happen when you encourage your spouse to co-lead with you. If you are married to a naturally strong and dominating spouse, then lovingly stand your ground and demand respect and consideration. Let them know that you want to share decision-making, and you won't be controlled or disrespected. You may need to seek Christian counseling, but don't be unkind or unrighteous. Be firm, treat control as a serious issue, and remember that people will treat you the way you allow them to.

Dear Father, I want to act in the way You created me to be. Holy Spirit, temper and work with my personality. In Jesus' name, Amen.

What is the difference between including your spouse in decisions and excluding them?

I WILL only use technology in ways that support my marriage.

Technology is a great servant but a terrible master.

Never let loyalty and faithfulness leave you.
Tie them around your neck;
write them on the tablet of your heart (Proverbs 3:3 CSB).

When it comes to faithfulness in marriage, it's not just about avoiding romantic relationships with others. In today's world, technology has made it hard to have alone time. This can pose a significant problem for marriages and families. While technology can be a useful servant, it can also be a terrible master. If you find it difficult to disconnect from your phone, tablet, or computer, then you and your marriage might be in bondage. It's crucial to set aside technology-free time each day to connect with your spouse without any interruptions. Shockingly, many divorces are caused by technology and social media. Remember, your marriage should take priority over all other relationships. Protect your spouse, prioritize their needs, and make time for intimacy and communication that does not include technology.

Dear Father, make me aware of the ways I use technology. Holy Spirit, give me wisdom and discernment as I access electronic media. In Jesus' name, Amen.

Ask your spouse's opinion about your use of technology. Be willing to adjust your habits based on the response you get.

Day 26

I WILL treat sex as a spiritual experience created by God.

Sex is a sacred spiritual experience with incredibly serious consequences that we must understand.

Flee sexual immorality. Every sin that a man does is outside the body, but he who commits sexual immorality sins against his own body (1 Corinthians 6:18 NKJV).

The primary reason sexual sin fails to generate true intimacy is because sex is fundamentally a spiritual experience. It only produces intended results when it is treated as sacred. In our culture, sex has been stripped of its spiritual context. We must remember that God created sex solely for marriage. By disregarding the spiritual aspect and disconnecting sex from its intended purpose, it falls short of fulfilling us. Sex is a sacred, spiritual encounter with significant consequences. Engaging in sexual acts establishes enduring spiritual connections. Our secularized society perceives sex casually, unaware of its spiritual nature and the profound implications it has on our bodies, minds, emotions, and spirits.

Dear Father, forgive me for anything I have ever done outside of the marriage relationship. Holy Spirit, convict me when my mind or heart strays from the intended purpose of sex within marriage. In Jesus' name, Amen.

Reaffirm to your spouse today that you commit to keeping sex within the purity of the marriage relationship.

I WILL protect the time and energy I need to serve my spouse.

The true priorities of your life and marriage are revealed by who you serve first and with the most energy.

Drink water from your own well—
share your love only with your wife (Proverbs 5:15).

When it comes to priorities, serving your spouse with energy and dedication is key. While it's important to give your first and best to God, it's not enough to just say it—your daily habits and disciplines prove your sincerity. In marriage, it's easy for good things to become harmful when they're out of priority. By giving your primary energies to your spouse, you can make your marriage work. Creating habits and traditions that prioritize your marriage are crucial. It's not about just making things happen, but *keeping* them happening. By establishing regular habits like date nights and times for intimacy, you can protect your relationship and invest in each other.

Dear Father, I want to keep my priorities straight as I serve my spouse. Holy Spirit, help me to keep my priorities in line so I can protect my marriage. In Jesus' name, Amen.

Do you ever get so busy serving others, including your children, that you neglect your spouse? Discuss how you can realign your priorities.

Day 28

I WILL (as a husband) guard my personal morality.

Sin can never be satisfied!

In view of all this, make every effort to respond to God's promises. Supplement your faith with a generous provision of moral excellence (2 Peter 1:5).

We are witnessing a growing problem of immorality in America, with men being the primary contributors. The massive pornography industry, generating billions of dollars annually, relies heavily on male support. Many marriages are battling the devastating effects of immorality, leaving a trail of tears in its wake. Romans 6:23 states that "the wages of sin is death." Take note that the death caused by sin is experienced in the present, not in the past or future. Sin deceives us, making promises it cannot keep. The devil, a habitual liar, always over-promises and under-delivers. His sole aim is to destroy your life and marriage, and he accomplishes it through sin. Stay vigilant and guard against his destructive influence.

Dear Father, I know You want me to be holy, just as You are Holy. Holy Spirit, deliver me from temptation and convict me of sin. In Jesus' name, Amen.

Have you seen husbands who have destroyed their marriages and sometimes careers because they have yielded to sin? What strategies do you use to avoid temptation and sin?

I WILL forgive my spouse as many times as necessary.

Unforgiveness is like a dead skunk in the basement: It makes the entire house stink.

If you forgive those who sin against you, your heavenly Father will forgive you (Matthew 6:14).

I f you've been around unforgiving people, you've seen the impact on their faces, words, and actions. Unforgiveness damages you more than it hurts those you hold it against. Unforgiveness toward anyone from your past negatively affects every aspect of your life, especially your marriage, unless you address it righteously. Forgiveness blesses and refreshes you when you let go of unhealthy thoughts and feelings. Follow these important steps to practice forgiveness every day in your marriage: (1) Release your spouse from judgment and stop replaying offenses. (2) Let your behavior reflect your forgiveness. (3) Bless and pray for your spouse with love and compassion. (4) Don't dwell on past offenses. (5) Repeat these steps until you genuinely release unforgiveness.

Dear Father, I want to forgive others, especially my spouse, as You have forgiven me. Holy Spirit, teach me to make forgiveness part of my daily life. In Jesus' name, Amen.

Is there any area of your marriage where you are still holding an offense? Start today to begin the process of forgiveness so you can restore health in your marriage.

Day 30

I WILL accept and respect my spouse's financial personality.

We realized we make better decisions because we are different. We both bring strengths to our conversations.

It is better to be godly and have little
than to be evil and rich (Psalm 37:16).

Have you ever considered that there are different personalities related to money? It's important to understand and accept that God may have wired your spouse to see money differently. Instead of judging and rejecting each other, respect each other's perspectives and make financial decisions together through communication, prayer, and compromise. You'll make better decisions together because of your differences. Share your financial concerns and opinions without judgment or punishment, but also recognize the weaknesses in each of your money personalities that need to be balanced. If both of you have the same money personality, then it's a good idea to seek financial counseling for balance and perspective. It's an advantage to have different financial personalities as long as you respect and communicate openly.

Dear Father, thank You for creating my spouse with a unique financial personality. Holy Spirit, help me to listen to what my spouse is saying about money. In Jesus' name, Amen.

How are you and your spouse different in your approaches to money? What is one good thing you see in your spouse's financial personality?

I WILL take personal responsibility to do what God wants me to do.

If we look to God for guidance in our decision-making, He will never lead us to a place of death.

For we must all stand before Christ to be judged. We will each receive whatever we deserve for the good or evil we have done in this earthly body (2 Corinthians 5:10).

Your primary responsibility is to honor and obey God. Your Creator has the authority to guide you and set boundaries. While personal rights are valued by our culture, they must be balanced with personal responsibility, starting with our responsibility to God. Sadly, many are rejecting personal responsibility and demanding greater rights, even among Christians who are influenced by the spirit of the age. Some justify affairs or divorces with claims of the "right to be happy," disregarding the impact on their loved ones. It's time to mature, seek guidance from the Bible, and reject distorted reasoning. Regardless of the cost, we are completely responsible to obey God, knowing His instructions are for our good.

Dear Father, You are my Creator, and You know what is best for me. Holy Spirit, help me to take responsibility for my thoughts and actions. In Jesus' name, Amen.

What reasons do you hear from people who want to excuse bad behavior? How are those excuses different from what God requires?

Day 32

I WILL expect God's blessings
and not give up on my marriage.

*For a marriage to be healed, there must be one spouse in the
marriage who will do the right thing and trust God for the results.*

"Love your enemies! Do good to them. Lend to them without expecting to be repaid. Then your reward from heaven will be very great" (Luke 6:35).

Have you struggled in your marriage even when you thought you were doing everything right? You may be tempted to give up. Jesus tells us to love our enemies, and sometimes our spouses can almost fit that description. Jesus promises if you show undeserved love and kindness, His grace will abound to you in return. If you're experiencing serious marriage problems, then you're in a vicious cycle of bad behavior. It's easy to justify your own actions because of what you partner has done. To heal your marriage, do the right thing and trust in God for the results.

Dear Father, walk with me even during tough times in my marriage. Holy Spirit, fill me with patience, perseverance, and love for my spouse. In Jesus' name, Amen.

Have you gone through a difficult time in your marriage? How can you trust more in the Lord to help you through hard times?

I WILL eliminate "mine" and "yours" from my vocabulary and replace them with "us" and "ours."

Marriage is designed by God to be a total sharing of life between two people.

Then make me truly happy by agreeing wholeheartedly with each other, loving one another, and working together with one mind and purpose (Philippians 2:2).

In marriage, the words "mine" and "yours" can create problems, while "us" and "ours" can solve them. No matter how valuable something is to you, ask yourself if it is worth sacrificing your marriage. God designed marriage to be a complete sharing of life, a bond that can only be exceeded by your eternal relationship with Jesus. It may seem like a high price, but it pales in comparison to the loneliness and disillusionment that comes with selfishness and self-protection. Do not let the enemy deceive you into putting yourself first. Surrender everything to God and your spouse, and you'll discover that this is God's wonderful plan for marriage.

Dear Father, I want to be unified with my spouse, even to the point of changing my vocabulary. Holy Spirit, guard my thoughts and my tongue as I speak about my spouse and our life together. In Jesus' name, Amen.

Have you found yourself claiming sole ownership in your marriage? Focus on changing the way you speak and think about your relationship with your spouse.

Day 34

I WILL guard my tone when I speak with my spouse.

So, in everything we say to our spouses, we must vigilantly watch our tones and make sure they are communicating respect, care, and value.

Let everyone see that you are considerate in all you do. Remember, the Lord is coming soon (Philippians 4:5).

Effective communication goes beyond words and includes tone. The same words can convey different meanings based on the tone you use. Pay attention to your tone so you can convey respect, care, and value when you communicate with your spouse or children. Men and women have differing needs, which should be met accordingly. Women require security, while men need honor. When you talk with your children, you should consider their different sensitivities. This is particularly important during discipline. Always be aware of the tone you use when communicating and make sure it aligns with your intended message.

Dear Father, I want to speak with a tone of care and respect. Holy Spirit, I want You to season my words and their tone with kindness and respect. In Jesus' name, Amen.

Ask your spouse if they feel you communicate with a tone that shows care and respect. Agree that you will pay attention to tone when you speak to each other.

I WILL, along with my spouse, seek God's guidance to meet the needs of my children.

We are their protectors and providers. We are
the lovers of their souls and their judges.

Children are a gift from the LORD;
   they are a reward from him (Psalm 127:3).

S uccessful biblical parenting means recognizing the four critical needs of your child: identity, security, purpose, and acceptance (all of which only God can fully satisfy). Children rely heavily on their parents to fulfill their needs, especially in their formative years. During this time, you symbolize God to them, playing the role of protector, provider, and judge. As a parent, it's critical for you to comprehend this crucial role in addressing your child's deepest needs. The aim should be to gradually transition them from your care to the care of God. Whether you realize it or not, that is your true purpose as a parent. Remember, your child's perception of God and His nature is strongly influenced by your character and how you treat them.

Dear Father, You have given me the incredible responsibility of helping to pro-
vide for my children's needs. Holy Spirit, teach me how to be sensitive and atten-
tive to my children, always pointing them to the Lord as the ultimate Provider.
In Jesus' name, Amen.

How can you help fulfill your children's needs of identity, security, purpose and acceptance?

Day 36

I WILL embrace the Holy Spirit's supernatural love.

God's agape love is the highest form of love, and it will transform any person, relationship, or marriage under its influence.

Beloved, if God so loved us, we also ought to love one another (1 John 4:11 ESV).

Here's an important fact many people don't realize: without the Holy Spirit's power, no one has the ability to truly love. God gives you the capacity to love supernaturally when you surrender to Him. People who don't know God can't experience His agape love, which is stable and unchanging. Many use the word "love" for fleeting desires or passion, but agape love is committed and sacrificial, like Jesus' love for you. His love is constant, no matter what you think, say, or do. When you say "I love you" to your spouse, consider if it's a passing feeling or an enduring commitment. Embrace the Holy Spirit's supernatural love, which will transform your marriage, making it stable and dependable. God's agape love has the power to change marriages and families for the better.

Dear Father, Your perfect love has changed my life forever. Holy Spirit, help me to love my spouse the way You love me. In Jesus' name, Amen.

How has God's agape love changed you? How will it change your marriage?

I WILL (as a wife) not allow fear to dominate my relationship with my husband.

Satan's number one weapon to incite women to sin is fear.

You are [Sarah's] daughters when you do what is right without fear of what your husbands might do (1 Peter 3:6).

A s a woman, you have a sin nature that resists your husband's leadership influence, which Satan tempts you to rebel against through fear—fear of pain, fear of loss, fear of the unknown, etc. This fear does not come from God, but He can certainly help you overcome it. Ask the Lord for guidance in keeping your focus on Jesus so that when your husband makes mistakes, you can overcome the urge to control everything. This does not mean you should tolerate abuse or destructive behavior, but rather you can learn to accept your husband's differences in approach. Instead of constantly correcting him, let him fail. Reject fear, as it opposes faith, love, and peace, and submit yourself to God. Trust in His Word, and your marriage will prosper greatly as you place your faith in Him.

Dear Father, I refuse to allow fear to dominate any part of my life. Holy Spirit, thank You for giving me a clarity and hope every day. In Jesus' name, Amen.

In what ways have you let fear control you in the past? How will you act differently now?

Day 38

I WILL work toward a common purpose with my spouse.

Couples grow apart because they are apart.

I appeal to you, dear brothers and sisters, by the authority of our Lord Jesus Christ, to live in harmony with each other (1 Corinthians 1:10).

Have you ever considered that in marriage, you and your spouse should be of one heart and purpose? If you desire to live an independent and selfish life, then marriage may not be the best choice for you. Marriage works only when you are together, and it's fulfilling when you have a common purpose that binds you together. Couples grow apart when the purpose of their lives is separated, and they foolishly believe that sharing a house, kids, or a bank account is enough to keep them close. However, intimacy and closeness in marriage have less to do with physical proximity and more to do with emotional interdependence. What is your "together purpose"? It must be something bigger than paying bills or making money. You must build your relationship around that purpose.

Dear Father, I want to be one with my spouse to follow Your purpose. Holy Spirit, let Your love bring us to unity. In Jesus' name, Amen.

Have you ever tried to work with someone who was at cross-purposes with you? What were the results?

I WILL (as a husband) guard my eyes and heart.

The only fulfilling sex that builds a strong marriage and family is with our wives and no one else.

"You have heard the commandment that says, 'You must not commit adultery.' But I say, anyone who even looks at a woman with lust has already committed adultery with her in his heart" (Matthew 5:27–28).

As a man, you are visually stimulated when it comes to sex. Women, on the other hand, prioritize your character and care over visual stimuli. It's normal and healthy, as God intended, for you to be attracted to your wife's naked body. However, the world is filled with alluring women and manipulative forces exploiting men's sexual instincts through explicit imagery. You must vigilantly guard your eyes and control what you watch. Resist the temptation to indulge in sexually explicit content or lust after women who are not your wife. Remember, God created sex, but meaningful intimacy is reserved for your wife alone. Give her your undivided sexual attention, as she is the only one who deserves it.

Dear Father, I believe You created me to experience and enjoy many things. Holy Spirit, keep my eyes and ears away from sin. In Jesus' name, Amen.

What do you do to stop negative things you see and hear from entering your mind?

Day 40

I WILL renounce the curse of dominance and control in my marriage.

As human beings we were created by God to relate to our spouses as equals. Control is against our design.

"Whoever wants to become great among you must be your servant" (Mark 10:43).

In most marriages, dominance is a common feature with a negative impact. The Law of Partnership is absolute in marriage, and you and your spouse must share everything as equal partners. Dominance is the number one enemy of partnership, as it destroys intimacy by seeking to control instead of sharing. God created you and your spouse as equals, and control is against your design as human beings. To disarm destructive dominance, you must remember God designed marriage as a relationship of ultimate pleasure and delight, and you and your spouse were created as complementary equals who share your lives in peaceful intimacy. However, rebellion against God caused the curse of dominance in marriage, leading to a constant struggle for control. To break this curse, you must repent and return to God's plan for your marriage.

Dear Father, I want to live the way You designed. Holy Spirit, help me lay down the desire to dominate and control. In Jesus' name, Amen.

Was one of your parents dominant or controlling? If so, what was the effect on your household growing up?

I WILL balance truth and love with my children.

Usher the child into an understanding and acceptance of Jesus Christ as Lord and Savior and meet the basic needs of the child.

Direct your children onto the right path,
and when they are older, they will not leave it (Proverbs 22:6).

As a parent, it's your role to create a nurturing environment of love and truth, leading to your child's understanding and acceptance of God. A child raised this way will more easily comprehend and accept the Lord, but an absent or abusive parent can hinder this understanding. Your dual responsibility includes guiding your child toward recognizing Jesus as their Savior and addressing their fundamental needs. These standards are the measure of success. When your child is ready to leave home, you should be able to affirm two things honestly and confidently: first, that you've revealed God's love and nature and led them to Jesus, and second, that you've faithfully and sacrificially met their crucial needs. Fulfilling these statements defines good parenting.

Dear Father, my greatest desire as a parent is for my children to know and love You. Holy Spirit, help me to create a healthy home environment of truth and love. In Jesus' name, Amen.

What can you do to point your children toward the Lord as you provide for their needs?

Day 42

I WILL believe in God's power to restore marriages.

Our marriage is testimony to the fact that there is nothing that is impossible with God.

"Humanly speaking, it is impossible. But with God everything is possible" (Matthew 19:26).

As Jesus hung on the cross, He forgave those responsible for His crucifixion, acknowledging their lack of understanding: "Father, forgive them, for they do not know what they do" (Luke 23:34 NKJV). Married people often make mistakes unknowingly, influenced by a lack of guidance and role models. It is essential to extend forgiveness to ourselves and our spouses for these errors. By putting our faith in God, we can seek restoration and intimacy in our marriages. Remember, God's miracles unfold when we act in faith. The devil may attempt to convince you that your situation is hopeless, but he is a liar. Reject his falsehoods and embrace the truth that nothing is impossible with God.

Dear Father, I believe you are the Creator and Sustainer of marriages. Holy Spirit, not only do we want our marriage to be strong, but we also ask You to bring healing and hope to other marriages. In Jesus' name, Amen.

How do you feel when you hear that with God nothing is impossible? What is an impossible situation you need God to change right now?

I WILL pray in faith for my spouse.

Faith gets our eyes off each other and the smaller issues and puts them on a big God.

Now faith is the substance of things hoped for, the evidence of things not seen (Hebrews 11:1 NKJV).

When you trust in God and His Word, amazing things happen. God responds to your faith and delights in your belief in His presence and good intentions for you. Instead of focusing on your spouse's flaws or the small issues that come up in any relationship, turn your eyes to the Lord. When you pray in faith, you not only witness God's miraculous answers but also find unity and peace during life's toughest storms. If you have ever tried to force change through harsh words or domination, you know it only leads to ruin. True transformation comes when you place your faith in God, follow His Word, and trust Him for the results. Remember, God cares about every detail of your life, including your marriage. So don't hesitate to pray, believe, and watch God work wonders in your relationship.

Dear Father, I believe You have great plans for my marriage. Holy Spirit, please give me the words to pray in faith. In Jesus' name, Amen.

What situation do you need to trust God for today?

I WILL (as a wife) not allow a difficult relationship with my father to dominate my marriage.

If you do not forgive your father, you will damage yourself and those around you much more than you will ever damage him.

"But if you refuse to forgive others, your Father will not forgive your sins" (Matthew 6:15).

Every young girl needs her father's affirmation and guidance to develop healthy self-esteem and the ability to depend on men. When a father is absent or unaffirming, a girl may grow up to be independent and opinionated, seeking unhealthy male affection and affirmation to fill the gap in her heart. This can lead to a dominant female/passive male relationship dynamic. To overcome these challenges, you must first realize the issues in your family system and forgive your father for any area in which he failed to measure up. Forgiveness is essential for your own healing. Embrace submission to your husband, allowing him to lead and make mistakes. Support him through prayer and trust in God's perfect healing and timing.

Dear Father, You are the perfect Dad. Holy Spirit, I choose to forgive my father for his mistakes, and I will encourage my husband as he grows and leads. In Jesus' name, Amen.

What kind of relationship do you have with your father? How does this compare with your relationship with your spouse?

I WILL treat sex in my marriage as a covenant sign.

*A covenant sign means we are honoring
our covenant relationship.*

Marriage *is* honorable among all, and the bed undefiled; but fornicators and adulterers God will judge (Hebrews 13:4 NKJV).

Sex is not merely for satisfying yourself or your spouse; it also serves as the covenant sign of your marriage. Engaging in sexual intimacy signifies your commitment and acts as a demonstration of good faith within your covenant relationship. As believers, it is important to regularly take communion as a way to show the Lord that you remember and appreciate the covenant you have with Him. Similarly, as husband and wife, having regular sexual intimacy communicates that you honor the sacred covenant you share and faithfully uphold it. When God sees you embracing the covenant sign, He pours out His blessings. Dedicate your bodies and sexual union as instruments of covenant blessings, fostering the beautiful intimacy designed by God.

Dear Father, unless I am physically unable, I want to show my ongoing covenant to my spouse through a regular sexual relationship. Holy Spirit, help us to keep our communication about sex clear and positive. In Jesus' name, Amen.

Have you considered your sexual relationship as part of your marriage covenant? Why or why not?

Day 46

I WILL give sacrificially to my spouse and my marriage.

You must obey God's design for marriage by faith before you can experience the blessings of love and fulfillment God has designed for all of us to enjoy.

"Give, and you will receive. Your gift will return to you in full—pressed down, shaken together to make room for more, running over, and poured into your lap. The amount you give will determine the amount you get back" (Luke 6:38).

God's design for marriage involves a sacrificial and serving husband alongside an honoring and caring wife. Their selfless love for each other is intended to create a lifelong relationship and perfect friendship. This kind of relationship does not fit many people's experiences, but it is attainable for anyone. Have faith in God's Word and trust that He holds the answers. Following God's design requires obedience and faith, which will lead to the abundant blessings of love and fulfillment. By giving generously, serving with humility, and laying down your life for your spouse, you can discover the marriage you've been searching for.

Dear Father, I want to be selfless and sacrificial in my marriage. Holy Spirit, show me how to serve my spouse. In Jesus' name, Amen.

What do you think about when you read the word "sacrificial"? What can you do to serve your spouse today?

I WILL (as a husband) win the battle for my mind by meditating on God's Word.

*A man can never overcome lust until he
has won the battle for his mind.*

We use God's mighty weapons, not worldly weapons, to knock down the strongholds of human reasoning and to destroy false arguments (2 Corinthians 10:4).

When you, as a man, encounter erotic images, epinephrine is released in your brain, permanently imprinting them. Satan manipulates this process to fill your mind with perverse images, weakening your marital bond. Overcoming lust starts with winning the battle in your mind. Replace unclean thoughts with the power of God's Word. Begin each morning by reading the Bible for at least five to 30 minutes. Load a Scripture verse or passage in your mind for the day. Throughout the day, reflect on what you read, especially when tempted sexually. You can't remove bad thoughts, but you can replace them. Understand that the battle against lust is fought in your mind, and Scripture equips you for victory. Trust in God's Word, not your own thoughts or willpower, to conquer every time.

Dear Father, You gave me Your Word to instruct and protect me. Holy Spirit, open the truths of the Bible to me. In Jesus' name, Amen.

What do you do to allow the Bible to have an influence in your life?

Day 48

I WILL take responsibility for my own behavior.

Don't focus primarily on your spouse; focus on yourself.

"And why worry about a speck in your friend's eye when you have a log in your own?" (Luke 6:41).

It's essential to focus on yourself rather than solely on your spouse. You can't control your partner's behavior, but you can change your own behavior with God's help. As Jesus explained, when we judge others, we attempt to remove a speck from someone else's eye while having a log in our own. Take responsibility for your words and actions and create an environment of purity and trust from your side first. You may be frustrated with your partner's selfish and insensitive behavior. Turn to the Lord and pray for your spouse to change when other attempts fail. Trust God to transform your spouse while you focus on your own behavior and weaknesses. It will alter the atmosphere and spirit of your marriage.

Dear Father, remind me that I have my own faults and weaknesses I need to address. Holy Spirit, convict me when I become critical of my spouse and remind me that I also must repent of sin. In Jesus' name, Amen.

Have you been focusing on your spouse's faults while dismissing your own? Ask God to show you a different way to respond.

I WILL strive for complete vulnerability and openness with my spouse.

There is no other relationship in life that affords the potential for as much "nakedness" as marriage.

Now the man and his wife were both naked, but they felt no shame (Genesis 2:25).

You may have never realized it, but you have a need for complete vulnerability and openness with your spouse, which cannot be fulfilled with any other person. God designed marriage as the singular place for us to fulfill the need for total exposure of our true selves. When we can undress ourselves in every area before our spouses without shame or fear, we are in a healthy place for an intimate relationship to develop. If we are unable to expose ourselves completely, it means we are hiding something that needs to be revealed. Though you may not be able to fulfill this inner desire for complete vulnerability in marriage at this time, it remains that God created a need in us for it to be met in marriage.

Dear Father, bring us both to the place where we can be completely open with each other. Holy Spirit, help us to be people who can trust each other completely. In Jesus' name, Amen.

Is there any area of your life you are withholding from your spouse? Talk to God about it.

Day 50

I WILL think about and focus on my spouse.

*Loving our spouse with our minds means we
think about them and focus on them.*

Finally, all of you, be like-minded, be sympathetic, love one another, be compassionate and humble (1 Peter 3:8 NIV).

Loving your spouse with your mind means you think about them and focus on them. You study them and learn their likes and dislikes. You freely share your thoughts with each other on a regular basis. You give each other the right to be honest and share openly without judgment or rejection. The thoughts you share should never be damaging to each other or done in spite. But some of your thoughts will inevitably be concerning negative things you are dealing with personally or even related to your spouse. Mental intimacy happens when you focus on each other and openly share your thoughts regularly and honestly. Having unhindered access to each other's thoughts is what results in mental intimacy.

Dear Father, I love my spouse and want to focus on them. Holy Spirit, help me to grow in mental intimacy with my spouse. Let them be first in my mind before anyone except You. In Jesus' name, Amen.

Do you think about your spouse before you consider anything else? How free are you as a couple about sharing your deepest thoughts?

I WILL take advice about my marriage from the Word of God.

When we read God's Word, it fills our minds with truth that works.

[The devil] was a murderer from the beginning. He has always hated the truth, because there is no truth in him. When he lies, it is consistent with his character; for he is a liar and the father of lies (John 8:44).

Jesus referred to Satan as "a liar and the father of lies." The devil specializes in filling our minds with disinformation to provoke negative emotions like resentment, fear, and rebellion. On the other hand, God's Word is filled with truth and wisdom that can solve your problems and make your life pleasant and productive. Don't believe anyone who contradicts God's Word. Take every thought captive to Christ, ensuring it aligns with His Word. Neglecting to do so will allow those thoughts to control you. Protect your precious marriage from the devil's lies by seeking truth in the Bible. Embrace God's Word, and you'll find stability and success as your reward.

Dear Father, I trust Your Word. Holy Spirit, help me to discern other voices that are not from You. I only want to hear Your voice. In Jesus' name, Amen.

Have you ever received marriage advice you knew was not from God? If so, how did you respond?

Day 52

I WILL (as a wife) not allow my parents' relationship issues to dictate how I relate to my husband.

When a young girl has been brought up watching her mother dominate her father, it creates many unhealthy images in her young mind.

The people will no longer quote this proverb:
"The parents have eaten sour grapes,
    but their children's mouths pucker at the taste" (Jeremiah 31:29).

When a girl grows up seeing her mother dominate her father, it can distort her perception of healthy relationships. You may have started believing that women should control men and developed disdain for your father's perceived weakness, perpetuating a cycle of female dominance in future generations. This is especially common in cultures where female dominance has been prevalent for a long time. Generational tendencies, known as iniquities, have a strong influence on our lives and marriages. It's important to recognize that our sins affect not only ourselves but also future generations until we break free from them. Both of you must decide to end the iniquities you received from your families and allow God to reshape your marriage.

Dear Father, I love my parents, but I recognize that they are not perfect. Holy Spirit, direct my steps as I lay down anything from my past that will not bless my marriage. In Jesus' name, Amen.

What lessons have you learned about marriage by observing your parents' relationship?

I WILL dream big yet realistic
dreams for my marriage.

*It's important that you set goals for your marriage
and keep your expectations high.*

And we are confident that he hears us whenever we ask for anything that pleases him (1 John 5:14).

For a thriving marriage, it's essential for you to set high goals. But along with these dreams, it's equally important to have grounded expectations. There's a risk in either of these two extremes: some couples unrealistically expect everything to be perfect, leading to disappointment, while others, possibly disappointed and jaded by past experiences, set their sights too low to avoid being hurt again. The secret is balance. Embrace big dreams for your marriage, but acknowledge that challenges will arise. It's during these times that you will grow closer, building trust and deepening intimacy. Be inspired to keep setting ambitious yet realistic goals for your marriage. Remember, you're meant for greatness, and God knows your desires.

Dear Father, I want to have big dreams, but I don't want to get ahead of Your direction. Holy Spirit, give me bold faith but keep me grounded in reality. In Jesus' name, Amen.

How do you feel about the statement that you should have big dreams, but they should also be realistic? How can you have faith while staying firmly grounded in reality?

Day 54

I WILL expect the best and work hard for it.

Big dreams and hard work are the magic
ingredients that create great marriages.

No matter what you do, work at it with all your might (Ecclesiastes 9:10 NIRV).

Happiness in marriage requires a combination of high expectations and a firm commitment to put in the necessary effort. It's like having the dream of owning a successful business. You get to be your own boss, but you also have to work hard and make sacrifices. The same principle also applies to wanting a healthy body—the desire must be supported by a commitment to eat right and exercise. Some couples think that if they have to work too hard at their relationship, something must be wrong. But the truth is, every healthy, successful marriage takes work. The key is to expect the very best *and* be willing to put in the effort and make the sacrifices to make it the very best. Expect challenges but don't fear them. With God's help, you can have the marriage of your dreams.

Dear Father, I believe You created marriage to reflect Your love. Holy Spirit, help me to keep believing the best and never give up. In Jesus' name, Amen.

What expectations about marriage did you have when you were a single person? How have those expectations changed?

I WILL do my best to transmit the right priorities to my children.

As parents, we must train our children through godly example to honor biblical priorities.

Train up a child in the way he should go;
even when he is old he will not depart from it (Proverbs 22:6 ESV).

Your children's sense of priority is shaped by how they perceive their position in your life. While all children face challenges, those who feel unloved and rejected by their parents endure greater difficulties and cause more heartache. Parenting is a demanding commitment that requires significant time and energy. Besides God and your spouse, nothing should hold greater value than your children. Make no compromises when it comes to dedicating time, attention, energy, and love to your kids. They need to tangibly experience their worth and importance to you. Remember, your kids' future happiness and success depend on God's favor, not solely on education, relationships, or income.

Dear Father, we thank You for blessing us. We want everyone in our home to honor Your priorities. Holy Spirit, show us how to love and teach our children to love You. In Jesus' name, Amen.

What are some ways you should let your children know they are a priority? How do you show them that God and your spouse are even higher priorities?

Day 56

I WILL show love to my spouse like I did early in our relationship.

Remember the joyous details of your happy and giving actions at the beginning when the relationship was so exciting and fulfilling.

"Look how far you have fallen!" (Revelation 2:5).

While feelings certainly have their place in a relationship, they shouldn't be the only foundation for your love. Always doing what you feel like doing can lead to confusion and pain. Instead, try making the decision to do what's right, even when it's tough. Take a moment to reflect on those happy and fulfilling moments at the beginning of your relationship. Remember how you honored and were sensitive to your partner's needs, and how you went out of your way to impress them. By maintaining this level of care and consideration, you can continue to build a loving and fulfilling relationship for the long haul. Work together to build your love to last a lifetime.

Dear Father, I want to show love for my spouse like I did when we first got together. Holy Spirit, reveal how I should recapture my love for my spouse. In Jesus' name, Amen.

What kind of loving things did you do when you first met your spouse? Which of those actions should you recapture?

I WILL (as a husband) refuse to give into the deception of sexual sin.

Today, millions of men live in sexual deception because they believe that monogamous sex in marriage isn't enough.

You should reserve it for yourselves.
Never share it with strangers (Proverbs 5:17).

Many men live in sexual deception, believing that monogamous sex in marriage isn't enough. They're deceived into thinking that pornography and adultery will bring satisfaction, but it's a lie. The truth is that the greatest sexual pleasure comes from a sexually pure, monogamous, loving relationship with your wife. By caring for her, pursuing her, and meeting her needs, true intimacy grows, as God designed. The world of sexual sin is driven by self-pleasure, the lack of love, and shaky commitment. It destroys marriages, families, and hollows out the souls of those bound to it. Reject the deception and embrace this truth: fulfillment lies within the context of a faithful and loving relationship with your wife.

Dear Father, I believe You provided sex as a good gift to be enjoyed in marriage. Holy Spirit, show me how to be faithful and loving to my spouse at all times. In Jesus' name, Amen.

How do you pursue your wife and let her know you are faithful only to her?

Day 58

I WILL openly and honestly share my emotions.

Emotional intimacy occurs as we are free to share our feelings with each other.

My lover is mine, and I am his.
He browses among the lilies (Song of Songs 2:16).

You will often hear people use the term "soulmate." Instead of searching for a singular person uniquely crafted by God for you, consider a different phrase: *an emotion mate.* Your genuine soulmate is not an external individual, but rather the spouse with whom you choose to share your deepest emotions and vulnerabilities. A profound level of intimacy comes from cultivating emotional openness within your marriage. Create a safe and accepting space where your spouse can freely express their feelings without fear of judgment or rejection. Embrace and celebrate honesty communicated with love. Effective communication involves not only sharing facts but also expressing your innermost feelings, so make it a habit to openly share your own emotions each day.

Dear Father, I know You are always open and honest with me. Holy Spirit, teach me to be emotionally honest with my spouse. Help me to be an emotion mate for them. In Jesus' name, Amen.

Do you share your emotions freely and honestly with your spouse? How can you change the way you communicate to be more emotionally vulnerable with your spouse?

I WILL give my attention to what God needs to do in my life before I focus on my spouse.

Pay attention to what God wants to do in your own life, and your spouse will become so curious that they will want to find out what is making life around your house so much better.

"You hypocrite, first take the plank out of your own eye, and then you will see clearly to remove the speck from your brother's eye" (Matthew 7:5 NIV).

When you attend seminars or read insightful marriage materials, it's tempting to say something like, "Did you hear what they mentioned about women submitting to their husbands?" or "Did you notice how men are supposed to love like Jesus?" However, that's not the intention behind any of our content. Don't use your newfound knowledge to point fingers or pressure your spouse. Instead, focus on how it can transform your personal life and attitude. If you genuinely embrace and live out these principles, your spouse might just become so intrigued that they'll want to dive into the material themselves, eager to discover what's bringing about the positive change in you.

Dear Father, I give You permission to work freely in my life. Holy Spirit, draw my attention to the transformation needed in my heart and mind. In Jesus' name, Amen.

How can you live in such a way that makes your spouse want to know more about God?

Day 60

I WILL (as a wife) surrender my personality to the Holy Spirit.

Some women are born with a naturally strong personality.

She brings him good, not harm,
all the days of her life (Proverbs 31:12).

If you are a woman with a naturally strong personality, such as a choleric temperament, then you may tend to be opinionated and aggressive by nature. There are many positive aspects to this personality type, such as the ability to think creatively, accomplish challenging tasks, and press through difficulties, but there are also specific dangers, especially in marriage. It's crucial for you to surrender your personality to the guidance of the Holy Spirit, restraining your innate desire for control. Respect your husband's opinions and treat him as an equal, refraining from using your forceful personality, dominance, or intimidation to manipulate situations. When your strong temperament is submitted to and led by the Holy Spirit, it can beautifully complement your husband's authority. However, if it goes unchecked, it can lead to undermining your husband's authority, causing significant damage to your relationship.

Dear Father, I believe You designed me to complement my husband in every way. Holy Spirit, I surrender my personality to You right now. In Jesus' name, Amen.

What kind of personality do you have? How does this personality lead you to interact with your husband?

I WILL seek God's wisdom about our sex life.

*We need to keep our sexuality
as an open conversation before God.*

You can ask for anything in my name, and I will do it, so that the Son can bring glory to the Father (John 14:13).

It is crucial for both of you to pray about sexual temptations, problems, and desires. Some may feel uncomfortable discussing sexual matters with God, but remember He is the creator of sex and is present with you during intimate moments. Sex is not repulsive to God; it is beautiful, and He wants you to experience joy in it. Therefore, maintain an open conversation with Him regarding your sex life together. Trust that God can increase your sexual desire if needed and believe in His power to heal any physical or emotional issues that may hinder intimacy. Sex is sacred to God, and He deeply cares about you. Including God in your sexual relationship will bring countless blessings.

Dear Father, I want You to help us in our sex life as a married couple. Holy Spirit, I trust You to heal us and guide us so we can be the best we can be for each other. In Jesus' name, Amen.

Have you ever prayed for God to help you in your sexual relationship? Make a commitment to involve God in every area of your life today.

Day 62

I WILL practice focus and discipline in my marriage.

Have clear priorities and protect them.

Dear children, let's not merely say that we love each other; let us show the truth by our actions (1 John 3:18).

Busyness and stress run rampant in today's society, but they are powerful enemies to your relationships with Jesus and your spouse. For a long-lasting, fruitful relationship, discipline and commitment to priorities are essential. You may declare God and family as your top priorities, but do your actions back this up? Or do activities like work, friends, sports, and online shopping consume most of your time and energy? Nothing should be so consuming that it depletes the resources needed for your relationships with God and your spouse. Remember, a successful marriage isn't accidental—it requires focus and discipline. You don't have to be perfect, but you do need to be intentional in what you say and do. It's crucial to identify your priorities and protect them fiercely.

Dear Father, You are a God of order. Nothing distracts You from Your relationship with me. Holy Spirit, help me to focus on the correct priorities—God, my spouse, and my family. In Jesus' name, Amen.

What is your plan to practice focus and discipline in your relationship with your spouse?

I WILL share control of finances with my spouse.

You are equal partners, and that spirit has to be present in all conversations and decisions.

Live in harmony with each other (Romans 12:16).

The Law of Partnership requires surrendering all assets and liabilities to the marriage, so nothing is individually owned or controlled, which establishes financial unity. Refusing to accept this truth leads to division and problems. Share ownership and control to prevent legitimate jealousy. When it comes to finances, it doesn't matter who has more expertise or manages it. You are equal partners, and that spirit should be present in all conversations and decisions. Exerting undue control over finances damages the relationship. One of the most harmful issues is withholding financial information. When making financial decisions, you need to solicit your spouse's input and agree on how much you can spend without each other's input. Significant financial decisions should be made together, and if you can't agree, seek counseling to prevent a wedge from coming between you.

Dear Father, we always want to cooperate with You and each other. Holy Spirit, keep us in unity as we discuss financial issues. In Jesus' name, Amen.

Have you ever had a heated conversation about money? What can you do next time to improve how you have those kinds of conversations?

Day 64

I WILL close all access points for the enemy to enter my marriage.

The devil only needs one good entry point to give him a stronghold.

So humble yourselves before God. Resist the devil, and he will flee from you (James 4:7).

In your own home, you must realize that a burglar doesn't require you to leave every door and window open to enter your house. All he needs is one way inside, and he can easily burglarize your entire home. Sin works in the same way. The devil doesn't need you to sin in multiple areas to destroy your life or marriage. He only requires one entry point to gain a stronghold and bring destruction. Some individuals have been devastated and marriages ruined because they allowed sin into just one area. Whether it's your sex life, finances, words, addictions, wrong priorities, selfishness, dominance, or anything else, you must understand that sin from that one entry point can harm you and your marriage. The longer it persists, the greater damage it can cause.

Dear Father, I want the devil to have no place in my life. Holy Spirit, reveal any areas of my life where the enemy has an entry point. In Jesus' name, Amen.

What have you done to make sure the devil has no entry point into your marriage?

I WILL refuse to return sin for sin.

Make up your mind that you are not going to sin in response to anything your spouse says or does.

Don't retaliate with insults when people insult you. Instead, pay them back with a blessing (1 Peter 3:9).

Revenge and retaliation won't solve any problem. They will only make matters worse. The only way to overcome a negative spirit is with the opposite spirit. Fighting fire with fire only leads to a bigger fire! Decide not to sin in response to your spouse's actions or words. The power of love and righteousness is greater than evil. If you're being abused by your partner, seek protection and address it immediately. However, even in imperfect marriages, we must choose to deal with things righteously and trust God for the results instead of justifying our bad behavior. Employ right behavior always and rely on God to reward you and change your spouse.

Dear Father, remind me that I have my own faults and weaknesses I need to address. Holy Spirit, convict me when I become critical of my spouse and remind me that I also must repent of sin. In Jesus' name, Amen.

Have you been focusing on your spouse's faults while dismissing your own? Ask God to show you a different way to respond.

Day 66

I WILL remove any sin in my life that prevents me from openness and vulnerability with my spouse.

Without a healthy respect for the deadly effects of sin, we are open targets for Satan's lies and destructive schemes against us.

For the wages of sin is death, but the free gift of God is eternal life through Christ Jesus our Lord (Romans 6:23).

Sin is the biggest obstacle to honest communication. God designed us for a pure relationship with our spouses. Sin is the greatest obstacle to purity, and it is always fatal. When we permit sin into our lives, we ingest a lethal poison, even in small doses. Without a healthy respect for sin's destructiveness, we are vulnerable to Satan's lies. Anything that violates our spouse or damages the relationship is sin. Spouses sometimes say or do things that are terribly painful and damaging. Even worse, the guilty person will often defend themselves and destroy the relationship further. Flee from sin for the good of your marriage and yourself.

Dear Father, I want nothing to do with sin because I know it separates me from You and my spouse. Holy Spirit, convict me of all sin and lead me to repentance. In Jesus' name, Amen.

Sin is a difficult area for us to admit. If possible, find a mature believer to talk with about any area in which you are struggling.

I WILL yield my marriage to God and expect His blessings.

In God's heart, marriage is a priority.

God saw all that he had made, and it was very good. And there was evening, and there was morning—the sixth day (Genesis 1:31 NIV).

If you asked God for a favor, would you ask Him to bless your marriage? Hopefully, that's high on your list, because marriage holds a special place in God's heart. Remember the story from Genesis? God created both man and woman and immediately sanctified their union. It's described as "very good." He blessed them, which means God empowered them for success, prosperity, and long-lasting joy. By God's grace, Adam and Eve were set up for unparalleled success. But the moment they strayed from God's guidance, their bliss turned to hardship. It's the same with marriages today. The quality of your bond isn't about God playing favorites. It's about choosing to align with His will. When you do, you invite blessings that mirror heaven on earth.

Dear Father, I choose to align my marriage with Your will. Holy Spirit, thank You in advance for the blessings that come from listening to You as I listen and obey. In Jesus' name, Amen.

What would you like God to do in your marriage today?

Day 68

I WILL (as a wife) not be an enabler for bad behavior.

When a person allows a loved one to behave in a destructive manner, they are "enabling" the other person to be what they are.

For each will have to bear his own load (Galatians 6:5 ESV).

You may wonder why some women naturally gravitate toward destructive men or find themselves in dependent relationships with unreliable partners. One answer is that these women are enablers. An enabler is someone who allows a loved one to engage in destructive behavior. But it goes beyond simply allowing—it also involves providing the resources or creating an environment that supports such behavior. Enabling may seem loving on the outside, but it's detrimental to everyone involved. A healthy wife refuses to witness the self-destruction of others, including her husband and family. She stands against bad behavior and refuses to enable or aid it. And if there is any abuse in a situation, a healthy wife draws strength and power from the Holy Spirit to confront it and figure out the best course of action.

Dear Father, You are a good Father who wants the best for me. Holy Spirit, reveal any enabling patterns in my life and show me how to make the appropriate changes. In Jesus' name, Amen.

What happens when you enable bad behavior from someone you love?

I WILL, as much as possible, honor our parents and nurture a friendship with them.

*One of the best ways to relate to your parents
is to view them as precious friends.*

"Honor your father and mother" (this is the first commandment with a promise) (Ephesians 6:2 ESV).

Consider your parents as cherished friends, deserving of your commitment and time. While your spouse should be your first priority (after God), it's still important to nurture your bond with your parents. If boundaries are over-stepped, address it as you would with any close friend to maintain a healthy relationship. While living with parents or in-laws may not always be feasible, step up to help the best way you can, especially when they are aging or in poor health. It's crucial to offer support and assist them in ways that respect both their needs and your boundaries. This not only honors them but also upholds your core values. Always ensure you and your partner remain understanding and supportive of each other during these times.

Dear Father, my parents have done so much for me, and I want to honor them. Holy Spirit, help me to bless my parents and let them know that I love and appreciate them. In Jesus' name, Amen.

What are some practical ways you can continue to build your bond with your parents?

Day 70

I WILL (as a husband) define success by my relationship to God and my family.

Success begins with God and family.

"For my yoke is easy to bear, and the burden I give you is light" (Matthew 11:30).

You may have been taught that you're only accepted if you perform. You may have been driven to achieve. This conditional love damages self-esteem. Parents should express love consistently, building a child's self-esteem and security. Seeking approval, children learn to perform for acceptance in society. Society's conditional acceptance, based on appearance and achievements, shouldn't dictate self-worth. Remember, God accepts you as you are, loving you unconditionally. Focus on doing what God tells you, rather than seeking man's approval. Jesus said His yoke is easy and His burden is light. Anything driving you and compromising relationships isn't from God. True success begins with God and family. Life becomes easier when we begin with that.

Dear Father, Your Word shows me how to be successful. You accept me and show me how to provide for my family according to Your will. Holy Spirit, keep me free from seeking the approval of other people more than You. In Jesus' name, Amen.

Many men have destroyed their marriages by seeking acceptance from someone other than God. What area of your life do you find the most temptation to exchange God's acceptance for the praise of other people?

I WILL admit my faults.

The heartfelt and sincere expression, "I'm sorry.
I was wrong. Will you forgive me?" can heal a
marriage quicker than almost anything else.

"Confess your sins to each other and pray for each other so that you may be healed" (James 5:16).

There's almost nothing that can heal a relationship quicker than an apology. However, if you refuse to apologize, you will suffer in your marriage. When both parties don't admit their faults, you're in trouble! The apostle John said that if we confess our sins, God will forgive us and make us right with Him (1 John 1:9 NIV). In marriage, when one spouse admits they are wrong, God restores the relationship. Even if your partner doesn't reciprocate or respond positively, you must confess your mistakes to be right before God. Humility and honesty are virtues that bring high rewards, while pride and selfishness create an atmosphere of fear and dread.

Dear Father, I know you don't want me to live with sin in my life. Holy Spirit, give me the courage to admit when I am wrong. In Jesus' name, Amen.

Do you find it difficult to admit when you are wrong? Ask God to show you what might be a barrier to acknowledging your faults.

Day 72

I WILL show my spouse I care about good communication.

It doesn't matter what communication techniques you may know and understand—if you don't care, it won't make a difference.

Kind words are like honey—
> sweet to the soul and healthy for the body (Proverbs 16:24).

Understanding communication techniques won't help if you're actually indifferent. Remember the early days when you and your spouse would chat for hours, sharing your hopes and dreams? Everything felt right because you genuinely cared. Many marriages lose that sense of caring. Less quality time, dismissive remarks, and a general disregard for your partner's feelings can disrupt your communication. You both have a need to feel safe and valued. You want to know your spouse genuinely cares. Show that you care through attentive eye contact, positive feedback, and openly valuing your spouse's input. When you genuinely care, understanding your partner becomes effortless. You'll not only mend the communication gaps but also reignite any lost romance.

Dear Father, I want to genuinely care about what is important to my spouse. Holy Spirit, please heal any places in my heart that are hurt from misunderstandings and help me to be an active communicator in my marriage. In Jesus' name, Amen.

How can you show your spouse that you care about what they have to say?

I WILL seek outside help for my marriage when necessary.

Getting help is not a sign of weakness;
it's a sign of wisdom.

Where there is no guidance, a people falls,
   but in an abundance of counselors there is safety (Proverbs 11:14 ESV).

Every couple has moments when they can't solve problems on their own. If you and your spouse are facing a long-term struggle and have come to an impasse over it, consider seeking external guidance and support. Now, seeking help does not mean venting about your problems on social media or complaining to friends through group texts. These actions only harm your relationship further. Instead, find a trustworthy authority figure who is grounded in biblical principles and can offer godly direction and wise insights to navigate your challenges. Cultivate a teachable spirit and embrace the mindset of success, recognizing that seeking wisdom and guidance is an integral part of your journey. Don't hesitate to reach out and learn from those who can help you overcome challenging times.

Dear Father, I am grateful that I don't have to go through hard times alone. Holy Spirit, help me to humble myself and accept godly counsel that will sanctify my marriage. In Jesus' name, Amen.

What difficult or complicated issues in your marriage could benefit from the advice of godly counsel?

Day 74

I WILL exercise faith every day.

God cares about every detail of your life, and He is ready to act on your behalf when you put faith in Him.

Faith shows the reality of what we hope for; it is the evidence of things we cannot see (Hebrews 11:1).

Every blessing you receive is a testament to your faith in God. It delights Him when you trust in His presence and provision. Your faith gets stronger as you trust in God's constant guidance and unyielding love. In your marriage, it's essential to exercise faith daily. It will change your focus from trivial matters to God's bigger plan. When you pray with faith, you not only see God working but also find peace in the middle of life's challenges. If you don't pray, anxiety can overshadow you, which may actually lead to increased conflicts in your marriage. Even when you are confronted with your spouse's flaws, trust God to work on them and stay faithful.

Father God, Your presence and provision sustain my life. Holy Spirit, help me to pray in faith instead of allowing anxiety to overtake my mind. In Jesus' name, Amen.

How can you exercise faith in God through your marriage?

I WILL only maintain friendships that build up my marriage.

Your close friends are some of the most important predictors of how successful you will be in life and in marriage.

Walk with the wise and become wise;
associate with fools and get in trouble (Proverbs 13:20).

Your friendships significantly influence your life and marital success. Researchers have revealed that couples who faced challenges but remained together had friends who supported their union. Disturbingly, patterns like divorce, infidelity, and substance abuse often appear in clusters among acquaintances. The adage "misery loves company" holds true; discontent can spread within communities. For a thriving marriage, surround yourself with friends who mirror your values. Although no one's perfect, it's crucial to have a supportive group urging you toward righteousness. Seek advice and prayers from faithful, principled individuals. Don't underestimate the corrosive power of bad company. Prioritize nurturing wholesome relationships, perhaps starting in your local church, where shared values pave the way for enduring marital success.

Dear Father, I want to have friends who will support and build up my spouse and my marriage. Holy Spirit, reveal any relationships I need to reconsider and change. In Jesus' name, Amen.

Take time to do a friend inventory. Are there relationships you need to change or end? Are there others you need to pursue?

Day 76

I WILL establish love as the highest virtue in my family.

Love is the only virtue that can guarantee success and positive generational transference.

"This is my commandment: Love each other in the same way I have loved you" (John 15:12).

S uccessful families prioritize people over money. If you convey to your family members that they are mere servants of money, a family business, a sports legacy, a religious institution, or anything that diminishes their inherent value, they won't embrace or perpetuate it. Love is the universal value cherished by all—across generations, cultures, political beliefs, and by God and people. Upholding love as the supreme value ensures success, while any other value system guarantees failure. Love, defined by the example of Christ, is selfless and serves others regardless of feelings or circumstances. When practiced authentically, it becomes the most powerful force on earth. Choose love as your guiding virtue, and you will experience success and positively impact future generations with your marriage.

Dear Father, You loved me through Your Son before I could ever love You. Holy Spirit, teach me to make love the guiding virtue in my marriage and family. In Jesus' name, Amen.

Have you ever seen someone value money over people? What were the results of that attitude? What are some practical ways to follow love as the highest virtue?

I WILL be aware that I can influence my spouse's words and behavior with my own.

When you notice attitudes, words, or behaviors in your spouse that make you unhappy, you need to consider the fact that to some degree you may be responsible for the negative behavior.

Don't be misled—you cannot mock the justice of God. You will always harvest what you plant (Galatians 6:7).

H ave you ever considered the principle of sowing and reaping in your life, especially in your marriage? Think of your words and actions as powerful seeds. What you say or do can profoundly influence your relationship, sometimes even more than you might realize. Your words and actions will inevitably bear fruit. Ever find yourself upset by your spouse's behavior? Pause and reflect if you might have contributed to that behavior. You reap what you sow, after all. But there's good news: you can change the harvest. By acknowledging any negativity you've spread and consciously choosing to sow positivity, you can pave the way for a brighter future in your marriage.

Dear Father, I never want to cause my spouse distress because of my words or actions. Holy Spirit, convict me when I say or do things that negatively impact them. In Jesus' name, Amen.

How can you be aware of when your words or behavior are having a negative impact on your spouse?

Day 78

I WILL be honest and admit when I am angry.

There is nothing wrong with anger. Even God gets angry.

> God is an honest judge.
> He is angry with the wicked every day (Psalm 7:11).

Acknowledging and allowing anger is important for a healthy relationship. Many families fear anger and suppress it, causing other problems, such as depression. Denying anger causes it to accumulate and become dangerous. Create a safe space in your marriage to express concerns. Forgiveness plays a key role in rebuilding trust and restoring intimacy. By imitating God's forgiveness, marriages reflect His redemptive plan. Forgiveness will strengthen your marriage covenant, exemplify biblical values, and promote personal growth. How you deal with anger also inspires others. While anger can arise for various reasons, expressing it isn't always justified. Couples must communicate openly, validate each other's emotions, and resolve conflicts positively. By addressing anger, your marriage can thrive and withstand challenges.

Dear Father, help me to become angry at the things that make You angry. Holy Spirit, I need Your voice to warn me about sin when I am angry. In Jesus' name, Amen.

What is your past history with anger? Did you express it in ungodly or godly ways? How can you express anger only in ways that are right?

I WILL choose to be a person of integrity.

To live a life of integrity means that every area of your life is in a generally healthy and morally sound condition.

People with integrity walk safely,
but those who follow crooked paths will be exposed (Proverbs 10:9).

Integrity signifies "wholeness" or "completeness." It's about making sure that every area of your life reflects godliness and health. Integrity doesn't demand perfection from you; rather, it emphasizes avoiding wrongdoing, deceit, or severe compromise. Consider this: a burglar requires only one open door or window to ransack an entire house. Similarly, a single lapse in judgment can pave the way for larger pitfalls in your life. Many couples have seen their relationship crumble due to just one unchecked issue, such as financial mismanagement or a detour from their shared values. You must be vigilant about keeping integrity in every aspect of your life. It will safeguard your relationship and wellbeing, ensuring that there are no open avenues for negative influences. Prioritize integrity and protect your future.

Dear Father, I want to be a person of integrity. Holy Spirit, show me any open doors in my life that the enemy might use to enter and cause chaos. In Jesus' name, Amen.

What aspects of your life are lacking complete integrity? How can you safeguard your marriage?

Day 80

I WILL make thoughtful financial plans with my spouse.

Every couple needs to sit down proactively and make a detailed budget of their finances.

Commit your actions to the LORD,
and your plans will succeed (Proverbs 16:3).

Have you and your spouse considered making a detailed budget? It's important to proactively do this together. If you feel like you don't have the skills or need help, consider going to a financial counselor who can help you. A budget helps you make decisions in advance and keeps both of you accountable. It also defines your values and what's most important to you. Having a real budget that you both agree with and honor is a huge step toward financial intimacy and partnership, giving you a clear roadmap for where you're going together. Without a budget, emotions are higher, and life is less certain, especially when you have too much debt. If you're facing major financial pressures, face them together with a proactive plan.

Dear Father, we understand that making a budget together is an act of faith. Holy Spirit, guide us with wisdom for how we should spend our finances. In Jesus' name, Amen.

Have you created a budget together? If not, decide today when you will sit down to make one.

I WILL (as a wife) submit to my husband as unto the Lord.

There is no Plan B.

For wives, this means submit to your husbands as to the Lord (Ephesians 5:22).

You may be resisting God's plan for your marriage because you don't like what it says about you. When you reject Ephesians 5, you're rejecting God's perfect plan for marriage. God's plan is clear. It's not about one partner dominating the other. Many women object to the idea of wives submitting to their husbands and that husbands should be the heads of their wives. But God's plan for marriage is about two humble-hearted, servant-spirited people who are both submitted to God and to each other as equals. Women need leadership, but they don't want to be demeaned or dominated. That's why husbands are commanded to be Christlike in their love and care for their wives. God's plan is not about subservience or domination. It's about two people working together, submitting to God and each other, and loving each other as Christ loves the Church.

Dear Father, I want to follow Your plan for marriage. Holy Spirit, show me how to submit to my husband in the Lord the way that Your Word teaches. In Jesus' name, Amen.

What do you think it means for a wife to submit to her husband?

Day 82

I WILL not justify my bad behavior when I am angry.

You aren't going to make any progress in resolving anger if you keep escalating it and perpetuating it with sinful words and actions.

"Be angry, and do not sin": do not let the sun go down on your wrath, nor give place to the devil (Ephesians 4:26–27 NKJV).

Paul tells his readers to "be angry," but then he then tells them not to sin. Many spouses justify bad behavior because of their spouse's actions. They might say something like, "I know I shouldn't have cursed and called you names, but you made me so mad." If you continue to escalate and perpetuate anger with sinful words and actions, you won't make any progress in resolving the issue. Dealing with anger requires putting your faith in God and believing that He will reward you for doing what's right. Trusting in Him enables you to manage anger in a healthy and godly way.

Dear Father, I want my words and actions to be pleasing to You. Holy Spirit, show me how to express anger or displeasure in a way that is pleasing to You. In Jesus' name, Amen.

When was a time you expressed your anger in a way you later regretted? What can you do differently the next time you encounter something that makes you angry?

I WILL connect my heart to my spouse with empathy.

Empathy is how we connect hearts.

Since God chose you to be the holy people he loves, you must clothe your-selves with tenderhearted mercy, kindness, humility, gentleness, and patience (Colossians 3:12).

When we practice empathy, we are better able to understand and share the feelings of others, which is essential for building deep connections with our spouses. When you're dating, empathy comes naturally. You watch how your words and actions affect your date. It doesn't have to stop there! By keeping empathy at the forefront of your relationship, you can create a caring environment that fosters deep romantic love. Maintaining empathy is crucial to keeping the spark alive throughout your married life. It's how you connect your hearts and ensure that your actions positively impact your spouse. By being sensitive to your spouse's needs and desires, you can create a strong and fulfill-ing relationship where both of your needs are met. If you find your relationship has gone off track, take responsibility for your actions and ask for forgiveness.

Dear Father, You loved me. Teach me to love my spouse with empathy. Holy Spirit, keep my heart soft and tender toward my spouse. In Jesus' name, Amen.

What are ways you can show empathy and keep your heart focused on your spouse?

Day 84

I WILL not confuse sex with intimacy.

Not understanding how God designed us, many people operate primarily in the physical dimension and wonder why they feel hollow and passionless.

Let your fountain be blessed,
and rejoice in the wife of your youth (Proverbs 5:18 ESV).

Confusing sex with intimacy has caused untold damage to many marriages. If you believe the lie that sex *is* intimacy, then you think the more sex you have, the more intimate your relationship will become. But it's simply not true. Physical intimacy is only a part of building closeness. Many people turn to pornography or casual encounters in an attempt to experience true intimacy, but these will never satisfy their longings. Operating outside of God's design leads to an endless and empty pursuit, where excitement diminishes with each experience. Understanding that sex is only one element of intimacy is key to experiencing genuine intimacy in your relationship.

Dear Father, I want to have real intimacy with my spouse, but I want it to be according to Your plan. Holy Spirit, teach me the ways to have intimacy with my spouse that go beyond just the physical. In Jesus' name, Amen.

Have you confused sex with true intimacy in your marriage? If you have, begin a conversation with your spouse about how to build closeness beyond your physical connection.

I WILL work to meet my spouse's unspoken needs.

*Pay attention to your spouse
and work to meet unspoken needs and desires they have
as you did in the beginning of your relationship.*

Let each of you look not only to his own interests, but also to the interests of others (Philippians 2:4 ESV).

Anticipating your partner's needs and desires and meeting them without being asked is one key to romance in your marriage. This thoughtfulness prevents the relationship from becoming stagnant or declining over time. When you first start a relationship, naturally you want to impress your partner by paying attention to their likes and dislikes. Over time, complacency becomes easy, so you stop doing the things that made the relationship great. Your spouse may start feeling unwanted and unattractive. Focus on your spouse's needs and be proactive. While it may require effort and consistency, it is worth it. By doing so, you can rekindle the dynamic love you really want and keep your relationship strong.

Dear Father, keep me aware of my spouse's needs even before they ask. Holy Spirit, keep my heart soft and attentive to my spouse's needs. In Jesus' name, Amen.

What is the last thing you did for your spouse before you were asked? What is the next thing you plan to do?

Day 86

I WILL demonstrate what I value by my priorities.

Our priorities are our values.

"Wherever your treasure is, there the desires of your heart will also be" (Matthew 6:21).

Your priorities reflect your values. When you prioritize God, it shows you highly value Him. On the other hand, when something else takes precedence over God, it reveals that you value that thing more than Him. The same principle applies to your family; prioritizing them shows that you highly value the people you love. Professing that someone is our priority but failing to live it out with our actions is really hypocrisy. Sadly, many people fall into this trap, which leads to disappointment and disharmony because our words and actions don't match. True love requires us to align our priorities with our values. By living out our priorities with integrity, we honor our commitments and experience the blessings that come from aligning our values with our actions.

Dear Father, I value You and my spouse. Holy Spirit, I want to do marriage Your way. Help me to keep my priorities in order. In Jesus' name, Amen.

What do you value most? Are your values demonstrated through your actions? If not, what can you do to change your priorities to reflect your values?

I WILL have a healthy dependency on God.

Each one of us is dependent because God created us that way.

The LORD *is* my shepherd;
I shall not want (Psalm 23:1 NKJV).

In today's culture that promotes personal independence, it's crucial to remember that God created us to be dependent beings. Each of us relies on God because that's how He designed us. Independence is a deceptive and perverse distortion of God's plan. We see this dependence illustrated in the analogy of sheep in the Bible. Sheep are vulnerable, lacking self-protection and provision. God compares us to sheep, emphasizing our need for Him. Understanding our weaknesses and turning to Christ for guidance, protection, and provision leads to a blessed and fulfilled life. Accepting our dependence upon God is vital for a successful Christian life—a daily reliance on Him for our significant needs. By trusting in Christ as our Faithful Shepherd, we embrace our true purpose and find contentment.

Dear Father, I am completely dependent on You. I trust You for guidance in every area of my life. Holy Spirit, give me wisdom to follow Your voice as You lead me. In Jesus' name, Amen.

What do you feel when you hear that God wants us to be dependent rather than independent? How does that idea go against our culture?

Day 88

I WILL speak the truth in love.

*Every successful relationship
must be balanced with truth and love.*

We will speak the truth in love, growing in every way more and more like Christ, who is the head of his body, the church (Ephesians 4:15).

Every successful relationship needs a balance of truth and love. Think of truth as the essential ingredient that sets the standard and protects you from moral decay. Love, on the other hand, values and uplifts your heart connection. Truth and love go hand in hand, like inseparable partners. But truth alone can be harsh and unyielding, like a strict boss with no loyal followers. And love alone is like a cheerleader without a team—it lacks definition and strength. Relationships based on truth without love dry up, and relationships based on love without truth blow up. But relationships based on both truth and love grow up. So strive for a balanced relationship. Be direct and honest while also nurturing a deep and compassionate connection. When you embrace truth and love together, your marriage will blossom.

Dear Father, Your Word is the perfect balance of truth and love. Holy Spirit, show me how to ground my marriage in truth and love. In Jesus' name, Amen.

How can you embrace truth and love in your relationship?

I WILL embrace the value of an annual vision retreat.

You can get through any problem.
You have God on your side.

If you need wisdom, ask our generous God, and he will give it to you. He will not rebuke you for asking (James 1:5).

For you to have a successful vision retreat with your spouse, follow these guidelines: (1) Go alone and don't take the kids. (2) Put it on the calendar and plan to spend the money you need for the retreat. (3) Be patient with each other and don't get discouraged. (4) Seek God's will by faith and believe He will speak. (5) Respect the different ways each of you may receive the vision. (6) Make a list of what you will discuss. (7) Write down what you believe God is telling you. If there is something you can't resolve, then to go to a Christian counselor when you return home. To help you have the best retreat possible, Jimmy and Karen Evans have written *Vision Retreat Guidebook*, available at www.XOMarriage.com.

Dear Father, guide us as we prepare to hear from You. Holy Spirit, soften our hearts to hear from You and each other. In Jesus' name, Amen.

Ask your spouse today about planning a vision retreat for your marriage. Try to set a date as soon as possible.

Day 90

I WILL embrace redemptive love in my marriage.

The best choice to make when faced with hurt is to redeem your spouse through righteous, proactive behavior.

"Don't seek revenge or carry a grudge against any of your people. Love your neighbor as yourself. I am GOD" (Leviticus 19:18 MSG).

When your spouse says or does something hurtful, your reaction speaks volumes about your relationship. In that moment, you have choices. You might bottle up your emotions, turn away, or even seek revenge. However, the wisest choice is to be redemptive and seek to restore and heal. That is what God did through Jesus Christ.

Here are four tenets of redemptive love:

1. Even if wronged, avoid sinning. Hostility only escalates the problem.
2. Use loving speech rather than derogatory words.
3. Trust in God's plan. Righteousness will prevail.
4. Show love, even if it is not returned.

This doesn't mean tolerating abuse. For serious harm, seek help. But in typical marital conflicts, demonstrate the selfless love of Christ.

Dear Father, Your love saves and sustains my life. Holy Spirit, help me to show the same kind of love to my spouse each and every day. In Jesus' name, Amen.

How can redemptive love restore even the most broken relationship?

I WILL guard against pride.

When you're walking in pride, the devil is the least
of your worries; you've got God against you.

And he gives grace generously. As the Scriptures say,
"God opposes the proud
but gives grace to the humble" (James 4:6).

Recognize your vulnerabilities; without a doubt, you're capable of faltering without God's grace. Never arrogantly assume you can sidestep guidelines without consequences. Pride often blinds, thinking it can thrive without truly following God. Pride ignores warnings, never admitting its frailty or seeking guidance. It's unaware of the impending doom due to its arrogance. Admit to yourself the risk of stumbling. Surround yourself with God and His faithful followers. Be alert; there's always a lurking danger, especially if you're overconfident. When you're humble, God offers protection and dominion over evil. On the other hand, pride draws God's resistance. With pride, it's not just the devil you should fear but also facing God's opposition, which assures your downfall.

Dear Father, You oppose the proud and reward the humble. Holy Spirit, keep me away from the sins of pride and arrogance. In Jesus' name, Amen.

Who is the most prideful person you know? How has their lack of humility harmed their relationships? When have you given into the sin of pride? What were the results?

Day 92

I WILL regularly practice disciplines and traditions with my spouse.

Disciplines and traditions are crucial in ensuring that your marriage will remain strong for the rest of your lives.

Place me like a seal over your heart,
> like a seal on your arm.
For love is as strong as death (Song of Songs 8:6).

Establishing disciplines and traditions can help you keep a strong marriage. You may think a few special occasions are enough to keep your relationship fresh, but you need regular disciplines or you will likely fall back into old patterns. Consider adopting some of these practices: schedule weekly date nights, pray together, take walks or trips together, have regular face-to-face conversations, plan intimate moments when both of you are well-rested, resolve conflicts before bedtime, read marriage books or attend conferences together, watch romantic comedies together, and find mutual activities to engage in regularly. Prioritizing your relationship with these habits with enthusiasm creates a strong foundation for future generations.

Dear Father, help us to set aside the time to build disciplines and traditions. Holy Spirit, help me always to find joy in spending time with my spouse. In Jesus' name, Amen.

Take time to evaluate the disciplines and traditions you have developed with your spouse. What can you do to improve this area of your relationship?

I WILL seek God's vision for my marriage and family.

It is critical that we have a plan for our future and know what we are trying to accomplish.

Where there is no prophetic vision the people cast off restraint, but blessed is he who keeps the law (Proverbs 29:18 ESV).

Do you have a vision for your marriage and family? If not, it's time to seek God and ask Him for one. Pray and ask God about His plan for your life, marriage, and family. Persist in seeking God until you receive a specific answer or a sense of His guidance. Once you grasp what you believe is God's will, write it down and keep it as your life's mission statement. Without a vision for important aspects like our lives, marriages, families, finances, and ministries, we lack direction. Our behavior will become undisciplined. Living aimlessly for a long time leads to a meaningless life and the failure to pass anything positive onto future generations.

Dear Father, I know that my own vision for my marriage will be faulty if You do not guide it. Holy Spirit, we come to You seeking Your vision for our life together. In Jesus' name, Amen.

Have you specifically asked God to give you a vision for your marriage? If not, begin that discussion with God and your spouse.

Day 94

I WILL practice servanthood in my sexual relationship.

Selfishness and dominance kill sexual intimacy.

For you have been called to live in freedom, my brothers and sisters. But don't use your freedom to satisfy your sinful nature. Instead, use your freedom to serve one another in love (Galatians 5:13).

A servant spirit should characterize your marriage, especially in the bedroom. Ultimate sexual satisfaction comes from both of you having servant hearts. When both partners approach sex with a servant mindset, it becomes a win-win experience. Your focus is not selfish or centered on yourselves, but on ensuring the satisfaction of your spouse. Selfishness and dominance hinder sexual intimacy. If you fail to be a selfless and generous lover, you deprive your spouse of something truly significant. Take time to ask your spouse about their sexual desires and make it your mission to fulfill them unless they go against moral principles or cause harm. Remember, you can only sexually satisfy your spouse if you are willing to serve and make sacrifices.

Dear Father, thank You for sending Your Son to be a servant and to show us how to serve. Holy Spirit, give me the right attitude about sex in my marriage. In Jesus' name, Amen.

Have you ever thought about God's calling to servanthood in your sexual relationship? Why or why not?

I WILL abandon any generational iniquities so they will not affect my family.

We are experiencing the blessings of living as God intended, free from family iniquities.

I acknowledged my sin to you,
>and I did not cover my iniquity;
I said, "I will confess my transgressions to the LORD,"
>and you forgave the iniquity of my sin (Psalm 32:5 ESV).

In the Old Testament, the word "iniquity" means "to bend or twist," which refers to a sin tendency or bent we have because of the negative influence of our parents. As a result, God warned in Deuteronomy 5:9–10 that the iniquities of the fathers could be visited upon the children to the third and fourth generations. Dominant behavior is often learned from parents and generational family systems, which can perpetuate for generations. The solution to the iniquity of dominance is to repent, forgive your family for their part in it, and submit this area of your life to Jesus. You grew up bent because someone was disobedient to God's design. Submit to God's Word and you can be transformed.

Dear Father, I repent of the sins of my parents that I have repeated. Holy Spirit, reveal any iniquities in my life. In Jesus' name, Amen.

What negative behaviors (iniquities) did you pick up from your parents? What are you doing to address those?

Day 96

I WILL learn the difference between good and harmful vows.

Renouncing harmful inner vows can open us up to experience love and intimacy like we've always desired.

Don't make rash promises, and don't be hasty in bringing matters before God (Ecclesiastes 5:2).

You and your spouse made vows when you were married. Did you know that you probably made "inner vows" earlier in life? Unlike your marriage vows, these inner vows can sometimes be painful and harmful. For example, an inner vow to never be hurt by a friend can make you distant and detached. Inner vows can be promises of future pain for you, potentially affecting generations. The remedy is to recognize and renounce them. Healing your marriage comes when you admit to your spouse that you're influenced by an inner vow and are breaking it. You may have been unapproachable and irrational in an area affected by the inner vow. Now, however, you are asking for accountability. Welcome loving honesty from your spouse without retaliation.

Dear Father, help me to see the harmful inner vows I have made. Holy Spirit, I renounce them and open myself to Your healing. In Jesus' name, Amen.

What inner vows have you made in your life? Why did you make them? What would your marriage be like if you were free from harmful inner vows?

I WILL renounce any inner vows I have made so they will not become a barrier to the health of my marriage.

It is common for people to have many operative inner vows controlling their lives without even realizing it.

The tongue can bring death or life;
those who love to talk will reap the consequences (Proverbs 18:21).

S imilar to iniquities, inner vows bend us in the wrong direction, and they are self-vows we make to ourselves, typically in response to pain. You might have made a vow to never let anyone hurt you again or to never be poor again. These vows silently guide and control our lives without us realizing it. Inner vows are our highest loyalties, and they take Jesus out His position as Lord in that area of our lives. They make us unteachable and unapproachable, leading us to become imbalanced and controlling in our relationships. To break inner vows, you must repent of them and ask the Lord to heal your pain and lead you out of it. Don't let your inner vows control your life and your marriage.

Dear Father, I renounce and repent of any inner vows I have made. Holy Spirit, guide me so my first loyalties are to You and my spouse. In Jesus' name, Amen.

Have you made any inner vows because of hurt you experienced in your past? Are you ready to repent and renounce them?

Day 98

I WILL choose faith over fear in our marriage.

God invites us to trust Him, and allow Him to be all the security we need.

GOD met me more than halfway,
he freed me from my anxious fears (Psalm 34:4 MSG).

Every driven person has two deep-seated fears. First is the fear of failure. Second is the fear that even if you succeed, it won't be what you desired. Being driven is often rooted in fear, insecurity, and doubt. Driven people try to control every situation to counter their fears. Control can shatter relationships and lead families into turmoil. The devil uses fear to wreck families and shatter marriages. But faith is trusting God's will no matter the situation, that He will make everything right. It means knowing you don't need to react in fear or insecurity. Faith is recognizing you don't need to control everything because God has it handled.

Dear Father, I confess that at times I am driven by fear. Help me not to react in fear and insecurity, but rather to respond in faith and love so that intimacy can flourish in our marriage. In Jesus' name, Amen.

Do you find yourself driven to control situations out of fear? What do you think are your core fears? What does a faith-filled response say to those fears?

I WILL make my marriage the core of our blended family.

Regardless of what came first, marriage must be the center of the family.

For this reason, a man will leave his father and mother and be united to his wife, and the two will become one flesh (Ephesians 5:31 NIV).

A strong blended family requires intentional effort and unwavering commitment. Next to serving God, the best thing you can do for your blended family is to make your marriage the foundation. Like the nucleus of an atom, the relationship you have with your spouse brings stability, purpose, and direction to the whole family. So carve out quality time for your spouse and make communication and intimacy a priority. Seek wisdom from God's Word and involve Him in every decision. Remember, when God holds His rightful place in your marriage, His grace permeates every aspect of your family life. As you align with God's design, your family experiences genuine happiness and fulfillment. Regardless of how your family was formed, God desires healing and restoration for every person.

Dear Father, thank You for blessing me with an incredible blended family. Holy Spirit, remind me that when I follow God's order for relationship, my life is infinitely better. In Jesus' name, Amen.

What do you need to do to make your marriage the core of your blended family?

Day 100

I WILL make our home a fun place to be while upholding God's standards.

A successful family is a playground with a fence around it.

> Praise the LORD!
> How joyful are those who fear the LORD
>   and delight in obeying his commands (Psalm 112:1).

Your family is a playground surrounded by a protective fence. Your family should be a place of warmth, welcome, and fun, where everyone enjoys God and each other. Through intentional activities and prioritized relationships, your home becomes a sanctuary of joy and support—a true playground. To safeguard your family in their pursuits outside of the home, you need clear rules and parameters. These boundaries protect and maintain a safe atmosphere. Without grace, a family becomes a fence without a playground—imprisoning and lifeless. Without truth, it becomes a playground without a fence—chaotic and susceptible to tragedy. A successful family finds balance in grace and truth, guided by rules and nurturing relationships.

Dear Father, You created us to have joy within the boundaries of Your commands. Holy Spirit, help me to make home a fun and enjoyable place to be with a focus on serving You. In Jesus' name, Amen.

How would you describe your childhood home? Was it a joyful place to be? Was it a difficult place to be? How do you want your home to be the same or different?

I WILL recognize my spouse and I both need each other.

We must never give up in our search for harmony in marriage.

If one member suffers, all suffer together; if one member is honored, all rejoice together (1 Corinthians 12:26 ESV).

Both men and women are essential for human life and to reflect God's complete design for humanity. Men and women have unique abilities, perspectives, traits, and sensitivities given by God. When mutual respect of these gifts happens according to God's plan, both men and women are blessed. The ongoing "battle of the sexes" stems from long-standing frustrations and tensions. Misunderstandings, abuse, and rejection have caused many people to guard themselves against the opposite sex or even reject them entirely. Despite any tension or frustration, we must recognize our need for one another. Embracing our God-given differences while complementing each other in interdependence is crucial for our emotional wellbeing. The success of marriages hinges on trusting our spouses.

Dear Father, lead me to have a healthy dependence on my spouse. Holy Spirit, help me to be a reliable source of support for my spouse. In Jesus' name, Amen.

When you hear that spouses should depend on each other, how does that go against other messages you are hearing in today's culture? How would you respond to someone who believes spouses should be completely independent?

Day 102

I WILL not allow the enemy to manipulate my emotions.

The devil loves photographic thinking.
He loves to show up in the worst moments
of our marriages and take a picture of them.

Better to be patient than powerful;
better to have self-control than to conquer a city (Proverbs 16:32).

Have you ever found yourself reacting to your emotions in your marriage? It's a mistake because the devil loves to use them to convince us that things will never change and that we must find happiness elsewhere. Even if we give in to our emotions and seek someone else, the devil will follow us and heap on the regret until we are as miserable as before. Instead, we must be people of conviction and not let our emotions control us. Feelings are fickle and unpredictable. God blesses obedience, not emotions. Doing the right thing only happens for those who are guided by their love for God, dedication to each other, and conviction that doing the right thing will be blessed in the end.

Dear Father, I want to be guided by You rather than my emotions. Holy Spirit, help me to listen to Your voice as I resist the devil. In Jesus' name, Amen.

What can you do when your emotions begin to overwhelm you while you are making decisions?

I WILL rise above discouragement.

Discouragement is not a condition; it is a choice.

David found strength in the Lord his God. (1 Samuel 30:6)

The devil uses discouragement as a weapon, aiming to divert us from God's plan with thoughts like, *I can't do this* or *Things will never get better.* Even King David, the brave shepherd boy and conquering warrior-king, faced moments of deep discouragement. One day, he and his army came back home to discover their city burned to the ground and their wives and children captured. To make matters even worse, the men were so upset that they talked about stoning David. But in this dire moment when nothing was going right, this leader chose not to let discouragement consume him. Instead, he turned to his one constant Source of comfort. You, too, can make this choice. You can choose to rise above the chaos and fix your eyes on the Prince of Peace who is always with you.

Dear Father, when the enemy tries to weigh me down with discouragement, I will trust in Your infinite goodness. Holy Spirit, remind me to lift up my eyes to see where my true help comes from. In Jesus' name, Amen.

What source of discouragement in your life do you need to surrender to the Lord?

Day 104

I WILL discover my spouse's needs and work to meet them.

On an ideal day in any marriage,
both spouses should have their needs met.

Always be humble and gentle. Be patient with each other, making allowance for each other's faults because of your love (Ephesians 4:2).

Romance is necessary for both men and women, and it meets their basic marital needs differently. Women need security, open communication, nonsexual affection, and leadership from their husbands. Meanwhile, men need respect, sexual intimacy, friendship, and domestic support from their wives. To keep romance alive in your marriage, you must honor and accept each other's differences and strive to meet each other's needs. Successful romance happens when you understand and pursue your spouse's needs in their language and according to their needs, not your own. By becoming emotionally bilingual and speaking love in each other's language, you can experience a fulfilling and satisfying marriage.

Dear Father, I want my spouse to know my love from how I show my love. Holy Spirit, keep me attuned and responsive to my spouse's needs. Help me to be honest about my own needs. In Jesus' name, Amen.

Have you asked your spouse what needs they have that are not being fulfilled? Have you expressed your needs?

I WILL embrace love over comparison.

Comparison can cause us to do things that keep us from being the people God wants us to be.

For am I now seeking the approval of man, or of God? Or am I trying to please man? If I were still trying to please man, I would not be a servant of Christ (Galatians 1:10 ESV).

Comparison can take two forms—healthy and helpful or unhealthy and dangerous. Healthy comparison happens when you learn from the examples of others and implement positive changes in your own life. However, unhealthy comparison involves jealousy and negativity, leading you to doubt God, yourself, and others. This second type of comparison hinders you from becoming the individual God created you to be. Jesus' disciples had an intense rivalry that stemmed from insecurity and led to unhealthy comparisons. But Jesus emphasized that loving God comes before loving people. Love was the foundation of His ministry. In marriage, you must prioritize loving God above comparing your relationship to others. Comparison robs you of joy and purpose, but genuine love brings contentment and unity.

Dear Father, Your love is perfect. Holy Spirit, protect my mind against the pull of comparison. In Jesus' name, Amen.

How has unhealthy comparison hurt you in the past? How will love bless you in the future?

Day 106

I WILL keep grace and truth balanced in my marriage.

Grace and truth are inseparable partners.

And the Word became flesh and dwelt among us, and we beheld His glory, the glory as of the only begotten of the Father, full of grace and truth (John 1:14 NKJV).

Jesus is the expressed image of God. God also created you in His image, characterized by "grace and truth" (see Genesis 1:27). Being Christlike means embodying both grace and truth. A lack of grace or a rejection of truth is not Christlike. Healthy and successful relationships reflect God's imprint through the balanced operation of grace and truth. Regardless of your upbringing, God's Word is what defines Him. He is a perfect blend of grace and truth. To have a thriving marriage, you must examine your own personality for balance. As a spouse or parent, your ability to build healthy connections relies on maintaining a balance of grace and truth. Acknowledge and overcome any natural imbalances you may have.

Dear Father, I never want to be legalistic, but I do want to uphold the standards found in Your Word. Holy Spirit, teach me to balance grace and truth according to Your Word. In Jesus' name, Amen.

Can you think of examples of grace or truth being out of balance with each other? What were the results?

I WILL keep technology intrusions in my marriage to a minimum.

Make technology your servant and not your master.

Look straight ahead,
and fix your eyes on what lies before you (Proverbs 4:25).

Do you ever feel overwhelmed by the constant barrage of technology intruding into your life and relationships? You're not alone. The digital world, with its endless calls, texts, emails, and notifications, can often feel invasive. Remember those moments when you've had to pause a conversation because of an incoming call? Such interruptions can lead to feelings of frustration and rejection in marriages, making your partner feel sidelined. It's basic manners not to let a gadget disrupt your cherished moments. Let technology serve you, not dominate you. Remind yourself that it's okay to disconnect. Consider a "technology time-out" or an "electronic Sabbath." While staying connected is valuable, there are moments when you should prioritize real-life interactions. If your spouse complains about your technology use, they have probably waited a long time before mentioning it.

Dear Father, I never want my spouse to feel unwanted or ignored because of my habits with technology. Holy Spirit, help me to be attentive and aware about my habits with technology. In Jesus' name, Amen.

Has your spouse ever complained about your use of technology? How did you respond? How will you respond in the future?

Day 108

I WILL bring my fear into the light.

*Jesus literally took hell upon Himself
so we could have heaven.*

"I am the light of the world. Whoever follows me will not walk in darkness, but will have the light of life" (John 8:12 ESV).

Fear feeds on the darkness because it's the realm of the enemy. But fear loses its grip when exposed to light. Jesus is the light of the world, and when you bring your fears to Him, He heals and empowers you. Jesus is not frustrated or annoyed by fear. He understands what you are going through because He experienced fear too. In fact, Jesus experienced so much fear in the Garden of Gethsemane that He began to sweat drops of blood. Still, He overcame fear, and you can too. The key is to bring your fear into the light. Talk to the Lord, and talk to wise counsel (your spouse, close friends, or a trusted pastor). When you and your spouse face your fears together, you grow, both as healthy individuals and as a united, immoveable team.

Dear Father, I believe You did not design me to live in darkness. Holy Spirit, give me the courage to bring my fears into the light. In Jesus' name, Amen.

Why does bringing fear into the light make it lose its power?

I WILL address issues that cause me to be angry as soon as possible.

Today's anger is manageable.
Yesterday's anger is the problem.

And "don't sin by letting anger control you." Don't let the sun go down while you are still angry (Ephesians 4:26).

You may have heard someone say, "Don't go to bed angry." That person was paraphrasing the apostle Paul. Dealing with an issue that causes you to be angry today is a lot easier than waiting until tomorrow. Left unresolved, issues often get worse. One of the key disciplines in any marriage is to stay current with your issues and not let them accumulate. Make a commitment not to carry anger for many days. If you can't resolve an issue on your own, seek counseling until it is resolved. Constantly ending the day angry will change your thoughts and feelings toward your spouse—and not for the better. If you hold onto unresolved anger, it can take a negative toll on your relationship.

Dear Father, I don't want to be an angry person. Holy Spirit, help me to resolve any issues I have with my spouse as soon as possible. In Jesus' name, Amen.

Is there an issue that has made you angry and you continue to hold onto it? Decide to address and resolve that issue as soon as possible.

Day 110

I WILL honor our marriage as created by God.

Your marriage is about you, your spouse, and God.

The Lord God said, "It is not good for the man to be alone. I will make a helper suitable for him" (Genesis 2:18 NIV).

God made Adam and Eve for each other. Each had the qualities that the other needed to meet each other's needs and fulfill God's plan. This shows us that marriage is more than just two people falling in love. It is also about being bound together for a larger story. On your wedding day, God was present supernaturally binding you together. He is still with you, guiding your marriage into the purposes and plans He has for you. God brought you together. Take this opportunity to thank Him for His presence and help. Ask Him to help you see His eternal purposes in your story.

Dear Father, thank You for bringing my spouse and me together. Help me to see my spouse as the partner You created for me, and me for them. Help us both to remember that our story is part of Your larger story. In Jesus' name, Amen.

Why do you think God brought you and your spouse together? How does knowing that your story is part of God's larger story give you courage and strength?

I WILL be mindful of how my actions impact the generations that will follow us.

Our behavior today affects the next generation.

"I hold parents responsible for any sins they pass on to their children to the third, and yes, even to the fourth generation" (Deuteronomy 5:9 MSG).

Picture yourself in the Garden, just after eating from the Tree of Knowledge. Are you aware of the repercussions? This act, driven by the urge for immediate gratification, brought consequences for many generations. You might think your actions today are isolated, but remember: every choice impacts the future, especially for the next generation. Consider this: how will your decisions shape tomorrow's world? Deuteronomy 5:9 warns of sins impacting multiple generations. Your values, habits, and priorities leave an imprint on your descendants. Cherish and guide your children. While you're not perfect, God wants your commitment and sincerity. He supports and forgives, but it's up to you to responsibly shape the future.

Dear Father, all throughout the Bible You are committed to families and have directed Your people to be mindful of future generations. Holy Spirit, give me wisdom and strength and help me to lay the right foundation for those who follow me. In Jesus' name, Amen.

Discuss with your spouse the kind of legacy you want to leave to your children and the generations who follow after them.

Day 112

I WILL seek God's wisdom in all our financial decisions.

We never make a decision until both of us are in agreement and have peace about it.

"Seek the Kingdom of God above all else, and live righteously, and he will give you everything you need" (Matthew 6:33).

You should never make a financial decision until both of you agree and have peace about it. Submit your finances to God and always agree before acting. This will bring peace into your relationship. Colossians 3:15 says, "Let the peace that comes from Christ rule in your hearts. For as members of one body you are called to live in peace. And always be thankful." God's peace is an important way He guides us. When you face financial decisions that aren't a matter of right and wrong, but right and right, pray about it together. Without praying, anxiety will cause problems in your relationship. Surrender your financial decisions to God, pray together, and see the tangible results of being led by Him.

Dear Father, we want to seek Your will in all our decisions, including our finances. Holy Spirit, speak to us about how we use money for Your glory. In Jesus' name, Amen.

Have you asked God about how to manage your money before now? How did He speak to you?

I WILL seek unity of vision for our sex life.

It is very helpful to talk about sex openly when you aren't in bed.

How good and pleasant it is
when God's people live together in unity! (Psalm 133:1 NIV).

Married couples should prioritize annual vision retreats. One area that deserves your attention is your shared sex life. You should engage in prayer and seek a vision for this aspect of your relationship. It can be immensely beneficial to have open conversations about sex outside of the bedroom. Take the time to have in-depth discussions about your desires, preferences, and any concerns you may have. This may be the first time you've engaged in such conversations, but it holds great importance. By sharing your sexual desires and dislikes with one another, you can create a plan that focuses on pleasing both of you. Write it down and commit to following it. You will appreciate the positive impact of discussing these matters.

Dear Father, we want to be unified as a couple about our sex life. Holy Spirit, help us to listen to You and each other as we discuss this important issue. In Jesus' name, Amen.

Have you ever had a serious discussion with your spouse about your sex life? Plan today to be open in your communication going forward.

Day 114

I WILL provide a climate for total openness with my spouse.

There is no such thing as "private sin."

But now you must be holy in everything you do, just as God who chose you is holy. For the Scriptures say, "You must be holy because I am holy" (1 Peter 1:15–16).

Purity is for both spouses. Men must remember that purity isn't only important for women and children. Both spouses must be cautious about what they allow into their lives. Marriage is a special bond between a man and a woman, and everything you think, say, or do has an impact on your partner and the spirit of your relationship. You may have thought your bad behavior or sins aren't affecting your spouse, but that is simply not true. Harboring sin in your life will inevitably affect your spouse. It's vital to understand that your spouse has every right to be concerned about every aspect of your life, since anything you do will affect them.

Dear Father, I realize that when I sin, I do not sin alone. Holy Spirit, make me aware of the pain I cause my spouse when I sin against them. In Jesus' name, Amen.

Have you ever done something wrong and thought you were only hurting yourself? How did you come to realize others were hurt by your actions?

I WILL prioritize my marriage higher than anything except God.

God designed marriage to operate as the most important human relationship in our lives. It is only second in priority to our relationship with Him.

Therefore a man shall leave his father and mother and be joined to his wife, and they shall become one flesh (Genesis 2:24 NKJV).

God's first words on marriage, spoken after creating Eve and presenting her to Adam, established His standard for all marriages. The Law of Priority means that a spouse must take precedence over everything and everyone else, except for God. Prioritize your spouse before children, jobs, hobbies, friends, parents, or family members. If you neglect this priority, it will likely cause problems in your marriage. You have formed a unique covenant with your spouse that cannot be made with anyone else. So honor and love your parents, friends, and family, but never do those things at the expense of neglecting your spouse.

Dear Father, help me to keep my priorities in the right order. Holy Spirit, reveal any place in my life where my priorities are out of sync with Yours. In Jesus' name, Amen.

What is one action you can take today to show your spouse they are your top priority?

Day 116

I WILL (as a wife) believe what God says about my value.

According to God's Word, He thinks so much of you that He sent His only Son to die for you on the cross.

So do not throw away this confident trust in the Lord. Remember the great reward it brings you! (Hebrews 10:35).

For a woman with low self-esteem, the solution is to stop believing negative opinions from others, self-criticism, and the mirror's reflection. Instead, embrace what God's Word says about you. He valued you so much that He sent His Son to die for you. As a child of God, you are destined for a righteous and godly partner. However, this does not mean divorce is justified if your husband isn't perfect. No one is perfect; we all make mistakes, and we all need to grow more and more like Jesus Christ. Trust in God's Word for yourself and your family. Refuse to accept anything that does not align with God's Word. While your family may balk at any changes, over time they will learn to appreciate your loving boundaries.

Dear Father, You say I am worthy of love, and I choose to believe You. Holy Spirit, show me any part of my life where I have not believed in my God-given value. In Jesus' name, Amen.

What does God's Word say about your value?

I WILL pursue God's purpose for our marriage.

*The sacred union of marriage showcases
Christ's love for the church.*

And this is why a man leaves father and mother and cherishes his wife. No longer two, they become "one flesh" (Ephesians 5:32 MSG).

Marriage is a reflection of Christ's dedication to the Church. Your bond with your spouse is meant to mirror your bond with Christ. Marriage offers a peek into God's promise to humanity. Jesus gave Himself up for your sins. His side was pierced, and His blood shed, all to connect with you. Similarly, think of Adam: his side was pierced and blood flowed, to bond with Eve. Marriage pulls you into God's intimate embrace. It lets you engage deeply, even super-naturally, with God's divine essence. Through the sacrificial love and devotion that a husband and wife have for one another, marriage showcases God's glory. Through it, God declares His unwavering promise for everyone to witness. This is the essence of marriage. If you're married, this is the reason behind your union.

Dear Father, thank You that in marriage You have given me a picture of Jesus' relationship to us. Help us to pursue Your purposes for our marriage. In Jesus' name, Amen.

What is one way today that you can act out the love of Jesus to your spouse?

Day 118

I WILL create a place for emotional intimacy and purity in my home.

God wants us to be able to share and express our feelings like little children without being rejected or embarrassed.

Blessed are the pure in heart,
for they will see God. (Matthew 5:8 NIV).

God designed marriage for couples to be completely naked with each other without fear or shame. It is just as important to be emotionally naked as it is to be physically naked. God wants you to share openly with your spouse, expressing your feelings like a child without fear of rejection or embarrassment. In marriage, God also wants you to be spiritually naked, intimately praying and worshipping together. Seek God's will for your life and marriage. Go to Him daily for forgiveness and guidance. Each day, be honest, accountable, and forgiving toward each other. By respecting God's Law of Purity, you will witness a significant difference in the atmosphere and pleasure of your relationship.

Dear Father, I want to build intimacy with You and my spouse. Holy Spirit, show me how I can be honest and transparent with my spouse in every way. In Jesus' name, Amen.

What does emotional nakedness mean to you? What steps will you take to increase emotional intimacy with your spouse?

I WILL cultivate the heart of Jesus in my home.

*We need to be careful about how
we talk about and treat people.*

"And the King will say, 'I tell you the truth, when you did it to one of the least of these my brothers and sisters, you were doing it to me!'" (Matthew 25:40).

Be mindful of the ways you talk about and treat people outside your home. Your family members learn from you, absorbing qualities like being unmerciful, judgmental, prejudiced, and bigoted. However, they can also learn to be compassionate, kind, helpful, and considerate. It's essential to examine your attitudes toward others and make them align with the compassionate heart of Jesus. Even more, you must demonstrate love and kindness to people of all backgrounds. If they are lost, pray for them and share your faith. If they are in need, offer assistance. Regardless of their flaws or attitudes, you must be cautious in your treatment of others because you bear a responsibility for them.

Dear Father, I believe You love all people. Holy Spirit, guard my tongue and show me how I can minister to others. In Jesus' name, Amen.

Do you have a habit of speaking negatively about others? Are you willing to let the Holy Spirit change the way you communicate about other people?

Day 120

I WILL not allow the fear of rejection
to control my life.

*Two thousand years ago, God rejected His Son once and
for all so that He will never reject us again in eternity.*

He was despised, and we did not esteem Him (Isaiah 53:3 NKJV).

No one likes to be rejected, and the fear of being rejected by your spouse can make intimacy very scary. Rejection can make you feel isolated or alone, but you can take comfort in knowing that Jesus—God the Son Himself—was rejected too. In fact, from his birth to his death, Jesus was the most rejected human being in the history of the world. Still, He never allowed rejection to keep Him from fulfilling His purpose, even unto dying on the cross for our sins. The Father rejected His own Son so that we could be accepted as children of God forever. Fear never held Jesus back from doing the right thing. Imagine if you could approach your marriage relationship with that kind of courage.

Dear Father, I want to be more like Jesus every day. Holy Spirit, help me to be courageous even in the face of rejection. In Jesus' name, Amen.

How does knowing that Jesus was rejected for you affect your self-worth? When others reject you, how does knowing God accepts you make you feel?

I WILL refuse to make divorce an option.

There is great strength and security brought into a marriage when two people refuse to give up.

But for those who are married, I have a command that comes not from me, but from the Lord. A wife must not leave her husband.... And the husband must not leave his wife (1 Corinthians 7:10–11).

One of the most unsettling aspects of divorce is the shattered pledge of "for better or for worse ... till death do us part." This lifelong commitment, once a security blanket, seems less certain today with many people marrying without total dedication. Commitment, especially in tough times, and learning from failures are fundamental to a robust marriage. You should never forget that weathering the hard times of marriage yields the joy of fulfilling promises. A strong marriage is not a fairy tale; it's the result of two people's unwavering commitment to making the relationship succeed. Participation in marriage isn't enough; complete commitment is needed. This firm foundation ensures stability and success in your marriage.

Dear Father, I believe You designed marriage to last a lifetime. Holy Spirit, fill me with courage, patience, and hope to get through the difficult times. In Jesus' name, Amen.

How does taking divorce off the table change the way you approach disagreements and tense moments?

Day 122

I WILL not allow the devil to use my anger.

*Since the Garden of Eden, the devil and his minions
have been on an all-out campaign to destroy
the institution of marriage.*

Anger gives a foothold to the devil (Ephesians 4:27).

When you go to bed with anger, you give an opening for the devil to slander your spouse to you. The enemy operates stealthily and introduces troubling thoughts while you are consumed by anger toward your spouse. The devil despises your marriage. Demonic forces wait patiently for each of you to take anger to bed. Then Satan implants slanderous thoughts about your spouse in your mind. You awake the next morning oblivious to what just transpired. You have unwittingly received counsel from the enemy, yet you believe you've gained new insight about your spouse, and you try to impose those thoughts on them. You're convinced that you are right and if your spouse will only comply, all your problems will vanish. In reality, you're trying to make your spouse align with devilish ideas.

Dear Father, I don't want the devil to have any place in my life. Holy Spirit, teach me to close the door to the devil. In Jesus' name, Amen.

Have you ever let the devil slander your spouse or someone else to you? What kinds of thoughts did you have?

I WILL repent for not showing love to my spouse the way I once did.

We must turn around and think like we did at the beginning.

"Turn back to me and do the works you did at first" (Revelation 2:5).

If you find that you are losing the love you once had for your spouse, it's a sign to change your direction or actions. Repent and return to the mindset you had at the beginning. When Jesus instructs us to repent, He means we should recall the fervent actions and right attitudes we displayed at the start of the relationship. Evaluate your current behavior and attitudes and adjust them to align with those at the beginning. Real repentance involves acknowledging the truth, admitting your mistakes, and taking corrective action. If you feel that your love for your spouse is dwindling, then reflect on your actions and attitudes. Identify where you may be off course from the initial path and take steps to correct it. Only then can you rekindle the love you once had.

Dear Father, I repent to You and my spouse for not showing them love like I once did. Holy Spirit, keep convicting me about how I should love my spouse. In Jesus' name, Amen.

Do you need to repent to your spouse because you do not show love like you once did?

Day 124

I WILL ask God to let me see my spouse as He does.

God takes our small human efforts and turns them into supernatural blessings.

See how very much our Father loves us, for he calls us his children, and that is what we are! (1 John 3:1).

Go desires for you to see your partner with a renewed vision, seeing them as He does: created in His image and fashioned for a divine purpose. They are intricately designed to fulfill your core needs and desires. Your union is a magnificent gift from God. When you adopt this perspective, transformation occurs. You begin to treat your partner with deeper love, respect, and empathy. Patience, kindness, and forgiveness flourish, as you focus on their virtues rather than their flaws. Memories of your initial passion rekindle. As you embrace God's vision for your marriage, He will elevate your bond, revealing grander purposes and blessing your lives, unfolding His deeper vision for bringing the two of you together.

Dear Father, You have given me a spouse over whom You delight. Forgive me for when I have only seen faults. Help me to see my spouse as You do. In Jesus' name, Amen.

How would you describe to someone the ways in which God made your spouse to bless the world? In what ways can you honor that gift today?

I WILL express mutual concern and care to my spouse.

With every area of our hearts and lives, we must communicate daily to our spouses the fact that we care about them.

For this is the message that you have heard from the beginning, that we should love one another (1 John 3:11 ESV).

Effective communication in your marriage requires genuine care and concern for your spouse. This begins with recognizing their value and regularly expressing their importance. Your overall behavior serves as a testament to your affection. Consider these seven daily aspects to show your love:

1. Eye contact
2. Affectionate body language
3. Pleasant countenance
4. Soft voice level and tone
5. Frequent contact and emotional connection
6. Service-oriented attitude
7. Sensitivity to their needs, hurts, and desires

When consistently and positively displayed, these will make your spouse feel cared for and open lines of communication. When they are absent, it can imply a lack of empathy and hinder communication.

Dear Father, You demonstrated Your incredible love for me by sending Your Son to save me from my sins. Holy Spirit, reveal to me the best way to show love to my spouse. In Jesus' name, Amen.

What expressions of love does your spouse respond to the most?

I WILL give to the Lord's work according to His Word and will.

God will pass your test.

Bring all the tithes into the storehouse so there will be enough food in my Temple. "If you do," says the LORD of Heaven's Armies, "I will open the windows of heaven for you. I will pour out a blessing so great you won't have enough room to take it in! Try it! Put me to the test!" (Malachi 3:10).

G iving the first of your finances to the Lord is essential. Giving is not a new concept; it started long before the Old Testament Law was established. In Genesis 4, Abel brought his best offering to the Lord and was blessed, but Cain refused to bring his best and was not blessed. However, giving will invoke God's blessing on your marriage and finances. Even if only one of you wants to give, let them give and trust God to bless you both. According to Malachi 3:10, giving is the only area where we are allowed to test God, so give with faith and trust that God will honor His Word.

Dear Father, we want to obey Your Word. Holy Spirit, reveal to us Your plan for our giving. In Jesus' name, Amen.

Ask God how much He wants you to give to support His work.

I WILL speak with kindness to my spouse.

Kindness means you respect the high value and emotions of the person to whom you're speaking.

When she speaks, her words are wise,
and she gives instructions with kindness (Proverbs 31:26).

Kindness is a vital ingredient for a thriving marriage. When your spouse unintentionally hurts you, it's easy to respond in anger and be hurtful in return. However, belittling and demeaning words and actions contradict the spirit of kindness. Recognizing the value of your spouse, both in God's eyes and in your own, helps you control your emotions. Learn to choose your words carefully, monitor your tone, and show compassion in your expressions. Yelling, crude gestures, and hateful expressions have no place in a kind relationship. It is an ongoing commitment to speak words of encouragement, blessing, healing, affection, and kindness. Create a safe space where your spouse can express their feelings without fear.

Dear Father, Your Word says that kindness is a part of the fruit of the Spirit. I want to honor You and my spouse with every word that comes out of my mouth. Holy Spirit, guide me as I choose to speak with kindness every day. In Jesus' name, Amen.

How can you demonstrate that you value your spouse by the kind words you speak?

Day 128

I WILL not allow my parents to intrude in my marriage.

You must protect your spouse from your parents if they are intruding upon your marriage, exerting undue control, or disrespecting your spouse.

... and the two are united into one (Genesis 2:24).

Dealing with family and in-law issues can be challenging, especially with problem in-laws. They often neglect or disregard their own marriages and continue seeking emotional connections with their child after the child marries. This leads to resentment toward their child's spouse. The only person who can change this dynamic is the biological spouse. Closing the door is impossible if they keep opening it. Defend your marriage by standing up to your intruding parent. Lack of boundaries or the refusal to defend them is the main issue. Remember, you're not the answer to your parents' significant emotional voids. Encourage them to work on their marriage, start a hobby, make friends, or see a counselor. You must stop them from trying to force you back into the center of their universe.

Dear Father, I want to address problems before resentment builds. Holy Spirit, give me wisdom and courage to address anyone who tries to interfere in my marriage. In Jesus' name, Amen.

What can you do to resolve complicated relationships with family members, including your parents?

I WILL (as a husband) guard against greed as I provide for my family.

Some men work a lot or play a lot because of greed.

But people who long to be rich fall into temptation and are trapped by many foolish and harmful desires that plunge them into ruin and destruction (1 Timothy 6:9).

You may find yourself working excessively or indulging in excessive leisure activities due to greed. While you may believe that you're doing it for your family's benefit, the truth is that you should prioritize giving them your presence and time. Money or material possessions won't solve your problems if they come at the cost of neglecting your loved ones. Deep down, the motivation for overworking or indulging in excess rest is personal gratification and material rewards. When your wife urges you to slow down and spend more time at home, don't make excuses claiming it's all for her. It's actually greed that drives you. Similarly, some men prioritize excessive leisure activities. The only solution to greed is to repent. Turn your heart back to God and your family.

Dear Father, I want to serve my family as I serve You. Holy Spirit, keep my heart from greed. In Jesus' name, Amen.

Have material possessions or other activities taken precedence over your family? What can you do to realign your priorities?

Day 130

I WILL speak kindly and positively to my spouse, even in the middle of conflict.

Not only is talking negatively extremely damaging for spouses, but it is also very harmful to the children.

"My people will live in peaceful dwelling places,
   in secure homes,
   in undisturbed places of rest" (Isaiah 32:18 NIV).

Some couples live in homes where cursing, name-calling, and verbal intimidation are commonplace. Hurtful words do not have a place in a loving marriage. Verbal abuse is a dangerous habit. Between some spouses fights escalate into screaming, cursing, and belittling each other. In some cases, it may even escalate to physical abuse. Such toxic communication not only damages the relationship between spouses but also has a detrimental effect on children who witness their parents speaking negatively to each other. Parents have a crucial role in teaching proper communication and conflict resolution to their children. The prevalence of youth violence often stems from the hostility they experience at home. Don't give it a place in your home.

Dear Father, I want to be loving and kind to my spouse even in the middle of conflict. Holy Spirit, help me to always exhibit Your fruit as I interact with my spouse. In Jesus' name, Amen.

How was conflict handled in your home growing up? What habits did you need to break in your own home?

I WILL submit to God's Word regarding my marriage.

We are called to live according to our faith,
regardless of our circumstances.

Joyful are people of integrity,
who follow the instructions of the LORD (Psalm 119:1).

In Ephesians 5, Paul reveals the divine model for marriage: sacrificial love and submission. There isn't a disclaimer in that passage. God doesn't tell the wife to submit to her husband only when he deserves it. Nor does He say for the husband to be loving and sacrificial only after receiving respect. Your Christian journey isn't about reacting based on others' actions. It's about acting according to Scripture, no matter how you're treated. As a Christian, you strive to emulate Christ: turning the other cheek when wronged, treating others as you wish to be treated, and prioritizing their needs over yours. Your actions should reflect your faith, independent of others' choices or circumstances.

Dear Father, sometimes I only want to submit or sacrificially love when I feel like my spouse deserves it. I realize that is not the way of Jesus. Please forgive me and help me to emulate Christ in my marriage. In Jesus' name, Amen.

When is it most difficult for you to submit or love sacrificially? Consider when you are unworthy of Christ's love; how does He respond to you?

If you decided to treat your wife to three of her favorite things, would you know what they were? Watch her closely to see if you can spot a way you can tend to her needs.

Day 132

I WILL be one with my spouse.

Once you are married, you are no longer two but one.

The husband should fulfill his wife's sexual needs, and the wife should fulfill her husband's needs. The wife gives authority over her body to her husband, and the husband gives authority over his body to his wife (1 Corinthians 7:3–4).

When God instituted marriage, He made it so that two entities merge as one. This isn't just about the exclusive intimacy of marriage. It's deeper. You should both share everything and own nothing separately. Paul's words in 1 Corinthians show the depth of connection God intends through marriage. When you unite in marriage, you concede rights over your body to each other. This isn't a means for misuse but rather a mutual assurance. By God's design, withholding is not an option—you must give wholly to one another. To truly become one, both of you must surrender individual rights for mutual benefit. It's a union where individualism fades and unity thrives; where two become one in heart, home, and spirit.

Dear Father, Your purpose for marriage is to be the deepest human connection we have. Holy Spirit, help me to give all of myself to my spouse, holding nothing back. In Jesus' name, Amen.

What parts of yourself have been withholding from your spouse? What was your reason for doing so?

I WILL expect the enemy to attack, but I trust that God is stronger.

When God has done something wonderful in our lives, you know the devil will do whatever he can to spoil it.

"The thief comes only to steal and kill and destroy; I have come that they may have life, and have it to the full" (John 10:10 NIV).

When God grants you a blessing or a joyful moment, you should be aware that the devil will always look for ways to sabotage it. As highlighted in 1 Peter 5, it's crucial to remain vigilant and on guard against Satan's crafty plans, especially when it concerns something as sacred as your marriage. Understand that the very reason Satan targets marriage is because of its immense value in God's eyes. When the enemy comes against you, you can draw strength from a profound truth: the One residing within you is infinitely more powerful than any adversarial force in the world. You can trust God's strength and assurance.

Dear Father, I trust that You are infinitely stronger than the enemy. Holy Spirit, remind me to stand guard against any attacks on my marriage and help me to find strength in my relationship with the Lord. In Jesus' name, Amen.

What power does the Bible promise to those who love God and obey Him?

Day 134

I WILL manage stress in a healthy way.

To succeed in marriage, you simply must keep the stress in your life and household to a manageable level.

I am leaving you with a gift—peace of mind and heart. And the peace I give is a gift the world cannot give. (John 14:27).

In this fast-paced world, stress-related illnesses are prevalent, and financial problems and overburdened schedules can be particularly destructive to marriages. To succeed in your marriage, you must view stress as an archenemy that threatens to destroy your relationship. Begin each day with prayer and Bible reading, trusting God and seeking His guidance. Honor the Sabbath, setting aside time for spiritual, emotional, and physical renewal. Participate in a Bible-believing church. Avoid excessive debt and save money for the future. Schedule and protect daily time together without distractions to talk and relate, enhancing intimacy and reducing stress. Above all, keep Jesus at the center of your life. He is the Prince of Peace, the ultimate stress-buster. Worship and celebrate Him and watch how everything falls into place.

Dear Father, I need Your guidance to make it through each day. Holy Spirit, show me how to manage stress in a healthy way. In Jesus' name, Amen.

How would managing stress correctly affect you mentally, emotionally, and spiritually?

I WILL fully commit to my marriage regardless of past relationship failures.

You must also avoid the "natural" tendency to wade in cautiously, rather than diving in completely.

Commit your actions to the Lord,
and your plans will succeed (Proverbs 16:3).

Despite past pain and mistakes, you must anchor yourself in the present and fully commit to your marriage. Without this commitment, you risk falling into a cycle of doubt and reservation. If you constantly fear that the next disagreement will end your relationship, you won't invest fully, and your spouse may pull back too. This hesitance can become a self-fulfilling prophecy, leading to repeated failed relationships. However, you have the power to change this narrative by deciding to commit completely. Remember, no marriage is flawless. The best marriages still have challenges, but they succeed when both partners face issues together. Don't assume today's problems are permanent. If you commit and act rightly, God will bless your union. Commitment is the key.

Dear Father, You fully committed Yourself to me by sending Your Son to save me. Holy Spirit, help me to take a step of faith as I fully commit myself to my marriage. In Jesus' name, Amen.

How can you demonstrate to your spouse that you are fully committed to your marriage?

Day 136

I WILL avoid manipulation in my relationship with my spouse.

Manipulation is the use of dishonesty, partial truth, or truth for the purpose of one's own advantage.

The getting of treasures by a lying tongue
is a fleeting vapor and a snare of death (Proverbs 21:6 ESV).

A void manipulation in your relationship with your spouse. Unfortunately, many spouses resort to verbal manipulation to exert control and achieve their desired outcomes. Manipulation involves using dishonesty, partial truth, or even truth itself for personal advantage. Selfishness lies at the core of manipulation, as it seeks to tip the scales in its favor without revealing its true motives. Instead of engaging in honest and humble conversations that benefit everyone involved, manipulation distorts the truth. A relationship built on manipulation is a complex web of mistrust, dishonesty, and exploitation. It will erode the foundation of trust and undermine the authenticity and vulnerability of your marriage. Build your marriage on honest communication, mutual respect, and genuine concern for one another.

Dear Father, I know You give freely and honestly to me. I want to do the same for my spouse. Holy Spirit, guide my tongue to speak honestly and lovingly to my spouse. In Jesus' name, Amen.

How have you seen someone use manipulation to get their way? How did it erode your trust for that person?

I WILL take turns with my spouse to focus on our individual sexual desires.

We are different by God's design, and we both have different sexual natures and needs.

Don't look out only for your own interests, but take an interest in others, too (Philippians 2:4).

God uniquely designed both you and your spouse with different sexual natures and needs. The purpose of allocating specific times for focusing on each other is to ensure that your individual needs are fully met. One of you may require ample conversation and a slower, more romantic approach, with sex reserved for the culmination of the experience. The other spouse may prioritize sexual intimacy over romance. In a marital context, sex should be a win-win scenario, where neither partner is left out or relegated to second place. It is important to establish a frequency and style of sexual expression that guarantees fulfillment for both spouses. Achieving this will require concessions and compromises from both sides, fostering a mutually satisfying and harmonious sexual relationship.

Dear Father, I always want to consider my spouse first. Holy Spirit, guide us as we negotiate our sex life together. In Jesus' name, Amen.

Have you considered having times where you focus on one of you in your sexual relationship? Make a plan to start taking turns being the focus.

Day 138

I WILL follow God's Word as my instructions for marriage.

Marriage must be conducted according to God's specific plan if it is going to work.

"Anyone who listens to my teaching and follows it is wise, like a person who builds a house on solid rock" (Matthew 7:24).

In every aspect of life, precision is crucial for success. Golfers must putt with absolute accuracy. Airplane manufacturers must adhere to strict specifications to ensure safety. Medications must be produced with exactness to be effective and safe. Marriages also thrive when they align with a specific blueprint: God's plan. He conceived the institution of marriage. God's teachings offer guidance on how to love and support your spouse. However, many couples ignore God's instructions, choosing instead to navigate their relationships based on their own personal beliefs. You willingly board a flight because you trust in the precision of its construction. In the same way, you can guarantee the health of your marriage when God's plans are used to build it.

Dear Father, I love Your Holy Word. I know it is there to correct and guide me. Holy Spirit, shine Your light on the Bible so I can receive what You want for me. In Jesus' name, Amen.

How often do you read God's Word to understand His will for your life?

I WILL be God's instrument to show my spouse how special and important they are.

The truth is, you will never fall in love with a person who makes you feel bad about yourself.

Love is patient, love is kind, *and* is not jealous; love does not brag *and* is not arrogant, does not act unbecomingly; it does not seek its own (1 Corinthians 13:4–5 NASB1995).

Have you ever wondered why you feel love for certain people? There are two main reasons. First, you admire something about them. Second, they boost your self-esteem. This truth about love remains constant, even in your relationship with Christ. For instance, do you love Jesus because of your admiration for Him and what He has done for you? He gives you a sense of worth and security. You would probably never love someone who tore down your confidence. Remember the early stage of your relationship when mutual admiration was evident and abundant. If you stop building up each other's self-worth, your relationship will suffer. But when you actively recognize and share what you admire about your spouse, you can revitalize your connection.

Dear Father, thank You for the incredible security I have in knowing You. You are so faithful. Holy Spirit, guard my mouth to speak words that will build up my spouse's self-worth. In Jesus' name, Amen.

What qualities do you admire about your spouse?

Day 140

I WILL seek relationships that encourage our marriage.

People need community in order to survive.

"For where two or three are gathered in my name, there am I among them" (Matthew 18:20 ESV).

Never underestimate the role peer pressure plays in your life. It can be both positive and negative. This is why Christians are advised to unite with fellow believers. We are encouraged to bond with those of similar beliefs, to "spur" each other "toward love and good deeds," and to consistently meet together so we can lift each other. You need a supportive community to thrive. Surround yourself with those who resonate with your values, comprehend your challenges, and have walked in your shoes. Find those who assure you, "You've got this," "You can overcome," and "I trust in you." In such communities, the vulnerable grow resilient, and the resilient become more formidable.

Dear Father, thank You for providing through Your church, a community that can support us in our marriage. Help me to value positive relationships and seek to be with people who will support our growth in love together. In Jesus' name, Amen.

Do the relationships in your life pull you to positive or negative feelings and behavior? Who can you identify that would have a positive influence on your marriage?

I WILL do my best to lead my children to the Lord by modeling God's work in my life.

In leading our children to the Lord, the best thing we can do is love God and live a life that is pleasing to Him.

Repeat them again and again to your children. Talk about them when you are at home and when you are on the road, when you are going to bed and when you are getting up (Deuteronomy 6:7).

As you guide your children toward the Lord, the most important things you can do are to love God and live a life that pleases Him. Trying to instill a love for God in your children that you're not living out yourself is not effective parenting. Your character and behavior have much more influence on your children than your instructions. Consider how your own parents' values and actions impacted your understanding of God. Parents who genuinely live their beliefs are best positioned to guide their children. Your habits, attitudes, speech, friendships, involvement in church, and marital relationship matter!

Dear Father, I want to live a life that serves as a godly example for my children. Holy Spirit, direct my words and actions as I live out my faith in front of my children. In Jesus' name, Amen.

Why is it so important to model God's work in your life in front of your children?

Day 142

I WILL take the risk to forgive.

Everything that happens in a marriage—
good or bad—affects both people.

"Forgive us our sins,
as we forgive those who sin against us" (Luke 11:4).

In marriage, every experience is a shared experience. If something affects one person, then it affects the other, and vice versa. When a spouse repents for wrongdoing, transformation takes place in both spouses. It is as if an emotional prison cell is unlocked, setting both of them free. Now, there may be some initial resistance to forgiveness because of the fear that more interaction will lead to more hurtful exchanges. However, trust is necessary to begin the healing process. Instead of dwelling on past wrongs, forgiveness must be chosen, and that requires maturity and restraint. You must make a conscious decision to refrain from judgment and the temptation to exert control. The potential rewards of shared vulnerability outweigh the desire for vengeance.

Dear Father, thank You for forgiving me of my sins. Holy Spirit, please help me to forgive my spouse for their mistakes and give us grace as we move forward in our relationship. In Jesus's name, Amen.

What are some steps you can take to begin rebuilding trust with your spouse?

I WILL not (as a wife) confuse love with enabling.

You simply are loving him enough to keep him from destroying himself and those around him.

And call upon me in the day of trouble;
I will deliver you, and you shall glorify me (Psalm 50:15 ESV).

If you genuinely think you are showing love to your husband by enabling his self-destructive behavior or allowing him to abuse your children or yourself, then you're mistaken. While you should not sin against your husband, it's essential to lovingly stand up to him when he is involved in bad behavior and refuse to be complicit in his harmful actions. By doing so, you're not rebelling or withholding love from him; rather, you're demonstrating true love by preventing him from destroying himself and those close to him. It takes courage and strength to confront destructive behaviors, but it is an act of love that can lead to healing and growth for both of you.

Dear Father, Your Word gives me with the courage to do the right thing even when it's scary or difficult. Holy Spirit, help me to understand the difference between loving and enabling my loved ones. In Jesus' name, Amen.

Who in your life can provide wise counsel regarding the way you deal with difficult situations?

Day 144

I WILL (as a husband) give my wife and family priority over my career.

Many men simply believe their families are an outgrowth of their work.

For if a man cannot manage his own household, how can he take care of God's church? (1 Timothy 3:5).

H usbands with misplaced values and priorities regarding their careers should turn to the Bible. Jesus stated that the greatest commandment is to love God, followed by loving others. Loving work didn't even make the top ten. Repentance and making necessary adjustments to your lifestyle are crucial steps to redirect your heart toward your home. Regardless of what else you have accomplished, if your heart isn't there, it won't matter. When a man reaches the end of his life, he will face the reality of what he has built. True happiness and success lie in building a relationship with God, your wife, and family. This success isn't measured by your net worth or social status but by getting the two most important things in life right—God and family!

Dear Father, I want to serve my family as I serve You. Holy Spirit, keep my heart from greed. In Jesus' name, Amen.

Have material possessions or other activities taken precedence over your family? What can you do to realign your priorities?

I WILL strive for consistency
in my interactions with my spouse.

We must be careful in our relationships to
be consistent in communication.

Make every effort to be found living peaceful lives that are pure and blameless in his sight (2 Peter 3:14).

In dysfunctional homes, family members experience constantly shifting dynamics. One moment they will be praised and the next cursed. Parents, or even just one parent, can transition from kind to vicious, leaving family members uncertain and insecure. Consistency in communication is vital for healthy relationships. Some couples experience communication breakdowns due to one spouse withdrawing from hurt and mistrust. One spouse may stop opening up emotionally because the other spouse's mood swings can turn mean and hurtful. Create a positive atmosphere in your marriage and family relationships, regardless of your personal feelings. Address concerns in a healthy way without lashing out or using them as an excuse for unkindness and selfishness.

Dear Father, I believe you are consistent and want us to be consistent. Holy Spirit, I need You to help me manage my emotions and my words. In Jesus' name, Amen.

How have you experienced inconsistency in the moods of others? Did you have interactions like that in your home while growing up? How have those past experiences influenced the ways you deal with your emotions?

Day 146

I WILL focus on God's presence and love during hard times.

The more Jesus hurt, the more He prayed.
He kept His eyes on God.

Even though I walk through the valley of the shadow of death,
  I will fear no evil,
for you are with me;
    your rod and your staff,
    they comfort me (Psalm 23:4 ESV).

Psalm 23:4 speaks of finding comfort in God's presence even in the midst of hard times. Similarly, Jesus overcame fear by anchoring Himself in Scripture. In the Garden of Eden, Satan taunted Jesus with lies about death's power, but Jesus stood firm, declaring His focus on the Lord. He clung to the promise of joy and eternal life, refusing to be ensnared by fear. In marriage, fear threatens unity. The enemy seeks to wield fear as a weapon, pushing us toward despair. When fear looms over us, God's Word reminds us of His unchanging help. Courage in marriage isn't about fear's absence, but acting righteously despite fear's presence. By fixing our gaze on God, we receive supernatural courage to withstand every attack and scheme of the enemy.

Dear Father, thank You for always being with me. Holy Spirit, remind me to keep my focus on the Lord no matter the circumstances. In Jesus' name, Amen.

How has God brought you through difficult times in the past?

I WILL do what is necessary
to give my spouse reasons to trust me.

Trust is an essential element of intimacy
and goodwill in marriage.

Her husband can trust her,
> and she will greatly enrich his life (Proverbs 31:11).

Trust is vital for intimacy and mutual respect in your relationship. When you trust your spouse, you can be at ease. Instead of complacency, you have genuine comfort. With trust, many aspects of your relationship flourish. For instance, studies have shown that the most fulfilling sexual relationships aren't among singles but committed, married couples. Casual relationships often lack depth and lead to dissatisfaction. In trustworthy relationships, communication is straightforward, enabling deeper connections and mutual understanding. To reap the benefits of trust, act responsibly, consider your spouse's feelings, and apologize when necessary. Consistency is also essential. While forgiveness can mend wounds, trust rebuilds through consistent, responsible actions over time. Prioritize trust and witness the impact it will have on your marriage.

Dear Father, I want to be a trustworthy spouse. Holy Spirit, help me to consider my spouse's feelings and prioritize building trust through consistent communication and actions. In Jesus' name, Amen.

Have you ever given your spouse a reason not to trust you? How can you earn that trust back?

Day 148

I WILL commit to seeing our marriage as a team.

As a team, you can celebrate your differences and use them to your advantage.

Then make my joy complete by being like-minded, having the same love, being one in spirit and of one mind (Philippians 2:2 NIV).

Yﾟou and your partner possess unique strengths. The key to a resilient marriage is for both of you to act as a team, playing the roles your strengths have prepared you for. Because God made each of you unique, you have different strengths and weaknesses. Seeing your marriage as a team is a way that you can stay focused working together for the same goal. So stop seeing your spouse as strange and start to see your spouse as the ideal teammate in life. When you do this, you can let your partner assist you in tackling things where you are weak. This can help your marriage flourish and make your relationship deeper and more intimate. Both of you benefit immensely.

Dear Father, thank You for making us uniquely different so that we complement each other's strengths and weaknesses. Help me to remember that we are on a team and benefit each other through our differences. In Jesus' name, Amen.

How can seeing each other's strengths help your weaknesses so you can reach your marriage goals?

I WILL replace negative thoughts with God's truth.

Satan is a hurt whisperer.

We destroy every proud obstacle that keeps people from knowing God.
We capture their rebellious thoughts and teach them to obey Christ
(2 Corinthians 10:5).

Freedom can feel instantaneous, a divine touch empowering you to overcome adversities. However, for many, it's a gradual journey of replacing falsehoods with truth. Sometimes we bring these falsehoods into our marriages. You're equipped with Jesus' authority and the Word of God, but that means you must align your thoughts with God's truths. Beneath visible struggles like conflict and addiction lies a deeper issue: pain from past traumas. Pain often drives us to distractions or self-medication. You must recognize the deceptions rooted in these traumas, like believing you're unworthy or responsible for past hurts. These lies keep you captive. To truly find freedom, you must uncover these deceptions and embrace God's truths.

Dear Father, You know every pain and offense I have experienced in my life. I am tired of carrying these burdens. Holy Spirit, I give You my heart to heal and my mind to transform and guide. In Jesus' name, Amen.

Do you have pain or trauma that you have not addressed? Are you ready for God to uncover and heal these areas of your life?

Day 150

I WILL pursue my spouse with the same enthusiasm that I once did.

Once again invest your time and energy into the relationship, regardless of how you feel in the process.

Work brings profit,
> but mere talk leads to poverty! (Proverbs 14:23).

I f you start work on your relationship today, you will still face some difficulties. As you remain steadfast and obedient, these problems will decrease, and it will be easier to overcome them. This will be a massive change from before, and you will enjoy so much pleasure and blessings in your life because of the power and truth of God's Word working daily in your marriage. If you want to live in a marriage where love and satisfaction are the norm, reject the false notion of love that the world presents and commit to working on your relationship. Pursuing your spouse with energy and diligence will become a labor of love, and you will become addicted to it. You will realize that marriage gets stronger and more satisfying every day when you do it God's way.

Dear Father, inspire me every day to pursue my spouse. Holy Spirit, teach me how to love my spouse deeply. In Jesus' name, Amen.

How did you pursue your spouse at the beginning of your relationship? What can you do today to pursue them?

I WILL not (as a wife) let the fear of rejection keep me from doing the right thing.

Fear of rejection is typically one of our deepest fears.

"However, those the Father has given me will come to me, and I will never reject them" (John 6:37).

R ejection is a deep hurt that we all experience at some point in life, and the fear of rejection is one of humanity's greatest fears. Some women become enablers out of the fear of rejection and being alone. These wives endure abuse and tolerate serious problems in their loved ones. They choose silence as the price for love and acceptance. But fear is not from God. Instead of fearing people's reactions, have faith in God and stand up for what is right. Even if you face rejection, trust that God will protect and reward you. Our highest authority is God, and He will never reject us for doing what is right. Regardless of what others do or threaten to do, if we put our faith in Him, God will work powerfully on our behalf.

Dear Father, You have the power to work miracles on my behalf. Holy Spirit, fill me with faith as I choose to do the right thing when I'm afraid of rejection. In Jesus' name, Amen.

What right thing have you been avoiding out of fear of rejection? Will you step out in faith and do it today?

Day 152

I WILL (as a husband) not use work or friends to avoid conflict.

A man does not find the correct answer to his problem by turning away from home.

He must manage his own family well (1 Timothy 3:4).

When there is unresolved conflict between you and your spouse, it's common for you to shift your focus to work or friends. However, the longer you do this, the more your relationship suffers. Perhaps you don't feel honored or respected at home, but you find validation at work. Consequently, you're drawn to the workplace to fulfill your basic needs or protect them. Regardless of the reason, turning away from home won't provide the solution to your problems. If you're using excessive work as a means to escape family issues, it's time to repent and return home. Ask God for help in overcoming your problems and face them directly. Through prayer and perseverance, as you confront these challenges head-on, God will honor you, and you will find greater happiness.

Dear Father, I know You love me even when you have to talk to me about difficult things.. Holy Spirit, give me the courage and strength to deal with difficult situations with my spouse. In Jesus' name, Amen.

Did you grow up in a home that had a lot of conflict, or was conflict avoided? How has that influenced the ways you deal with conflict today?

I WILL seek total freedom for myself because it affects my marriage.

Only Jesus can save you, but He can also heal you and set you free.

"So if the Son sets you free, you are truly free" (John 8:36).

Total freedom begins with these three truths:

1. **God's Word is the authority.** Your freedom begins by placing trust in the authority of God's Word. If you have difficulty understanding it, ask a mature believer to help you.

2. **You need freedom.** Acceptance is key. Everyone, including you, carries the weight of sin from birth. This bondage has ramifications in your life. You bring it into your marriage. People often struggle to admit their limitations and sins. Acknowledging your need for freedom is not a sign of weakness; it's the first step toward true liberation.

3. **Your relationship with Jesus must be first.** Ultimate freedom isn't just about shedding chains but establishing a profound relationship with Jesus. Ensure nothing stands between you and Him, and freedom will follow.

Dear Father, I know there is freedom in Your Word. I was in such bondage before I invited Jesus into my life. Holy Spirit, make and keep me free. Reveal areas of bondage so that I can repent and renounce them. In Jesus' name, Amen.

What will you do to pursue ongoing freedom in your life?

Day 154

I WILL tear down strongholds in my mind because they affect my marriage.

God has equipped you with mighty weapons to destroy the enemy.

We use God's mighty weapons, not worldly weapons, to knock down the strongholds of human reasoning and to destroy false arguments (2 Corinthians 10:4).

The apostle Paul says we're battling mental strongholds—areas where negative emotions and deceptive thoughts dominate. Imagine the devil building a command center in your mind, causing fear, anger, or confusion. All of those will have a negative impact on your relationship with your spouse. Align your thoughts with God's. He's given you powerful tools; not physical weapons, but spiritual ones, capable of demolishing these strongholds. Understand this: God expects you to take initiative in your mind. Fortunately, he's given you authority. God's Word is your potent weapon against negative thoughts. Replace toxic thoughts with God's promises. By doing so, you'll find freedom and clarity, tearing down the devil's barriers and firmly establishing God's fortress in your mind and marriage.

Dear Father, I know the blood of Jesus frees me from the devil and his strongholds. Holy Spirit, I claim Your healing and deliverance today. In Jesus' name, Amen.

Where does God need to deliver you from strongholds? Have the courage to recognize and name them. Ask for help if you need someone to pray with you about it.

I WILL never give up on my marriage.

If we will keep doing what is right, regardless of what we see or in times of discouragement, God will honor us, and we will harvest the fruit of our labors.

Let us not become weary in doing good, for at the proper time we will reap a harvest if we do not give up (Galatians 6:9 NIV).

O n October 29, 1941, you would have heard one of the most concise yet impactful speeches by Sir Winston Churchill. He asserted, "Never give in! Never give in! Never! Never! Never! In nothing great or small, large or petty—never give in, except to convictions of honor and good sense." Such profound advice isn't just historic wisdom; it's also biblical. By persistently doing what's right, even in challenging times, you'll see that God honors your determination. But if you surrender, you don't solve any issue; you either postpone it or miss the potential rewards of victory.

Dear Father, it is tempting to give up on my relationship with my spouse when we face challenging moments. But I know You honor righteous determination. Holy Spirit, renew in me a love for my spouse that can withstand the hard times. In Jesus' name, Amen.

How has God honored your determination in the past? What are you trusting Him to do in the future?

Day 156

I WILL make honesty a foundation for my family.

A family based on denial and dishonesty is a house of smoke and mirrors that will eventually collapse.

The LORD detests lying lips,
>   but he delights in those who tell the truth (Proverbs 12:22).

In your marriage communication, honesty should be the foundation above all else. This doesn't require a blunt and insensitive disclosure of every detail, but rather a commitment to speak the truth and confront reality. As spouses, it means acknowledging your problems and avoiding emotional distance. Honesty plays an important role in creating harmony and intimacy. It will help you resolve conflicts. On the other hand, a family built on denial and dishonesty is like a house of smoke and mirrors that will eventually crumble. Embrace transparency and truthfulness within your family, as it will strengthen your bonds and create a solid foundation for genuine connections and growth.

Dear Father, I believe You are a God of truth and want Your children to be truthful. Holy Spirit, I never want to be dishonest because I am afraid. Help me always to be a truthteller. In Jesus' name, Amen.

Have you experienced people who don't tell the truth because they are afraid of the consequences? How do you think God can help us to be truthtellers?

I WILL be adventurous and creative in my sexual relationship with my spouse.

*Keep your sexual relationship pure
but have fun and be creative.*

Marriage *is* honorable among all, and the bed undefiled (Hebrews 13:4 NKJV).

You must avoid two sexual extremes. The first is falling into monotonous routines, always approaching sex in the same way. The second is feeling pressured to constantly change and experiment. You don't have to constantly come up with something new, but if you never try anything different, you may not be taking sex or your spouse seriously enough. Pray, reflect, and discuss everything with your spouse. If the Bible explicitly prohibits something, you should avoid it. However, if it's not addressed in the Bible, consider whether it is safe, mutually agreed upon, and won't harm your relationship or anyone else. If it meets these criteria, try it and see if you enjoy it. You don't have to share the exact same preferences to explore new things.

Dear Father, thank You for creating sex as a good gift to be enjoyed in marriage. Holy Spirit, help us to always be open to one another's needs and desires. In Jesus' name, Amen.

Have a discussion with your spouse about what it means to you to be adventurous and creative in your sex life together.

Day 158

I WILL dedicate time to communicating with my spouse.

Where the rubber meets the road in proving priorities is how much time we are willing to give to something on a regular basis.

Enjoy life with the wife whom you love, all the days of your vain life that he has given you under the sun (Ecclesiastes 9:9 ESV).

To show your spouse they are your priority, actions speak louder than words. The time you dedicate to something is the ultimate test of your priorities. Effective communication can be categorized into three types: proactive, personal, and intimate. Proactive communication involves planning and discussing the future, such as in a vision retreat. Personal communication involves setting aside protected time every day to connect and share about personal issues. Intimate communication involves expressing love, encouragement, praise, affection, and discussing sexual issues. Prioritizing and protecting communication is crucial to your marriage's success. Dedicate the proper amount of time to strengthen your partnership, protect your friendship, and grow your intimacy.

Dear Father, I want to set aside time to communicate with my spouse. Holy Spirit, help me to organize my life so that I can. In Jesus' name, Amen.

Have personal and intimate communication with your spouse. As you are talking, discuss when you can both spend extended time together for a vision retreat.

I WILL (as a wife) use my natural strength in my relationship with my husband.

Many women are born with a very sweet, laid-back personality.

She dresses herself with strength
and makes her arms strong (Proverbs 31:17 ESV).

You may have a sweet and laid-back personality, characteristic of the phlegmatic temperament. Your strength lies in your relational loyalty and sensitivity, and you make a wonderful friend. However, it's important to be aware of the potential to become an enabler. Your accepting nature may prevent you from confronting others when necessary. Even though it's rarely fun to confront someone, it's often important to do so for both your sakes. To navigate this, embrace your natural strength and use it to love others. At the same time, learn to stand up for yourself in love and express your true feelings. By speaking the truth in love, you can be both a loyal companion and an active partner. Balancing your gentle nature with assertiveness allows you to maintain deep, stable relationships while ensuring your own needs are met.

Dear Father, I believe Your design for me is unique and perfect. Holy Spirit, teach me how to use my natural strength to honor and bless my spouse. In Jesus' name, Amen.

What is your natural strength? How can you use it to benefit your relationship with your husband?

Day 160

I WILL exercise the authority God has given me in my life and marriage.

God is telling us to grow up into the authority He has given us.

"Look, I have given you authority over all the power of the enemy, and you can walk among snakes and scorpions and crush them. Nothing will injure you" (Luke 10:19).

There are four pivotal truths for you to take authority over the enemy in your life and marriage:

1. **The devil is real.** Many believers deny the devil's reality. If you dismiss his existence, he gains power to wreak havoc in your life and marriage.

2. **Jesus triumphed over the devil.** He already conquered the devil at the cross. The devil has no true power over you.

3. **Jesus gave you authority.** You possess dominion over the devil and all dark forces. Jesus entrusts you with this power. You are not helpless.

4. **You must exercise your authority.** God wants you to embrace this authority. When you understand His power is working in you, you can break chains and fend off the devil. Victory is in your grasp.

Dear Father, I know you have given me authority through Jesus. Holy Spirit, give me strength and wisdom to exercise that authority. In Jesus' name, Amen.

What will it mean for you to exercise God's authority in your life?

I WILL combine big dreams with hard work to create a great marriage.

*Big dreams and hard work are the magic
ingredients that create great marriages.*

Whatever you do, do well. For when you go to the grave, there will be no work
or planning or knowledge or wisdom (Ecclesiastes 9:10).

Here's an intriguing perspective on successful relationships: couples with high expectations for their partnerships often fare the best. However, lofty expectations can lead to disappointment unless they're paired with a realistic understanding of the effort required. It's like a musician who wants to be first chair in an orchestra. His great ambitions will take hard work and sacrifice. Many people overlook the concept in relationships, wrongly assuming that hard work implies something's gone wrong. But lasting relationships demand effort. Start with a shared vision of what you both desire. Pair this with dedication, sacrifice, and persistent effort. Remember, every challenge is a steppingstone to your ideal relationship. Embrace them, work together, and rely on each other's strengths to make your shared dreams a reality.

*Father God, You are with me through every success and challenge. Holy Spirit,
I submit my dreams to You and commit to working hard for Your glory and for
the strength of my marriage. In Jesus' name, Amen.*

What "big dreams" do you have for your marriage, and how will you accomplish them?

Day 162

I WILL have a gardener's mentality toward my spouse.

A gardener takes responsibility to do what is necessary to restore the plant to health.

A bruised reed he will not break,
  and a faintly burning wick he will not quench;
  he will faithfully bring forth justice (Isaiah 42:3 ESV).

Many people approach marriage with a consumer's mentality—they expect perfection, and when imperfections arise, they question their choices. But as a Christian, you are called to a gardener's mentality. When faced with a sick tree or shrub, a true gardener doesn't blame others or give up on the plant. Instead, they take responsibility and seek ways to nurture and restore it to health. To protect your marriage, ask yourself, *What can I do to help my spouse? How can I contribute to their growth and wellbeing?* If you approach your marriage as a consumer, you may grow impatient and frustrated with your spouse's problems. However, as a gardener, you remain optimistic and proactive. Your prayers and obedience are powerful tools for redeeming your spouse and helping them become the person God intended them to be.

Dear Father, my spouse is the most important person in my life. Holy Spirit, show me how I bless them in their spirit, soul, and body. In Jesus' name, Amen.

When challenges arise in your marriage, will you be a consumer or a gardener?

I WILL seek help from God and my physician if I am ever struggling with depression.

You don't have to live in bondage anymore.

To all who mourn in Israel,
  he will give a crown of beauty for ashes,
a joyous blessing instead of mourning,
  festive praise instead of despair (Isaiah 61:3).

You might find yourself turning to substances when you are seeking relief from the weight of discouragement and depression. Some people seek solace in food or alcohol, or they even mistreat others, as a means to find comfort in the midst of despair. Depression isn't just an emotion. Some forms of depression are biologically rooted, like postpartum depression after childbirth due to hormonal and chemical shifts. Always consult with a physician when you are depressed. God can use these situations in your healing journey. Emotional exhaustion can lead to depression, as can unresolved anger. Grieving for a prolonged time without healing can also wear on your emotions. Depression will impact your marriage, so address it as soon as possible.

Dear Father, You are compassionate and full of mercy and grace. Holy Spirit, if depression ever becomes overwhelming, lead me to the right people and professionals who can help me find hope and healing. In Jesus' name, Amen.

Do you or your spouse struggle with depression? Have you had honest conversations about its effects and ways to seek help?

Day 164

I WILL establish an emergency relief plan for my marriage.

Having an emergency relief plan for your marriage is as important as a hurricane route is for a community on the Gulf of Mexico.

Commit your actions to the LORD,
and your plans will succeed (Proverbs 16:3).

In many major southern cities in the US, local authorities have designated routes for natural disasters in order to save lives and prevent chaos. Similarly, couples need an emergency relief plan to navigate challenging times in their relationship. It's almost certain that at some point, you and your spouse will face an impasse about sex, children, finances, or any number of issues. An emergency relief plan means agreeing that if you can't work things out together, the two of you will seek and submit to pastoral or professional Christian counsel. This disaster preparation may not be needed often, but it can be the key to preserving your relationship and restoring peace. Establish your emergency relief plan today so you can be prepared to navigate any storm that comes your way.

Dear Father, I believe You are with me every moment of every day. Holy Spirit, give me wisdom to know what to include in our emergency relief plan. In Jesus' name, Amen.

What would you like to include in your emergency relief plan?

I WILL keep confidences
but never hide abuse.

*Successful families honor confidentiality, but
they don't cover up destruction.*

People who conceal their sins will not prosper,
> but if they confess and turn from them, they will receive mercy (Proverbs
> 28:13).

In your family, confidentiality is important, but when there is destruction, it's crucial to seek help. Instances of sexual abuse, spouse abuse, child abuse, or any illegal behavior require reaching out to someone outside the family, such as a friend, church leader, or even the authorities. Many children from abusive homes were silenced and trapped by the obligation to keep dark secrets, enduring severe violence or sexual molestation. However, successful families value confidentiality while refusing to cover up destruction. If you experience abuse or witness harmful behavior within your family, remember that real love seeks help. We should never demand that our family members enable self-destruction or harm others while protecting us. Love means keeping confidentiality but exposing abuse and destruction for the sake of the family's wellbeing.

Dear Father, make our home a place that does not need to keep dark secrets. Holy Spirit, help me to keep confidences but never to hide sin or abuse. In Jesus' name, Amen.

What have been the results of people hiding abuse? When the truth is discovered, what have been the consequences?

Day 166

I WILL help my children develop their God-given identity.

All of us have a deep need to feel unique and significant.

Direct your children onto the right path,
and when they are older, they will not leave it (Proverbs 22:6).

Everyone craves a sense of uniqueness and significance. You start this process of instilling identity in your children by emphasizing their individuality. Don't draw comparisons between your child and their siblings or impose strict adherence to family systems. Instead, encourage them to express themselves freely within a loving and structured environment. As your children mature, their feelings and opinions should increasingly guide their paths. Don't grant them a liberty that leads to self-destruction, but do allow them the space to become who God intended within secure boundaries and His will. Since training isn't just teaching or telling, be sure to model the right behaviors. Finally, approach each child's upbringing individually, and don't try to shoehorn them into a one-size-fits-all mold.

Dear Father, You created each of my children with their own unique identity. Holy Spirit, help me to appreciate their individuality and allow them the right amount of freedom to express themselves. In Jesus' name, Amen.

What makes each of your children unique?

I WILL protect the right order of priorities in my marriage.

We need to be firm in our commitment to keep our priorities right.

The instructions of the LORD are perfect,
  reviving the soul.
The decrees of the LORD are trustworthy,
  making wise the simple (Psalm 19:7).

Protecting your established priorities is essential. While avoiding legalism, maintain a firm commitment to keep them in order. Temporary work demands may require extra time, but avoid letting it become a long-term habit. Occasionally missing church due to vacation or illness is understandable, but be cautious not to form a habit. Priorities are eternal principles, not exact science. God doesn't demand rigid conformity but expects honest commitment to doing what's right and being willing to repent and change. Successful families have consistent practices, habits, and traditions that require intentional effort. Daily dedication to living rightly brings blessings for your marriage and family. Make a commitment to God and your family, placing them where they belong, and a life of blessings will follow.

Dear Father, I want my family to follow Your laws and Your priorities. Holy Spirit, guide us as we commit to keeping our priorities in the correct place in our lives. In Jesus' name, Amen.

How can you protect the right priorities without becoming legalistic? What are some examples?

Day 168

I WILL not (as a wife) respond to my husband's distraction with my own distraction.

Just as a man needs to turn his heart toward his wife and home, a woman must learn to do the same thing.

Don't love money; be satisfied with what you have. For God has said,
"I will never fail you.
I will never abandon you" (Hebrews 13:5).

God's presence and attention are constant and unchanging. He promises to never abandon or turn His heart away from you. This assurance brings comfort in the midst of even the most difficult times. Similarly, marriage is a commitment never to abandon or turn your heart away from your spouse. You promise to remain physically present in and emotionally focused on your relationship. Many wives react to their husband's distractions with their own distraction, leading to an all-around lack of effort in fighting for the marriage. But it doesn't matter who started the problem, because you have the power to make a change. By turning your heart back to your husband and actively working to strengthen your connection, you can help restore the heart of your marriage.

Dear Father, Your constant love is my greatest source of joy. Holy Spirit, show me new ways to turn my heart toward my husband. In Jesus' name, Amen.

What distractions have disrupted your marriage? How can you strengthen your connection?

I WILL bring my thoughts into obedience with God's Word.

People of the Word live in victory and freedom.

For we are God's masterpiece. He has created us anew in Christ Jesus, so we can do the good things he planned for us long ago (Ephesians 2:10).

When you discern the devil's influence, you'll quickly spot his attempts on your thoughts. It's essential to counter these and uphold freedom for your mind. Constantly align your thoughts with God's Word. Reject ideas influenced by the enemy and submit them to Christ's authority. Jesus is your guide for distinguishing right from wrong. If tempted to believe there's no consequence for sins, remember such lies have ancient origins, like the serpent's deceit to Adam and Eve. The effects of giving into deception impact not only you but also your spouse. Anchor your life in God's truth, not cultural trends. The path to freedom comes from mastery over your thoughts, deepening your bond with Jesus, and grounding your mind in God's Word.

Dear Father, I believe Your Word is true and Truth. Holy Spirit, keep bringing me back to the power of the Bible. In Jesus' name, Amen.

How can you be more of a "person of the Word"? What will you do to make God's Word more of a force and factor in your life?

Day 170

I WILL remain willing to change.

Real change happens when I choose to be the one who can change.

Throw off your old sinful nature and your former way of life, which is corrupted by lust and deception. Instead, let the Spirit renew your thoughts and attitudes (Ephesians 4:22–23).

You must understand that the only thing you can change is yourself. When you change, your marriage changes too. To initiate this transformation, you need to abandon the thought pattern that says, "My spouse is the problem, and when they change, everything will be good." Have you considered your own issues? You probably chose a partner who mirrors you in both strengths and weaknesses. Both you and your spouse may think that if the other changes, everything will be fixed. However, change really begins with you. Recognizing your strengths and weaknesses, as well as those of your spouse, is invaluable to enhancing your marriage. In the light of God's grace, ask yourself tough questions about yourself, and be prepared to act on the answers.

Dear Father, shine Your light into my heart and help me to see where I can change. Holy Spirit, I receive Your power to grow in grace and maturity. In Jesus' name, Amen.

Identify one habit you can change that would enhance your spouse's life. Can you begin making that change today?

I WILL work toward building a positive atmosphere in our home.

A person's spirit opens up when praised,
but closes when criticized.

Enter his gates with thanksgiving;
    go into his courts with praise.
    Give thanks to him and praise his name (Psalm 100:4).

In your family, communication will thrive when the atmosphere is one of emotional brightness, positivity, and encouragement. Just as the Psalms teach us about approaching God's presence with thanksgiving and praise, we also open our hearts to those who radiate positivity and close them to negativity. Praising and affirming one another is vital within your family. Husbands should cheer for their wives, wives for their husbands, and parents for their children. Building a positive, affirming atmosphere in the home will give everyone a sense of being valued and cherished. The devil knows that a dark and poisonous environment will ruin intimacy. To counter this, discipline yourself to practice daily praise, starting with your relationship with the Lord.

Dear Father, I want my mouth to be filled with praise, beginning with praising You. Holy Spirit, help me build an atmosphere of positivity and praise in our home. In Jesus' name, Amen.

Do you praise more than you criticize? How do you plan to reduce the number of critical remarks while increasing words of praise?

Day 172

I WILL be a "Spirit-filled" spouse.

With the help of the Holy Spirit, we can fulfill our roles as husbands and wives.

"But you will receive power when the Holy Spirit comes upon you. And you will be my witnesses" (Acts 1:8).

God infused the Holy Spirit into Adam and Eve. Their bond remained Spirit-filled until they turned away from God. He designed you and your spouse as equals, albeit with distinct roles. With the Holy Spirit's guidance, you can fulfill these roles as a husband or wife. Women are fashioned to assist, akin to the Holy Spirit's role. Men's roles resemble Christ's. Forget the flaws of your parents' relationship; love as Christ does. Without the Holy Spirit, you can't fully love your spouse. As a husband, your roles mirror Jesus: the prophet, priest, and king. As a prophet, seek God's guidance. As a priest, be sensitive, caring, and supportive. As a king, lead with humility, putting her first.

Dear Father, I will need Your Spirit to help me as a spouse. Holy Spirit, I want to love as Christ does. Guide me to be more like Jesus. In Jesus' name, Amen.

How do you know when the Holy Spirit is guiding you? How do you distinguish His voice from other voices, including your own?

I WILL recognize that romance is necessary in my marriage all day long.

It is critically important in sex and all other areas of marriage to accept and celebrate the inherent differences we have.

You have captivated my heart, my sister, my bride;
you have captivated my heart with one glance of your eyes,
with one jewel of your necklace (Song of Songs 4:9 ESV).

Sex doesn't begin when you get in bed; it starts when you wake up in the morning and greet each other. Sex is not just about the physical act but also about the overall intimacy in your relationship. When a husband loves his wife sacrificially and with sensitivity throughout the day, it becomes the ultimate form of foreplay. However, if he neglects her needs and ignores her, then it will negatively impact their connection in the bedroom. On the other hand, when a wife honors her husband, meeting his needs throughout the day, it prepares him for intimacy on all levels, including sexually. Actions throughout the day set the stage.

Dear Father, I want to have a sexual relationship with my spouse that shows I deeply love and care for them. Holy Spirit, remind me to show love to my spouse all day long. In Jesus' name, Amen.

What efforts do you make every day to show your spouse you love and care for them?

Day 174

I WILL (as a husband) express love and admiration for my wife.

Every woman is a reflection of her husband.

You are altogether beautiful, my love;
there is no flaw in you (Song of Songs 4:7 ESV).

When you express your love to your wife by speaking uplifting words and addressing her concerns with support and friendship, you meet one of her deepest needs. A wife radiates love when she is surrounded by praise and respect. Neglect or constant criticism, on the other hand, will drive her to seek validation somewhere else. While never justifiable, affairs can occur when women feel valued and special by someone outside their marriage. Don't let anyone else fill your position as your wife's biggest cheerleader. As her husband, you should be her primary source of praise. This not only blesses her, but it also reduces the likelihood of outside temptation. Follow these guidelines: speak positively every day, compliment all areas of her life, avoid sarcasm, be careful with words of correction, and embrace romance. Let love and respect flourish, building a secure and fulfilling bond in your marriage.

Dear Father, I want my spouse to know how grateful I am for her. Holy Spirit, show me how to speak her love language. In Jesus' name, Amen.

How does your spouse like to receive love? Is this the way you have been giving it?

I WILL reorganize my priorities
when they become misplaced.

God made marriage as something sacred and beautiful,
and it will stay that way if we prioritize it properly.

"But seek first the kingdom of God and His righteousness, and all these things shall be added to you" (Matthew 6:33 NKJV).

God is the top priority, and your spouse comes second, only after Him. Allowing anything or anyone to intrude into your marriage violates your sacred union, and any sense of violation should prompt you to reestablish God's priorities in your life. Prioritizing God and your spouse is crucial to a happy and fulfilling marriage, and it fits His design. Sacrificing time and energy for lower priorities is acceptable, but only after your first two priorities are met. This may present challenges, but honoring the Law of Priority brings great rewards, because marriage is designed as something sacred and beautiful by God.

Dear Father, I want to follow Your order for my life and marriage. Holy Spirit, keep my heart and ears open to hear your conviction when I get things out of order. In Jesus' name, Amen.

Is God at the top and your spouse second only to Him? What can you do to correct your priorities and keep them in the right order?

Day 176

I WILL (as a wife) strive to balance motherhood with making my husband my top priority.

Give your children the time and energy they need but give your best to your marriage.

Wives should always put their husbands first, as the church puts Christ first. (Ephesians 5:24 CEV).

The first law of marriage is priority. Placing anything above your spouse is a sure way to breed jealousy. Men often make the mistake of prioritizing their careers over their wives, while women often prioritize their children over their husbands. These choices can stem from a husband's emotional detachment or the demands of motherhood on a wife. It harms both the marriage and the children's understanding of relationships. Remember, children are temporary. They will only live in your home for about 18 years, and then they will begin their own adult lives, leaving you alone with your spouse. While your children are growing up, the primary factor in their emotional security is the health of your marriage. Make your marriage a priority as you refocus on your husband and give your relationship the right amount of time and energy.

Dear Father, I need Your help keeping my priorities in the correct order. Holy Spirit, guide me to be the best wife and mother that I can be. In Jesus' name, Amen.

How can you prioritize your husband while also taking care of your children?

I WILL (as a husband) strive to make my wife feel secure.

Although security is a very broad term and general in meaning, nevertheless, it is a woman's greatest need.

In the same way husbands should love their wives as their own bodies. He who loves his wife loves himself (Ephesians 5:28 ESV).

As a husband, you must understand that security is your wife's greatest need. Whether she's with her parents or living with you, she desires to feel safe and provided for in every aspect. While God fulfills her deepest need for security, you have a role in meeting her sense of security. Communicate four essential things to her: prioritize her above all else after God, show care and attentiveness, seek her feedback, and be fully committed to meeting her needs unconditionally. Don't fear her response when you make yourself available to meet her needs; instead, she will respond positively to an atmosphere of security created by your sacrificial care. True authority and manhood are built upon humble, sacrificial servanthood, not ego. Remember, meeting her needs will bring harmony and fulfillment to your marriage.

Dear Father, You give me security. Holy Spirit, help me to show my wife I care about her by giving her security. In Jesus' name, Amen.

Ask your wife how she defines "security." Discuss any differences you may have in your definitions.

Day 178

I WILL meditate regularly on God's Word.

*When we read God's Word, we load our
minds like a powerful weapon.*

He sent out his word and healed them,
snatching them from the door of death (Psalm 107:20).

Do you know the Bible's guidance in every part of your life? It isn't just religious nonsense but a manual for all humanity. Biblical meditation isn't about emptying but about filling your mind and soul. The term "ruminate" embodies this: chewing on God's Word repeatedly until it becomes a part of you. When doubts arise, turn to Scripture for clarity and strength. Use quiet moments to reinforce God's teachings in your mind. Instead of dispelling negative thoughts, replace them with powerful Scriptures. They will provide insight into how to live in a healthy relationship to your spouse. Your path to freedom lies within God's Word; embrace it to navigate life's journey for you and your spouse.

Dear Father, I want Your Word to be on my heart and mind constantly. Holy Spirit, help me as I read the Bible, and then help me to think about it all day long. In Jesus' name, Amen.

How often do you think about God's Word in your daily life? What can you do to increase your commitment to reading, understanding, and meditating on Scripture?

I WILL close ranks with my spouse.

You and your spouse must be a united front.

"If a house is divided against itself, that house cannot stand" (Mark 3:25 NKJV).

Success in marriage does not require people who are perfect, but it does require spouses who are willing to close ranks. Originally a military term, to close ranks means that troops would unite to meet the onslaught of an enemy. Envision yourself and your spouse as guards whose mission is to protect your family from intruders. The wider the gap between the two of you, the more vulnerable your family becomes to infiltration by the enemy. However, when you choose to close ranks, standing shoulder to shoulder or even face-to-face, you become an impenetrable fortress. Nothing can come between you or defeat you when you are united. Your relationship is a haven of love, protection, and strength under the leadership of King Jesus.

Dear Father, I want my relationship with my spouse to be a safe place. Holy Spirit, show me how to close ranks in my marriage as I reject any spirit of division that tries to come against my home. In Jesus' name, Amen.

What are some ways you can close ranks with your spouse on a daily basis?

Day 180

I WILL manage our finances with my spouse with planning and discipline.

Begin right now to get your financial house in order.

A prudent person foresees danger and takes precautions.
The simpleton goes blindly on and suffers the consequences (Proverbs 27:12).

Financial consultants often share that couples facing significant monetary difficulties usually lack a budget. This makes sense because financial stability in your relationship largely depends on budgeting and planning. Engage in this process together to gain a sense of direction and prevent problems. Don't think of budgeting as restrictive; it's a tool for better money management. Don't overlook estate planning either. Seek professional advice if needed, especially on wills, insurance, retirement funds, and savings plans. Always keep your partner informed and involved in all financial decisions, even uncomfortable ones, such as death or disability preparations. Remember, long-term financial success requires discipline and prompt action. As you organize your finances, not only will your marriage strengthen, but you'll also continue to enjoy God's blessings.

Dear Father, my heart's desire is to be a good steward of the resources You have blessed me with. Holy Spirit, direct me to me to make wise financial decisions with my spouse. In Jesus' name, Amen.

What is the state of your finances? Do you follow a budget? If no, are you willing to make one and adhere to it?

I WILL be open, honest, and intimate as I communicate with my spouse.

I heard this saying once: "Trust is earned in drops and lost in buckets." I believe that is accurate.

The heart of her husband trusts in her,
   and he will have no lack of gain (Proverbs 31:11 ESV).

Effective communication with your spouse requires a deep level of trust, which can be built by consistently doing and saying the right things. Vulnerability is key to honest and intimate sharing, but it also requires responsibility and care in your words and actions. Trust can be lost in a moment of insensitivity or irresponsibility, but it can also be regained through repentance and true change. To build trust and maintain it, keep promises, remain faithful and pure, be accountable for your behavior, be attentive to your spouse's needs, validate their feelings, treat them as equals, protect them from negative influences, and maintain a positive attitude. With trust, your communication can be open and fearless.

Dear Father, I want my spouse to always trust me. Holy Spirit, work in our marriage to rebuild any trust that either of us has broken. In Jesus' name, Amen.

As you look at the ways to build trust, what is one area you would like to give special attention to today?

Day 182

I WILL confess and confront the sin of rebellion when it manifests in my life.

When we try to live independently from the Shepherd, we simply can't do it.

All of us, like sheep, have strayed away.
   We have left God's paths to follow our own.
Yet the LORD laid on him
   the sins of us all (Isaiah 53:6).

A rebellious nature and desire for independence invite the devil to wreak havoc in your life and marriage. It's our rebellion that necessitated Jesus' sacrifice. Like sheep, we are vulnerable and lost without guidance. Left alone, we're directionless, defenseless, and burdened. God envisions us needing His guidance. From Genesis to Revelation, He desires to coexist with us in harmony. But the devil tempts us, causing us to stray. If you succumb, believing the falsehood that independence from God leads to freedom, you'll find yourself trapped. Remember, sin's allure is deceptive; its long-term consequences are devastating. Many have been misled, their lives shattered by its effects. By recognizing these deceptions and turning to Christ, true freedom and fulfillment can be found.

Dear Father, I submit to Your authority and to that of those You have placed over me. Holy Spirit, convict me rebellious attitudes. In Jesus' name, Amen.

Do you think of yourself as naturally rebellious? What can you do to see rebellion as a sin and not a personality trait?

I WILL (as a wife) do what I can to manage stress.

Since our time and energies are limited, we must pay the most important people first.

Search for the LORD and for his strength;
continually seek him (Psalm 105:4).

S tress is an epidemic in today's society. It's the main reason people visit doctors and rely on prescribed drugs. You have only 24 hours in a day, and just as you budget your money, it's crucial to budget your time and energy wisely. Prioritize the most important people—your spouse and children—over other commitments. Safeguard your family from anything or anyone trying to steal their time and energy. If you're overwhelmed, ask yourself where you can reduce demands to protect your health, wellbeing, marriage, and family. Consider if your job is worth the stress it brings. Even if your income drops, quitting might improve your life, even if it means downsizing expenses. Remember, don't be driven through life. Take control and cut back on lesser priorities.

Dear Father, I want my life to demonstrate Your peace and joy. Holy Spirit, open my eyes to see anything I can do to remove stress from my life. In Jesus' name, Amen.

What are the top three stressful things in your life? What can you do to reduce that stress?

Day 184

I WILL honor my parents but sever any ties of authority they have in my marriage.

When you get married, you must sever the ties of authority your parents have in your life.

Honor your father and mother. Then you will live a long, full life in the land the LORD your God is giving you (Exodus 20:12).

Understanding the balance between honor and authority is crucial for your marriage, especially as it concerns parents or in-laws. While always respecting and honoring your parents is important, their direct authority diminishes once you marry. This doesn't mean cutting ties; you can seek their advice and even work for them. However, their influence should never compromise your marriage. Unwarranted interference, whether through manipulation or financial control, can strain your relationship. It's essential to establish clear boundaries in your marital life. While staying independent, make sure you continue treating your parents with love and respect. Although their guidance is valuable, remember that the final decisions in your married life are yours to make with your spouse.

Dear Father, thank You for my parents and all they have sacrificed for me. Holy Spirit, direct me as I seek to honor them while establishing clear boundaries for my marriage. In Jesus' name, Amen.

What boundaries do you need to set and enforce to keep a healthy relationship with your parents?

I WILL strive for unity of vision with my spouse.

Remember, division occurs because we have two visions.

"Any kingdom divided by civil war is doomed. A family splintered by feuding will fall apart" (Luke 11:17).

In a marriage, division arises when you and your spouse have two different visions. Without a singular vision from God, couples can become divided and ultimately defeated. God's financial provision is linked to His vision for your marriage. Once you receive God's vision for your marriage, He will provide everything you need to make it a reality. Going on a vision retreat with your spouse and surrendering your marriage to God annually is a huge step toward unifying your marriage under His authority and provision. Unity is not about imposing your will on your spouse but about submitting to God's will and purpose for your marriage. As God adjusts your perspectives into His vision, you'll begin to live in harmony and peace. Unity is the sacred prize for couples who humble themselves before God and each other, under the covering of His will.

Dear Father, I want the same vision for marriage as my spouse has, and that is Your vision. Holy Spirit, help us to stay unified. In Jesus' name, Amen.

Have you ever experienced divided visions? What were the results?

Day 186

I WILL (as a husband) sacrificially love and serve my wife.

There is no alternative.

For husbands, this means love your wives, just as Christ loved the church. He gave up his life for her (Ephesians 5:25).

Ephesians 5 directs men to serve their wives sacrificially and selflessly as modeled by Jesus. His appeal as a leader for billions of people worldwide lies in His unparalleled character and reliability. He is not an authoritative taskmaster, but a humble servant-leader who washed the feet of His disciples. Similarly, a Christian husband must embody the same spirit of selflessness and humility. Most women embrace this proposition fully. As a husband, you are to submit to God and your wife by loving and caring for her sacrificially as your equal. As a wife, you are to submit to God and your husband by honoring him as you would the Lord and serving him accordingly. A Christian marriage that follows this standard shows honor to both spouses' needs.

Dear Father, I want to follow Your plan for marriage. Holy Spirit, show me how to sacrificially love and serve my wife like Jesus did for us. In Jesus' name, Amen.

What do you think it means for a husband to sacrificially love and serve his wife?

I WILL put God first in my life and marriage.

In marriage, both spouses have moral obligations to God and to each other to protect their relationship from being violated by people or things of lesser priorities.

"Do not worship any other god, for the LORD, whose name is Jealous, is a jealous God" (Exodus 34:14 NIV).

Not all jealousy is negative. God created us to love Him above everything else and becomes jealous when other gods, such as money, pleasure, or fame, threaten our relationship with Him. It is legitimate jealousy when we allocate time, energy, or resources rightfully belonging to Him to anything else. The Law of Priority in marriage applies to our relationship with God, too, as we must have no other gods before Him. When we do, He becomes jealous to safeguard His relationship with us. God's love prompts His jealousy, as He fights to hold on to us and allows us to prioritize our spouses when we put Him first.

Dear Father, I want You to be first in my life—You, and You alone. Holy Spirit, show me when I am putting other things in front of God. In Jesus' name, Amen.

Make a note to pray this question to God throughout the day: "Lord, what can I do today to show You that You are first?"

Day 188

I WILL seek a clear understanding from God for the reasons He brought us together.

We are doing things for a specific purpose, and we aren't wasting our efforts or just going through the motions.

Listen to my voice in the morning, LORD.
Each morning I bring my requests to you and wait expectantly (Psalm 5:3).

Why did God bring you and your spouse together? Many Christian couples say God put them together, but they don't have a clear understanding of why. Imagine having complete clarity about God's purpose for you as a couple. How can you measure your success without knowing the goal? Think of a carpenter building a structure without a blueprint. Even though the carpenter knows how to do the job, there is no clear purpose for it. Many couples come together in a home, have children, pay bills, raise kids, and go through the motions, but they don't have a clear vision. Vision brings clarity, so you don't waste your time or simply go through the motions.

Dear Father, we want to have the same heart and purpose. Holy Spirit, help us to clarify the vision You want for our family. In Jesus' name, Amen.

Have you taken the time to talk about your vision as a couple? Have you considered taking a vision retreat to discuss and pray about it?

I WILL practice regular habits to give my marriage consistency and stability.

A successful marriage is not about what you can make happen once.

Let your wife be a fountain of blessing for you.
Rejoice in the wife of your youth (Proverbs 5:18).

Developing a thriving marriage isn't about finding a quick fix or a one-time solution. Resolving issues and maintaining a strong relationship require ongoing effort. The key is to get your marriage on track and keep it there. An important way to do this is to establish habits that prioritize quality time and energy for your spouse. Set aside a dedicated night for a date, pray together, take walks, plan short trips, have focused conversations without distractions, make time for intimacy, resolve conflicts before bedtime, read marriage books as a couple, attend conferences, enjoy romantic comedies, and find activities you both love to do regularly. Building healthy practices into your marriage ensures that both of you have your needs met consistently and passionately.

Dear Father, I want my marriage to be healthy and joyful. Holy Spirit, please give me wisdom to know what disciplines and traditions will be a blessing to my marriage and family. In Jesus' name, Amen.

What disciplines and traditions would you like to create with your spouse?

Day 190

I WILL break free from generational iniquities.

We don't want to transfer iniquities to our children and grandchildren.

I confess my iniquity;
I am sorry for my sin (Psalm 38:18 ESV).

In Hebrew, an iniquity means "to bend or twist." Just as a plant may grow crooked due to external forces, you too might have been influenced by your parents' sins. To break the cycle of iniquities in your life and prevent their negative impact on your marriage and children, follow these steps:

1. Take responsibility for your own behavior without blaming others.
2. Specifically identify the problem.
3. Repent sincerely, confessing your sins to God.
4. Forgive your parents.
5. Break the iniquity's hold by surrendering it to Jesus.

Pray a simple prayer to break the iniquity over yourself, your spouse, and future generations. Then be a righteous example by repenting, behaving responsibly, and showing love and care.

Dear Father, I believe You want my marriage and family to be free from iniquities. I especially want to avoid passing them down to the next generation. Holy Spirit, reveal any sinful attitudes and actions I may have inherited. In Jesus' name, Amen.

When you think about your family tree, what iniquities have been passed down to you?

I WILL embrace faith as the antidote to fear.

*Jesus felt fear, but He faced His fear by faith,
and He will never be afraid again.*

The LORD is my light and my salvation;
whom shall I fear?
The LORD is the stronghold of my life;
of whom shall I be afraid? (Psalm 27:1 ESV).

Jesus prayed three times in the Garden of Eden to let the cup of suffering pass from Him, but He ultimately faced His fear by faith. In the same way, you will encounter moments of fear in your marriage. It would feel wonderful if God simply removed any fear of rejection, vulnerability, or the unknown, but that doesn't always happen. Sometimes, God will empower you to confront the fear. Consider Jesus' arrest. He could have run away and hid, but He stood firm. After His resurrection, He greeted His disciples with "Peace to you." His fear was transformed into peace through His faith. If you find yourself in a situation where you have to face your fear head-on, be confident the Lord will give you the strength and resilience to conquer it.

Dear Father, I believe You know exactly what I need. Holy Spirit, fill me with supernatural courage to face my fears. In Jesus' name, Amen.

What fears is God preparing you to face today?

Day 192

I WILL encourage healthy humor in our home.

We need to plan times to enjoy each other and laugh.

A cheerful heart is good medicine,
   but a broken spirit saps a person's strength (Proverbs 17:22).

Humor in families is often overlooked, but holds significant importance. God's mercy often blesses each family with a comedian, bringing joy into our lives. We should be grateful for those who bring laughter and respect their positive influence. However, humor must never be crude or at someone's expense, and sarcasm, rooted in anger, can be harmful. Pure and clean humor is essential. It should not replace necessary discussions during difficult times but be used sensitively, considering others' emotions. Keeping humor in perspective helps us navigate challenging situations. Plan enjoyable activities with your spouse, such as game nights, outings, trips, or couple dates to maintain a spirit of enjoyment and fun. Marriages should be filled with a wholesome sense of humor, preserving our joy amid life's pressures and problems.

Dear Father, You are a God of joy, and Your joy is my strength. Holy Spirit, show me how to keep my marriage fun and enjoyable. In Jesus' name, Amen.

How often do you and your spouse share humor and laugh together? What kinds of activities would give you more joy as a couple?

I WILL, with my spouse, learn to lean on each other.

Men and women need each other to achieve their greatest potential in God.

The human body has many parts, but the many parts make up one whole body. So it is with the body of Christ (1 Corinthians 12:12).

You must lean on God in your weak moments through these five areas of reliance:

1. **God's Presence:** Maintain absolute reliance on God. Your connection to God is deeply reflected in your prayer life.
2. **Respecting the Opposite Sex:** Seek wisdom and insight from the opposite sex, particularly your spouse.
3. **God's Anointed Advisers:** Respect and listen to the guidance of spiritual mentors.
4. **Close Friends:** We must have godly companionship in our lives.
5. **Wise Counselors:** Consistently seek wisdom from counselors. There is great value of informed advice.

Recognizing and embracing these areas of dependence will guide you toward true success and spiritual growth.

Dear Father, I want to achieve and receive all You have for me. You have given my spouse to me to help me follow You and do great things for Your Kingdom. Holy Spirit, reveal Your amazing plan for our lives and our marriage. We want to join You in this great adventure. In Jesus' name, Amen.

How difficult is it for you to rely on other people, including Your spouse?

Day 194

I WILL not allow my emotions to dictate the atmosphere for my marriage.

True love is the choice to do the right thing for the object of your affection regardless of negative circumstances or the other person's behavior.

Jesus Christ is the same yesterday, today, and forever (Hebrews 13:8).

In marriage, you have two options for your relationship's thermostat: emotion or decision. You must choose if your feelings will dictate the atmosphere or if you will do the right thing, regardless of how you feel. Building your marriage on the thermostat of decision doesn't mean emotions aren't important; it means you act positively and proactively, even when negative emotions arise. Love is a decision, not just an emotion. It's the choice to do what's right for your partner, regardless of circumstances or behavior, and it's a commitment that remains unwavering through all phases and challenges of marriage. Don't let emotions rule your marriage; instead, let God's love be your standard. His love is stable and constant, through all life's ups and downs. Worship Him, and let His love guide your decisions.

Dear Father, I want my marriage to glorify You. Holy Spirit, help me to love my spouse the same way You love me. In Jesus' name, Amen.

Has your marriage been guided by decisions or emotions? How can you choose to love your spouse today?

I WILL (as a wife) monitor relationships outside my marriage.

While we all need these other relationships in our lives, they must be monitored carefully.

A wife should put her husband first, as she does the Lord (Ephesians 5:22 CEV).

For many women, relationships with friends, parents, and family members can pose a threat to their marriage. While these relationships are important, it's crucial to monitor them carefully to ensure they don't undermine your relationship with your spouse. Excessive phone time, overly close bonds that replace your spouse, and spending too much time at their homes or yours can all cause problems. To establish and protect a strong connection with your spouse, make sure to prioritize daily time and energy for them. Don't sacrifice your marriage for the sake of others, even if it may hurt their feelings. If you're seeking outside relationships due to marital issues, be mindful not to let them interfere with actively supporting and praying for your husband.

Dear Father, I am grateful for all the wonderful relationships in my life. Holy Spirit, give me wisdom to make sure my relationship with my spouse is the one receiving the most care and attention. In Jesus' name, Amen.

What relationships do you need to monitor and perhaps reevaluate?

Day 196

I WILL give God the glory for His vision and provision in my marriage.

God imparts vision and provision to you and the result is victory.

And my God shall supply all your need according to His riches in glory by Christ Jesus (Philippians 4:19 NKJV).

The grand prize of having a vision is victory. When you surrender to the Lord and pray for Him to reveal His will to you, He imparts vision and provision to you, resulting in victory. God doesn't bless good ideas; He blesses His ideas. The process of having a vision retreat for your marriage is about getting God's plan for your marriage in writing and in detail. It's about coming together as a couple and proactively planning, rather than reacting and living defensively in the dark. Do yourself a favor and have an annual vision retreat. When God gives the vision for your marriage, give Him glory often for His guidance and supply. He is good and wants good for your marriage.

Dear Father, I give You thanks and praise for the vision and provision You have given to our marriage. Holy Spirit, thank You for speaking clearly to us. In Jesus' name, Amen.

Have you stopped to give God the glory for bringing you this far in your marriage? If not, begin today!

I WILL embrace friendship with my spouse.

*Friendship is the glue that keeps marriages
from getting old and stale.*

The heartfelt counsel of a friend
is as sweet as perfume and incense (Proverbs 27:9).

Some people might be surprised to think of a married couple as friends. But this is something that God intends for marriage. Some of a wife's deepest needs are security, nonsexual affection, and open and honest communication. Some of a husband's deepest needs are respect and friendship. These needs complement each other. Men grow in friendships through fun experiences that help them become emotionally open and vulnerable. Women desire to be secure in their relationship and to receive affection that goes beyond sexual. When wives take interest in their husband's activities and when husbands respect and affirm their wives, friendship blossoms.

Dear Father, thank You for providing us with a deep and abiding friendship through our marriage. Though we will have other friends, help us to see the friendship in our marriage as the most valuable friendship we have been given. In Jesus' name, Amen.

Have you taken time to consider your spouse as your best friend? If you were to imagine what you need most in a friend, what would it be? What interests and activities can you begin to share to enhance your friendship?

Day 198

I WILL have a Godward mindset
toward my marriage.

*Having a Godward mindset
means focusing your mind toward God.*

I know the LORD is always with me.
I will not be shaken, for he is right beside me. (Psalm 16:8).

In the beautiful book of Psalms, David's songs stand out as gems of worship. He penned 73 of these 150 individual songs, and he composed many of them during the most challenging moments of his life. These psalms resonate with so many believers because they offer comfort and encouragement, especially when you are facing tough times of your own. David's secret is that he consistently directed his thoughts toward God. This Godward perspective contrasts starkly with the devil's ploy—a godless mindset in which we focus on the giants, the mountains, and the problems. God is ever-present, but your attitude and state of mind determine whether you acknowledge His presence. When you have a Godward perspective of your circumstances, you will find strength even in the midst of overwhelming challenges.

Dear Father, thank You for Your presence that brings peace in the midst of chaos. Holy Spirit, help me to direct my thoughts toward God on a daily basis. In Jesus' name, Amen.

How does having a Godward mindset change the way you view challenges?

I WILL never give up on making my sexual relationship with my spouse the best it can be.

Sex is a beautiful gift from God.

Love never gives up, never loses faith, is always hopeful, and endures through every circumstance (1 Corinthians 13:7).

If you find yourself facing physical or emotional barriers that prevent you from being sexually open with your spouse, then take it seriously and seek help. When one of you has a problem, it becomes a shared problem. Ignoring it can leave your spouse feeling disconnected and cause significant harm to your marriage. Whether it's sexual guilt, past trauma, unresolved conflicts, or physical difficulties, it's crucial to address the issue head-on. Don't let any challenge derail the intimacy and sacredness of your marriage. Communicate to your spouse that you are committed to fighting for your marriage and meeting their needs, no matter the obstacles. Sex is a beautiful gift, meant exclusively for the covenant of marriage. Face your challenges together and you will cultivate a profound and enduring intimacy that will bind you together on the deepest level for a lifetime.

Dear Father, I never want to give up on my spouse or our sexual relationship. Holy Spirit, guide me to the right solutions for any difficulties we face. In Jesus' name, Amen.

Have you ever felt like giving up in the past? What did you do to keep going?

Day 200

I WILL be a channel of healing.

Embrace biblical principles to transform your marriage into a journey of healing.

Some people make cutting remarks,
but the words of the wise bring healing (Proverbs 12:18).

You may notice that attraction to your mate has a purpose, and marriage can be a healing journey when approached correctly. God has given you inherent traits to fulfill your spouse's needs, and using these to serve and love them not only meets their needs but also heals past wounds. You can find understanding of men's and women's basic needs in the Bible, like men's need for respect and women's for security, as seen in Ephesians 5. These are healing gifts spouses can give each other. Embracing these principles empowers you to nourish and cherish your relationship, making it a true healing journey. Your marriage becomes better because you each become more healed, and you fall more in love with your spouse as a channel of healing.

Dear Father, thank You that I can be a channel of Your healing for my spouse. Holy Spirit, guide me to serve my spouse like You serve me. In Jesus' name, Amen.

How can you meet your spouse's need today? What happens inside of you when your spouse meets your needs? Can you share that with each other?

I WILL prioritize my relationship with my spouse, even over my relationship with my children.

If you don't teach your children to respect your marriage, you won't have one.

Children are a gift from the LORD;
   they are a reward from him (Psalm 127:3).

C hildren are a gift from God, but they can present a challenge to any couple's priorities. Without boundaries, children can consume all your time and energy, leaving little for your spouse. Teach children to respect the marriage, so that they understand your marriage relationship takes precedence over them. Becoming a "helicopter parent" or "supermom/dad" and centering your lives around your children can erode your marriage. Remember that children are a temporary assignment, while your marriage is permanent. Encourage your children to respect marriage and model for them how they should love their future spouse. Don't allow your children to disrupt your priorities. If you've made this mistake, then apologize to your spouse, set boundaries with your children, and teach them to respect your marriage.

Dear Father, I believe You joined me together with my spouse in an unbreakable bond. Holy Spirit, keep us united as we raise children together. In Jesus' name, Amen.

Plan to have a conversation with your spouse about how God wants you to relate to your children. If you don't yet have children, now is a good time to talk about this issue.

Day 202

I WILL celebrate other people's blessings instead of being resentful.

Comparison keeps us mistrustful of God and offended at Him.

Rejoice with those who rejoice (Romans 12:15 NKJV).

When you compare yourself to others, you begin to obsess about people who seem wealthier, smarter, happier, or in better relationships. This creates a wedge not only between you and your spouse but also between you and God. You begin to doubt His love for you, and this can create an offense against the Lord in your heart. To find peace and freedom in your relationship with God, you must genuinely appreciate who you are, where you are, and what you have. In marriage, this means focusing on the spouse God gave you and not anyone else's. If you can't rejoice in others' blessings, it's time to examine your heart. Ask the Lord to show you how to celebrate the blessings He gives to the people around you. Recognize that His love for you is unique, and He has a special purpose just for you.

Dear Father, I believe You are a Father who loves to bless His children. Holy Spirit, reveal to me any resentment in my heart. In Jesus' name, Amen.

Do you find it difficult to be happy for other people? What can do you to grow in this area?

I WILL not (as a wife) allow my emotions to lead me.

Although feelings sometimes are good and helpful, they are completely unreliable as a primary source of direction.

They are the kind who work their way into people's homes and win the confidence of vulnerable women who are burdened with the guilt of sin and controlled by various desires (2 Timothy 3:6).

There can only be one leader in your life. When you are led by your emotions, you are not led your convictions, and you become an easy target for the enemy's lies and deception. Remember Eve disregarded God's command because she was emotionally manipulated by Satan, which lead to destructive consequences for herself, her marriage, and her descendants. While feelings have their place, they are unreliable as your primary guiding factor. Make God's Word your authority, not your emotions. Choose to do what's right, whether you feel like it or not. By breaking free from the grip of your emotions, you allow God to control your life, and His plan is always the best plan.

Dear Father, I give You full control of my life. Holy Spirit, be my comforter and teacher when my emotions try to dictate my words and behavior. In Jesus' name, Amen.

How can your emotions be a healthy influence? How can they be a dangerous influence?

Day 204

I WILL establish a healthy emotional distance from my parents and in-laws.

Although it may be difficult at first to make a change or to stand up to your parents or in-laws, everyone concerned will be better off in the long run if you take action now.

This explains why a man leaves his father and mother and is joined to his wife, and the two are united into one (Genesis 2:24).

When you get married, your spouse should become your top priority, even over your parents or in-laws. This reprioritization requires a healthy distance from extended family, allowing you to forge your own identity and bond with your spouse. Continuous interference from or the constant presence of family members can prevent this bonding and hinder the formation of your distinct marital identity. It's crucial that you set appropriate boundaries. While your parents and in-laws remain an essential part of your life, you must ensure that their involvement doesn't overshadow God's plan for your marriage.

Dear Father, I understand that my closest relationship should be with my spouse. Holy Spirit, give me wisdom to set an appropriate distance between my marriage and any other family members. In Jesus' name, Amen.

What kind of relationship do you have with your parents and in-laws? Do you need to make any changes to protect your marriage?

I WILL be physically affectionate with my spouse.

Outside of the bedroom we need to be physically affectionate people.

Let him kiss me with the kisses of his mouth—
for your love is more delightful than wine (Song of Songs 1:2 NIV).

P hysical intimacy isn't solely about sex; it includes nonsexual affection, which is needed by both women and men. Beyond the bedroom, it's important to demonstrate physical affection as part of your marriage. Not only will it strengthen your marriages but also benefit your children, who are encouraged by witnessing their parents' love for each other. It helps teach them how to treat their future spouses with care and respect. Regardless of where you currently stand in your marriage journey, don't give up. Work to experience physical intimacy because God designed marriage as the place for you to experience it.

Dear Father, I want my spouse to know that I love them in every way. Holy Spirit, help me to experience physical intimacy with my spouse in nonsexual ways. I want to have a deep and intimate relationship with my spouse. In Jesus' name, Amen.

Do you give you spouse nonsexual physical intimacy on a regular basis? Have a conversation with your spouse about how to give physical intimacy in a way that is appreciated and accepted.

I WILL (as a husband) communicate
my faithfulness to my wife.

*A man's heart must remain faithful, not just when
his wife is present but also when she is absent.*

Drink water from your own well—
share your love only with your wife (Proverbs 5:15).

Jesus taught that even desiring another woman in your heart is akin to adultery. As a married man, flirting with other women is inexcusable. To maintain faithfulness, you must make it clear to everyone that your wife is the sole object of your desire. Inappropriate watching of other women, whether through media or in real life, is dishonoring and sinful. It damages trust and causes insecurity. Avoid using threats of adultery or divorce in anger or frustration, as they harm your relationship and give the devil an opportunity to meddle in your marriage. Diligently create an environment of trust and security. As you demonstrate sexual purity and restraint, you allow your wife to feel safe and secure. Choose love, fidelity, and honor to build a lasting marriage that is free from the damaging effects of infidelity and divorce.

Dear Father, I want to be a faithful husband. Holy Spirit, show me any areas of my heart that do not honor my spouse. In Jesus' name, Amen.

What is your spouse's communication style? How do you best communicate with each other?

I WILL build intimacy by intertwining my life with my spouse's life.

True intimacy is created when two people so intertwine their lives with each other that one cannot determine where one life ends and the other begins.

A person standing alone can be attacked and defeated, but two can stand back-to-back and conquer. Three are even better, for a triple-braided cord is not easily broken (Ecclesiastes 4:12).

Investing everything in your marriage enables you to share everything and belong to each other entirely, creating a profound sense of intimacy. True intimacy arises from intertwining lives to the point where you cannot tell where one of you ends and the other begins. Prioritizing personal independence hinders intimacy. Godly intimacy requires selflessness, giving, and sacrifice. While many seek intimacy, few are willing to pay the price. To achieve oneness, consider whether you are separating yourself from your partner, withholding anything, or controlling them. Confess any violations to your spouse and to God. Eliminate this sin, because it poses a grave threat to any relationship.

Dear Father, I want to have complete oneness with my spouse. Holy Spirit, convict me when I try to withhold anything. In Jesus' name, Amen.

Take a mental inventory of your life to see if you are withholding any area from your spouse. What actions will you take to remedy the situation?

I WILL seek out healthy friends who support my marriage.

Your friends are your future—good or bad.

Do not be misled: "Bad company corrupts good character" (1 Corinthians 15:33 NIV).

It's hard to keep your marriage pure when your main friend group is made up of people who are impure. You don't have to be legalistic to recognize that you need to be careful about your environment and close relationships. You will become like those you surround yourself with. Your friends shape your future. Sadly, adultery and divorce often happen within friend groups. When you're around people who are engaging in sin, they can become a support system for your own sin. You need friends who will uplift you and love your spouse, rather than advising you to leave your spouse when you face problems. You don't need friends who will tempt you to sin. You need friends who set a good example and encourage you to do the right thing. A healthy local church is a great place to find those kinds of friends.

Dear Father, help me to choose my friends wisely. Holy Spirit, lead me to friends who will honor You and support my marriage. In Jesus' name, Amen.

Do you have godly friends who support your marriage? What are some of the things they do to show you they respect marriage?

I WILL accept my God-given destiny.

You can only be you; you cannot be someone else.

You saw me before I was born.
>Every day of my life was recorded in your book.
Every moment was laid out
>before a single day had passed (Psalm 139:16).

G od designed each person on this earth with a distinct identity and destiny. It's futile to measure yourself against the careers, wealth, fame, or appearance of others. The key to success lies in embracing who God made you to be. His love for you is unwavering, and He expresses it through the unique path He has set for you. Psalm 139:16 says that your days were written in God's book long before they came to be. Comparison traps you in the illusion that you must become someone else to feel worthy and accomplished. But the most certain way to miss out on happiness is to ignore your unique calling and identity. Striving to change your unchangeable self always leads to failure. God made you to be you and only you, and His plan is perfect.

Dear Father, thank You for Your design for my life. Holy Spirit, show me the best way to walk about my destiny. In Jesus' name, Amen.

What excites you the most about God's unique plan for your life?

Day 210

I WILL forgive those who have hurt me in past relationships.

Forgiveness is the most important factor that determines a person's emotional health and ability to relate to people properly.

"You have also heard that our ancestors were told, 'You must not break your vows; you must carry out the vows you make to the LORD.' But I say, do not make any vows!" (Matthew 5:33–34).

Divorce and break-ups from serious relationships are profoundly painful, often feeling more enduring than other kinds of grief. In their hurt from a breakup, many people might not process emotions well, leading to unresolved feelings. Essential to healing is forgiveness, but it's challenging when you've been hurt by an ex. You might carry diminished trust and heightened expectations when you enter a new relationship. Many people also form "inner vows" like "No one will ever hurt me again," reflecting self-protective promises. However, these vows can harm future relationships because you try to control everything instead of giving it to God. Without true forgiveness, past pains can overshadow future relationships.

Dear Father, I do not want to allow pain from my past to stop me from enjoying new relationships. Holy Spirit, I need Your comfort and guidance as I choose to forgive by faith. In Jesus' name, Amen.

Whom do you need to forgive from your past in order to move forward?

I WILL be content in what God provides for us.

True contentment means that we will be thankful if we just have adequate food and covering.

So if we have enough food and clothing, let us be content.
But people who long to be rich fall into temptation and are trapped by many foolish and harmful desires that plunge them into ruin and destruction (1 Timothy 6:8–9).

Contentment is appreciating what you have and patiently waiting on God's timing for anything more. Today's culture often breeds discontent, pushing us to accumulate more things and forcing many people toward financial ruin. Commit to a lifestyle that values contentment, no matter what your financial status is. Practice gratitude, find peace in what you currently have, and humbly present your dreams to God. This will safeguard you from greed and discontent. The apostle Paul says the love of money can breed a lot of trouble (1 Timothy 6:10). Don't let wealth control you; instead, use your finances as God guides. Remember, your happiness hinges on your relationship with Jesus, not your financial status.

Dear Father, You give me everything I need exactly when I need it. Holy Spirit, teach me how to be content and grateful. In Jesus' name, Amen.

How does contentment with your current situation affect your relationship with your spouse and family?

Day 212

I WILL be a faithful gatekeeper.

Who you are today has been decided by you and what gate you opened.

I will give you the keys of the kingdom of heaven; whatever you bind on earth will be bound in heaven, and whatever you loose on earth will be loosed in heaven (Matthew 16:19 NIV).

As a gatekeeper, you have the God-given authority to determine what comes into your marriage. Be intentional about what you allow your eyes to see. Protect your ears from gossip and foul language. Watch over your mouth and choose to speak words that encourage instead of tear down. Align your mind with the truth of God's Word. Invite God's presence and guidance into your spirit. Keep the desires of your flesh within the covenant of your marriage. Filter your emotions with love and grace. Be vigilant in guarding your eyes, ears, mouth, mind, spirit, flesh, and emotions. You alone are responsible for these gates, and with the help of the Holy Spirit, you can be a faithful gatekeeper.

Dear Father, I want to be a good gatekeeper for my marriage. Holy Spirit, help me to be wise about what I should and should not allow in my relationship. In Jesus' name, Amen.

What harmful things do you need to stop allowing through your gates?

I WILL fight against the true enemy of my marriage.

Satan hates marriage, and every couple will come under spiritual attack.

So let God work his will in you. Yell a loud *no* to the Devil and watch him make himself scarce. Say a quiet *yes* to God and he'll be there in no time (James 4:7–8 MSG).

Satan detests marriage and battles against every couple. It's crucial for you to pick the right battles. Direct your fight toward the real adversary, not your partner. The enemy's disdain is because he knows how significant it is to God. Since Genesis 3, marriage has been under assault. If the devil dismantles marriage, then he knows society crumbles. He knows children thrive in intact families. Marriage offers healing and support. God designed marriage for mutual aid and social cohesion. Satan despises those benefits of marriage. Even so, you possess authority. Don't fear the devil, but recognize he is a liar. He attacks through anger and division. Jesus granted you the authority stand against the enemy in faith and truth.

Dear Father, empower me to fight the enemy every day. Holy Spirit, help me to know when the devil is trying to attack my marriage. In Jesus' name, Amen.

What do you think is the best way to recognize and combat the enemy?

Day 214

I WILL submit all my fears to God.

*When you submit your fear to God, fear
no longer tells you what to do.*

"Not My will, but Yours, be done" (Luke 22:42 NKJV).

S ubmitting your fear to God means acknowledging your feelings without being ruled by them. Though fear may knock, you don't have to open the door. Instead of acting on what you feel or even think, your behavior is determined by what aligns with God's Word. Decisions rooted in fear always lead to regret. Your emotions are real, but they're not necessarily what's right or best for you or the people you love. Jesus demonstrated this truth in the Garden of Eden when He acknowledged His fear but surrendered to God's will. To live beyond your emotions, you must choose to reject fear's control and act on faith. As you and your spouse submit your fears to the Lord, He will bless your marriage, guide you on the right path, and fill your future with hope.

Dear Father, I submit all my fears to you. Holy Spirit, help me to live by the unchanging truth of God's Word instead of my fickle feelings. In Jesus' name, Amen.

How would your life be different if you made decisions based solely on God's Word instead of your feelings?

I WILL approach my marriage as an "owner" rather than a "renter."

An owner's mentality demonstrates a commitment to the relationship regardless of the circumstances.

Little children, let us not love in word or talk but in deed and in truth (1 John 3:18 ESV).

Do you approach your marriage with an "owner's mentality" or a "renter's mentality"? Imagine renting a house and the landlord demands you pay $50,000 for repairs. You'd likely refuse because it's not your long-term investment. However, if you owned the property, you'd be more inclined to invest in its upkeep. A renter's mentality in marriage can be harmful. When challenges arise or flaws surface, doubt creeps in. You might wonder if you chose the right person. You become passive during critical moments, waiting for your spouse to make repairs. You may start looking elsewhere. Owners are committed. They are "all in." Problems become shared responsibilities. Instead of being passive, you're proactive. Co-owners both work to benefit the relationship.

Dear Father, I want to be "all in" as an owner of my marriage. Holy Spirit, keep me from halfway commitments to my spouse. Forgive me for doing things that would cause my spouse to doubt my commitment or to feel insecure. In Jesus' name, Amen.

How can you show your spouse you are "all in" today?

Day 216

I WILL appreciate my role and giftings in my marriage.

Do not give up impact for influence when
God has called you to impact.

The human body has many parts, but the many parts make up one whole body. So it is with the body of Christ (1 Corinthians 12:12).

Just as the human body's different parts serve distinct purposes, you and your spouse possess strengths and qualities that complement each other. It is crucial to value your role and giftings within marriage. Instead of comparing yourself against one another, choose to appreciate the beauty of your distinct contributions. In the human quest for significance, it's common to crave influence over impact. However, impact is often more profound and necessary. Consider a teacher's limited influence on their students versus a mother's intimate impact on her own children. In marriage, the impact you have on your spouse's life far outweighs the influence of external forces. So celebrate your uniqueness and prioritize the impact you can make on your spouse's life as you cherish the beautiful connection that defines you as a couple.

Dear Father, I want to have a positive impact on my spouse. Holy Spirit, direct my words and my actions every day. In Jesus' name, Amen.

What are three ways you and your spouse complement each other?

I WILL (as a wife) place faith over my feelings.

The woman without faith is unwilling to take God at His word.

And it is impossible to please God without faith. Anyone who wants to come to him must believe that God exists and that he rewards those who sincerely seek him (Hebrews 11:6).

Do you let temporary emotions guide your decisions? God's Word is life's final authority, but many people place greater faith in their feelings than His eternal promises. It's not a sin to wrestle with questions or even struggle with doubt. But hard-hearted unbelief is not just a minor problem—it is actually a sin. The only solution is to repent and obey God's Word. No matter how you feel about God or His instructions for your life, what truly matters is what you *do*. Refuse to let your feelings control you and start exercising your will through faith. As you do so, you will witness remarkable improvements in your life and marriage.

Dear Father, I choose to trust that You know what exactly what I need. Holy Spirit, show me how to build my faith so that I am no longer controlled by temporary emotions. In Jesus' name, Amen.

When your feelings seem too strong, what can you do to stop them from dominating your behavior?

Day 218

I WILL (as a husband) communicate my dedication to providing financially for my family.

A wife needs the assurance that her husband is committed to providing for her financially.

But those who won't care for their relatives, especially those in their own household, have denied the true faith. Such people are worse than unbelievers (1 Timothy 5:8).

As a husband, you must prioritize your wife's financial security. You can show your commitment in four ways: praying together for God's guidance, actively seeking the best employment, being a hardworking and faithful employee, and being a wise money manager. Make decisions together, valuing her input and avoiding domineering behavior. Act as a team, whether both of you work outside the home or not. Your wife needs to know you're dedicated, honest, and dependable, as instability creates insecurity. Sacrificing income or benefits should never compromise her security. Remember, financial responsibility is a joint effort. In our home, we make significant financial decisions together, and my wife handles bill payments. Find what works best for you, but always prioritize unity and teamwork.

Dear Father, everything we have comes from You, and I want to be a wise steward of Your blessings. Holy Spirit, guide me through every financial decision, both large and small. In Jesus' name, Amen.

How do you demonstrate that you are committed to your family's financial wellbeing?

I WILL embrace my spouse's differences.

Spouses have differences from one another by divine design.

May the God of endurance and encouragement grant you to live in such harmony with one another, in accord with Christ Jesus, that together you may with one voice glorify the God and Father of our Lord Jesus Christ
(Romans 15:5–6 ESV).

Are you caught up in a painful dance of expectations and disappointments? There is good news: you can change your world. The journey commences with embracing and respecting the intrinsic differences within your spouse. This doesn't imply that your spouse or marriage never needs to change. Yet, it does mean that attempting to change your spouse's God-given differences is a swift route to disappointment. The undeniable reality is that both you and your spouse are intentionally unique, crafted by divine intent. The longer you are married, the more these differences between you and your spouse will come to light. Often these differences represent unique gifts and strengths your spouse possesses. Honoring these differences can help you fulfill one another's needs, and savor your marriage.

Dear Father, You have made us with unique strengths. Help me to see and honor those differences. Help me to receive my spouse's strengths and to share my strengths to fulfill my spouse's needs. In Jesus' name, Amen.

What strengths do you see in your spouse that you do not have? How can you use your strengths to serve your spouse?

Day 220

I WILL openly address issues
and conflict rather than avoid them.

Silence in a marriage and family is a dangerous thing.

"If another believer sins against you, go privately and point out the offense. If the other person listens and confesses it, you have won that person back" (Matthew 18:15).

Instead of addressing issues and finding resolutions together, some couples choose silence as a way to punish or intimidate each other. When tension or conflict arises, it's important to take a healthy approach and engage in open dialogue before things spiral out of control. This is especially critical when anger is present; the sooner you bring it to the surface and diffuse it, the better the outcome. Silence poses a grave danger within a marriage. It takes a toll on the relationship and prolongs the problem. Many adults experienced lifelong emotional pain due to growing up in homes where one or both parents used silence as a way to punish and control. If that is you, break the cycle in your marriage.

Dear Father, I believe You are always open and honest with me. Help me to be transparent with my spouse. Holy Spirit, convict me when I fall into unhealthy communication patterns. In Jesus' name, Amen.

Has someone ever given you "the silent treatment"? How did that make you feel?

I WILL acknowledge the qualities I admire in my spouse.

One of the most crucial roles you play in your husband's or wife's life is to be God's instrument in revealing to them that they are very important and special.

Pleasant words *are like* a honeycomb,
Sweetness to the soul and health to the bones (Proverbs 16:24 NKJV).

In the early days, you and your spouse were smitten with each other's special qualities and the way they made you feel. But over time, it's easy to stop showing admiration and appreciation for each other. Feelings of love can start to fade, and you find yourself wondering, *What happened to our spark?* Don't be afraid, though—you have the power to reignite that spark. Begin today by making a conscious effort to acknowledge and affirm your spouse. Let them know what you like about them! As your spouse feels cherished, your love will flourish, and your relationship will once again be joyful and fulfilling. Let Christ's love guide you as you grow in love and admiration for each other day by day.

Dear Father, thank You for the wonderful gift of my spouse. Holy Spirit, remind me to express how much I appreciate and admire them. In Jesus' name, Amen.

What qualities do you admire most about your spouse? How will you verbalize this admiration today?

Day 222

I WILL discern good fear from bad fear.

*God has a good plan for your future. He will never
prophesy gloom and turmoil to control your life.*

And His name will be called Wonderful, Counselor, Mighty God, Everlasting
Father, Prince of Peace (Isaiah 9:6 NKJV).

Fear acts as a navigation system in your relationship. Good fear is like a
trusted advisor that says, "Hold on," "Change course," or "Keep going." It
helps you make wise choices that lead to a better future. On the other hand, bad
fear acts like a doomsday prophet, filling your mind with negativity. It predicts
a doomed marriage, financial ruin, unpopularity, and despair. But remember,
God has a wonderful plan for your life, and He will never use fear to control
you. Jesus is the Prince of Peace, and His presence will bring harmony in your
marriage and serenity in your life. In this divine partnership, you'll find comfort
and fulfillment as you place your trust in God's unchanging plan for your future.

*Dear Father, I believe You have a wonderful plan for my life. Holy Spirit, thank
You for Your peace that guides me every day. In Jesus' name, Amen.*

How does good fear help you make wise choices? How has bad fear hurt your
marriage in the past?

I WILL recognize and address any seeds of comparison in my heart.

If you really love someone, you want something good for them. If you don't love them, you resent them when something good happens to them.

You shall love your neighbor as yourself (Matthew 22:39 ESV).

Comparison can spring up from surprising sources. A lack of self-acceptance may seem like humility, but it will hurt your relationship with God and your spouse. On the other hand, if you rely on your status or position or the approval of others, you will always be disappointed. An orphan spirit craves excess, and an entitlement spirit believes it deserves what others have. Consider whether you hold a distorted view of God. True love desires the best for others, but a spirit of rejection causes resentment to build when others are blessed. Covetousness, jealousy, and envy will sour your heart and your relationships. To uproot these seeds, you must choose to trust in God's provision and care, both for you as an individual and for your marriage.

Dear Father, I trust You to provide and care for me. Holy Spirit, open my eyes to any roots of comparison that needs to be removed from my life. In Jesus' name, Amen.

What sources of comparison is the Holy Spirit bringing to your attention to deal with?

Day 224

I WILL genuinely listen to my spouse.

Whenever our spouses are speaking to us,
we should listen carefully.

Spouting off before listening to the facts
is both shameful and foolish (Proverbs 18:13).

Hearing and truly listening are different. Hearing is physical, while listening involves intellectual engagement. When your spouse speaks, it's vital to listen carefully, as they often convey more than just words. If you don't genuinely listen, they'll notice and may look for someone who will. If you're unable to concentrate, then address it honestly, because regular communication is key. Demonstrate active listening by asking relevant questions, providing brief comments, and maintaining eye contact. Despite everyday distractions, make sure to dedicate exclusive time for meaningful conversations with your spouse. After your spouse speaks, respond appropriately, even if it's a simple acknowledgment. Be cautious about harsh words or distant looks, as they can put up a roadblock to effective communication.

Dear Father, I love knowing that You hear me when I speak to You. Holy Spirit, teach me how to be a great listener so that I can honor my spouse. In Jesus' name, Amen.

What are some verbal and nonverbal cues you can use to let your spouse know you are really paying attention and listening to them?

I WILL deal with conflicts in a positive manner.

Spouses should begin conflict resolution by stating their love, admiration, and commitment to each other.

A gentle answer deflects anger,
>   but harsh words make tempers flare (Proverbs 15:1).

Deal with conflicts positively. When you address your emotions promptly, you gain an advantage. Resist the temptation to start resolving issues with threats or hostility. For instance, if a troubled couple begins arguments by shouting about the possibility of ending their marriage, then you can expect one day they will make good on the threat. Negative name-calling doesn't lead to change. To effectively resolve conflicts, begin by affirming your love, admiration, and commitment to your spouse. Feeling loved makes it easier to tackle problems. Defensive reactions are common when confronted with anger and aggression. Remember, avoid calling names and instead provide affirmation. Positive communication will lead to conflict resolution and reinforce your love for your spouse.

Dear Father, even when we have displeased You, Your love remains. Holy Spirit, help me always to affirm my love for my spouse, even when I am angry. In Jesus' name, Amen.

Have you tried to address a difficult issue by first affirming your love for your spouse? If not, try it the next time you have a disagreement.

Day 226

I WILL take the "right path" in my marriage, even when it seems difficult.

When you get to the difficult times in your life and marriage, you must forgive, commit, and give of yourself in spite of your negative emotions.

The LORD says, "I will guide you along the best pathway for your life. I will advise you and watch over you" (Psalm 32:8).

At pivotal moments in your marriage you'll face choices. Will you forgive or hold onto bitterness? Will you face challenges or flee from them? When your partner upsets you, will you seek solace elsewhere or fight for your relationship? Every relationship faces challenges; it's the perseverance and selflessness during hard times that make a difference. Temptations might lure you with seemingly easier paths, and sometimes, people might push you toward them, arguing against what you know is right. Remember two things: First, the "easy way" often hides unforeseen challenges. And second, the right path, although daunting at first, offers more rewards as you progress.

Dear Father, I know You can give me the strength to do difficult tasks with righteousness and integrity. Holy Spirit, keep speaking to me so that I might not sin against You. In Jesus' name, Amen.

What can you do better to stay true to your promise to stand by your spouse through difficult times?

I WILL overcome rejection through the power of the Holy Spirit.

Jesus overcame rejection on every level, and He has empowered us to do the same.

"If the world hates you, remember that it hated me first" (John 15:18).

R ejection hurts more than almost anything else. Satan often tries to use rejection as his primary control point, but by following Jesus' example, you can put a stop to this evil manipulation tactic. Jesus never permitted the fear of rejection to stop Him from obeying the Father's will. He never allowed it to influence His attitude or His interactions with people. Jesus was willing to die the most painful and shameful death imaginable and be the ultimate sacrifice for us. Why? Because He refused to allow Satan to control the way He made decisions, the way He treated people, and whether or not He would do God's will for His life. Even if you are struggling in your marriage today, you can decide to surrender all decisions to the lordship of Jesus Christ. He has good plans for you *and* your spouse. He can be trusted.

Dear Father, I surrender control of my decisions to You. Holy Spirit, thank You for giving me the power to overcome rejection. In Jesus' name, Amen.

What decisions do you need to surrender to the Lord?

Day 228

I WILL be a faithful steward with our finances.

Faithfully working and wisely planning over many years will be how we establish financial security.

The trustworthy person will get a rich reward,
but a person who wants quick riches will get into trouble (Proverbs 28:20).

Beware of tempting get-rich-quick schemes. Con artists capitalize on greed, knowing that it can drive people to make irrational choices they wouldn't normally make. Realistically, very few people get rich overnight. For the vast majority of people, financial security comes from consistent work and intelligent planning over the years. As one financial expert said, "Spend less than you earn, and do it for a long time." Avoid chasing instant financial solutions. Just as losing weight requires disciplined, healthy living over time, so does attaining financial stability. By faithfully and consistently managing your finances well, you'll achieve security and success. Don't gamble on quick fixes. Stay faithful to God's Word daily; what you attain will be yours for life.

Dear Father, I don't want anything to distract me away from diligently managing the finances You have blessed me with. Holy Spirit, help me to make wise decisions that will bless my family. In Jesus' name, Amen.

What is your plan to avoid the temptation of get-rich-quick schemes that sound too good to be true?

I WILL prioritize my relationship with Jesus.

Everyone has to have their own relationship with Jesus—and it's from that relationship that a good marriage will grow.

"Remain in me, and I will remain in you. For a branch cannot produce fruit if it is severed from the vine, and you cannot be fruitful unless you remain in me" (John 15:4)

One of the greatest gifts you can give to your marriage is the foundation of your own relationship with Jesus. It is not enough to rely on your spouse's faith or your shared experiences in church. You must personally know and follow Christ. He is the anchor that holds you steady through storms and the source of wisdom and guidance for every decision. Your relationship with Jesus shapes your character, instills selflessness, and teaches you forgiveness and grace. It empowers you to love your spouse sacrificially. As you draw closer to Christ, you become a better spouse, creating a solid foundation for a thriving and fulfilling marriage.

Dear Father, thank You for the gift of Your Son, Jesus. Holy Spirit, help me to prioritize my relationship with Jesus above anything else. In Jesus's name, Amen.

How does your relationship with Jesus impact your marriage right now? What impact would you like to see in the future?

Day 230

I WILL trust God's work in my spouse's life.

If you do not let God bless other people the way He wants to bless them, He will not bless you the way you want Him to bless you.

For where jealousy and selfish ambition exist, there will be disorder and every vile practice (James 3:16 ESV).

God cares for you and your spouse equally. However, every person is a unique creation, so His blessings for you may look a bit different from His blessings for your spouse. It's so important to guard your heart against jealousy and bitterness. Even though you love your spouse, you may be tempted to interfere with God's work in their life. Here's a crucial truth to understand: if you don't allow God to work in your spouse's life as He intends, He may not work the way you desire in your life either. Loving your spouse means you genuinely support their success and achievements, both individually and within the marriage. Let God be God as He blesses your spouse as He sees fit.

Dear Father, I believe You know exactly what my spouse and I need. Holy Spirit, reveal anything in my heart that would try to interfere with God's plan. In Jesus' name, Amen.

How can you show love and support to your spouse today?

I WILL (as a wife) rely on God's Word for self-discipline.

Learn now to discipline yourself and to put some parameters on your life.

No discipline is enjoyable while it is happening—it's painful! But afterward there will be a peaceful harvest of right living for those who are trained in this way (Hebrews 12:11).

Some people had very laid-back, permissive parents who never enforced responsibilities or provided consistent correction. If you grew up without proper discipline, then you may have learned to do as you pleased without considering what was right or wise. A woman who lacks personal discipline must understand that while her parents may not have disciplined or held her accountable, God will. Start now to discipline yourself and set boundaries in your life. The Word of God will be your greatest parameter. As you strive to follow God's guidance, He will forgive your mistakes as you learn to overcome temptation. Don't give up! God loves you and will empower you to succeed as you seek Him and pray for His grace.

Dear Father, I know I need Your Word to be my guide. Holy Spirit, teach me and discipline me according to God's grace. In Jesus' name, Amen.

What was discipline like in your home as a child? How has that influenced you today?

Day 232

I WILL work hard to make joint decisions with my spouse.

Resolve that you will never make important decisions without talking and praying together.

Two people are better off than one, for they can help each other succeed (Ecclesiastes 4:9).

God's vision for marriage was to create an unbeatable and unbreakable bond between two: a man and a woman. Achieving this "oneness" means you have to function as a cohesive unit. Start by making sure neither of you dominates the other, because dominance hinders unity and intimacy. You will build unity when both of you align under Jesus Christ's Lordship, letting His will be your guide. It's critical that decisions, especially major ones involving finances, children, jobs, or family, are made jointly. Respect each other's views and always consult one another. Remember, unity thrives when you prioritize teamwork and mutual respect. Commit to never making significant choices without discussing and seeking guidance together.

Dear Father, I want to make decisions with You and my spouse as my partners. Holy Spirit, forgive me for being independent in my actions and help me to consider You and my spouse going forward. In Jesus' name, Amen.

How can you make sure that both of you consider one another in decision-making? If you have been independent in your decisions, ask for forgiveness and commit to unity going forward.

I WILL avoid sexual activity that is not permitted by God.

God has told us in His Word how we can fulfill our need for sex while avoiding the sensual destruction everywhere around us.

Flee from sexual immorality. Every other sin a person commits is outside the body, but the sexually immoral person sins against his own body (1 Corinthians 6:18 ESV).

To fully embrace and enjoy intimacy in marriage, it's essential to know what is and isn't permitted by God. Here are the six sexual behaviors God warns against:

1. Engaging in sex outside marriage.
2. Intimate relations with someone of the same gender.
3. Intimacy with a family member.
4. Relations with minors.
5. Intimacy with animals.
6. Fantasizing about someone other than your spouse or indulging in pornography.

God isn't restrictive; He designed intimacy for pleasure. God also knows the harm certain behaviors bring. In marriage, you can pursue sexual fulfillment with trust and respect for God's guidelines. If you wonder about practices not mentioned in God's Word, then such decisions rest between you and your spouse.

Dear Father, You created sexual intimacy to be enjoyed within the covenant of marriage. Holy Spirit, I will not do anything that is not permissible according to God's Word. In Jesus' name, Amen.

Why do you think God warns against certain sexual behaviors?

Day 234

I WILL remember love
is an act of will and not only a feeling.

God's love endures the tests and trials of life.

"This is my commandment: Love each other in the same way I have loved you" (John 15:12).

When the New Testament speaks of the love that God has for His people, it uses the Greek word *agape*. This word is distinct from other words for love in Greek that denote sexual attraction, parental and sibling love, or the kind of love in a community of friends. The love of God is absolute, unconditional, and eternal. It is not a fleeting emotion. This love is entirely disinterested in self. The love that God has for you is an unchanging resolution, not a feeling. This is the kind of love that God intends to be in your marriage. You must choose to love each other. It is made possible because we are secure in God's unwavering love for us.

Dear Father, I am humbled that Your absolute love is extended toward me. Because I am secure in Your love, I can make the same choice to love my spouse every day. In Jesus' name, Amen.

When you said "I will" at your wedding, did you express only a feeling or did you express a decision? How does your spouse need to experience love from you today?

I WILL rely on the Holy Spirit to give me the capacity to love my spouse the way God wants.

We don't have the ability to really love without the power of the Holy Spirit.

But the fruit of the Spirit is love, joy, peace, forbearance, kindness, goodness, faithfulness, gentleness and self-control. Against such things there is no law (Galatians 5:22–23 NIV).

Here's a truth about love: without the Holy Spirit's influence, truly loving someone becomes almost impossible. True love—the kind God grants—is called *agape* in the Bible. It's unwavering and consistent. In contrast, what many people label "love" might be driven by lust or fleeting passion. Such feelings can vanish, leading some to declare they're out of love and exit relationships. But *agape* love? It mirrors Jesus' love for us: steadfast and unwavering. When you say, "I love you," is it a fleeting sentiment or a commitment that endures regardless of circumstances? The most resilient relationships are rooted in the Holy Spirit's influence, underpinned by this divine, unwavering love. This *agape* love has the power to revolutionize any relationship.

Dear Father, Your love is perfect. It never fails me. Holy Spirit, revolutionize my relationship with my spouse to reflect God's amazing love. In Jesus' name, Amen.

How can you demonstrate *agape* love to your spouse?

Day 236

I WILL (as a husband) provide soft, nonsexual affection to my wife.

An essential need of all women is nonsexual affection.

Likewise, husbands, live with your wives in an understanding way (1 Peter 3:7 ESV).

Nonsexual affection is an essential need for all women. By showing physical affection to your wife without any request for sexual intercourse, you fulfill this important emotional, mental, and physical need, and you set a positive example for your children. Make it a habit to touch and caress your wife in gentle, nonsexual ways throughout the day. Hug her, hold her hand, and be physically close. These expressions of love benefit both of you. Take the time to ask your wife what kind of affection she desires and make an effort to fulfill her requests. Meeting her needs in this area strengthens your relationship and develops a deeper connection. Remember, by showing nonsexual affection, you create a loving and secure environment for your marriage and your family as a whole.

Dear Father, help me be attentive to every need my wife has. Holy Spirit, give me wisdom as I do my best to be a godly, caring husband. In Jesus' name, Amen.

Do you know what forms of nonsexual touch your wife enjoys? If not, how can you find out?

I WILL create and follow a plan
to manage stress in our family.

*To succeed in marriage, you simply must keep the stress
in your life and household to a manageable level.*

You will keep in perfect peace
    all who trust in you,
    all whose thoughts are fixed on you! (Isaiah 26:3).

Stress is one of the most formidable adversaries to marriage in today's fast-paced world. Did you know that most doctor visits stem from stress-induced illnesses? Stress not only drains your time but also depletes your emotional and physical energy.

Consider these strategies to manage your stress:

1. Start your day with prayer and Bible reading. Give God your concerns and seek His direction.
2. Observe the Sabbath. It's spiritually, mentally, and physically beneficial for you.
3. Steer clear of unnecessary debt. While tempting, it adds an underlying layer of stress.
4. Carve out distraction-free moments with your spouse.

Remember, placing Jesus at the center of your life infuses it with peace. Embracing His presence can be your ultimate stress relief.

Dear Father, I believe You want me to be peaceful, not stressed. Holy Spirit, show me what strategies I need to implement in order to manage the stress of living in this world. In Jesus' name, Amen.

How does placing Jesus at the center of your life help to reduce your stress level?

Day 238

I WILL approach difficult conversations with humility.

Pride is one of the most deadly forces in a relationship.

Live in harmony with each other. Don't be too proud to enjoy the company of ordinary people. And don't think you know it all! (Romans 12:16).

When you address an issue with your spouse, is your main goal to win or to resolve the problem? But what if *you* are the problem? When approaching conflict, embrace a spirit of humility. This allows for an objective examination of both sides. It enables you to take responsibility for your own actions. Winning becomes less important than redeeming the relationship and safeguarding the emotions of your spouse. Pride, however, can be one of the most destructive forces in a relationship. It seeks dominance rather than peace, refusing to accept fault and demanding others shoulder the blame. If you are ready for conflict resolution, then you must crucify your pride and embrace humility. Begin from a place of mutual service and not from one of domination, intimidation, or manipulation.

Dear Father, Jesus is my model for service and humility. Holy Spirit, convict me of the sin of pride whenever it raises its head in my life. In Jesus' name, Amen.

How dangerous is pride? Can you give an example of pride causing great damage in a relationship?

I WILL work to help my children feel secure.

*Children feel secure when they are in an
atmosphere of stability and love.*

But you must remain faithful to the things you have been taught. You know they
are true, for you know you can trust those who taught you (2 Timothy 3:14).

A child's sense of security is greatly influenced by the stability of their parents and family. When strife exists in the home, even if not explicitly discussed, your child will intuitively feel insecure. Recognize your child's natural sensitivity and emotional vulnerability. Arguments may not mean divorce to you, but to your child, they breed insecurity. Show love and service to your spouse in your child's presence. Provide patient instruction to your child and communicate about their fears and other issues. Children feel secure in a stable, loving environment, so you must diligently work to create this atmosphere by setting boundaries and applying loving discipline. This balance of accountability and acceptance will make your child feel loved and secure.

Dear Father, I want everyone in my home to safe, loved, and secure. Holy Spirit, reveal to me anything that I do or say that might make my child feel insecure. In Jesus' name, Amen.

What boundaries should you set for yourself and your family to promote feelings of security and stability?

Day 240

I WILL actively pursue accountability.

When people plan on doing something good or godly, they don't mind others watching.

Loners who care only for themselves
spit on the common good (Proverbs 18:1 MSG).

When you avoid accountability, you prioritize personal desires over God's calling. This path can lead to many pitfalls. Accountability isn't just a shield against wrongdoings; it offers invaluable insights and can help you grow spiritually. Imagine being a leader known by thousands and recognized everywhere; wouldn't you appreciate the heightened sense of responsibility? Think of the advantage of having so many observing you. Embracing too much independence can be disastrous. Personal failures come from evading accountability. Those who succeed seek guidance and are open to feedback. They live in the light and avoid darkness and deception. If you act honorably, you won't fear scrutiny. Valuing righteousness means embracing accountability. Avoiding it suggests questionable intentions. True moral integrity demands accountability.

Dear Father, You created me to have relationships with other people. I need them to help me live according to Your will. Holy Spirit, lead me to the people who can point me to righteous living and correct me when I am in error. In Jesus' name, Amen.

Who do you have in your life to keep you accountable to God and your spouse?

I WILL turn my doubts over to God.

You will never resolve your doubts until you turn them over to God.

I am the way, the truth, and the life (John 14:6).

There will be times in your marriage when doubt sneaks in. You might start to wonder, *What am I doing with my life? Have I made the right choices?* It's tempting to try to hide your doubts from God, but there's no need to fear. God isn't your adversary—He is your most loyal friend. God doesn't mind your questions or struggles because He knows they're a part of life. When Jesus was on this earth, He never once lashed out at those who questioned Him with pure, honest intentions. In Mark 9:24, the father of a demon-possessed boy was brutally honest with Jesus when he said, "I believe; help my unbelief!" (ESV). Jesus responded with love and mercy, and He will respond to you the same way today.

Dear Father, teach me how to turn all doubt over to You. Holy Spirit, remind me that You are my closest companion and that You are always ready to guide me through moments of uncertainty with love and grace. In Jesus' name, Amen.

What doubts do you need to turn over to God today?

Day 242

I WILL keep faithful to the fundamental principles that make a marriage successful.

*As difficult as things may be, there is an answer,
and it's probably not that complicated.*

Those who love your instructions have great peace
and do not stumble (Psalm 119:165).

Consider this: No matter how tough things might seem, there's a solution, and it's likely simpler than you think. Here are some fundamental principles to enhance any marriage:

- Your relationship with Jesus Christ is paramount in a marriage.
- Always place your marriage as your top priority.
- Marriage takes effort.
- It's about teamwork and giving up some things for the greater good.
- Overpowering your partner erodes intimacy and mutual respect.
- Acknowledge and respect the inherent differences between genders. Strive to meet each other's unique needs.
- Address any anger daily; never let issues linger overnight.
- Trust in your journey requires faith.
- Even if it's just one of you, placing trust in God and acting righteously can transform the toughest marriages.

Dear Father, I want to be successful in my marriage. Teach me how to respond to my spouse in ways that build up our relationship. Holy Spirit, keep speaking to me about how to be a good spouse. In Jesus' name, Amen.

Which of these principles resonates most with you? Which of them are areas where you know you need to do some additional work?

I WILL faithfully support my spouse through grief.

Grief does not have to destroy your marriage.

"Comfort, comfort my people," says your God (Isaiah 40:1 ESV).

Grief can shake your marital foundation. In fact, many say that the death of a child often leads to divorce. Yet, grief doesn't have to be the end of your marriage. Life will bring loss, but don't let one of those losses be your relationship.

1. **Recognize Your Differences:** Men and women grieve differently.
2. **Discuss Your Feelings:** Create a safe space for sharing emotions.
3. **Cultivate Empathy:** Step into your partner's shoes.
4. **Seek Spiritual Support:** Lean on your faith, pray together, and seek God's wisdom and comfort.
5. **Know When to Seek Help:** Consider professional counseling specializing in grief.

Choose to navigate together for a stronger relationship.

Dear Father, You are with me through every pain and loss. I trust Your compassion and comfort to help me when I am suffering. Holy Spirit, be present for me and lead me to the right people who can help me cope with loss and grief. In Jesus' name, Amen.

Have you or your spouse suffered losses or the death of loved ones? Ask your spouse how you can support them when they are experiencing the effects of loss and grief. How can your spouse more effectively help you?

Day 244

I WILL do my best to listen to my spouse, even when I don't like what I hear.

*One of the reasons conflicts are never resolved in families
is that the members simply will not listen to each other*

Understand this, my dear brothers and sisters: You must all be quick to listen, slow to speak, and slow to get angry (James 1:19).

If you feel so threatened that you refuse to sit down with someone and listen to their grievances about you, there may be something wrong with you. It's important for every man to ask his wife about his shortcomings and what changes she would like to see in him. Most women are fair, relational, and intuitive, and their insights hold value. But more importantly, their words need to be heard and actively listened to by their husbands. By listening, we can address issues that could otherwise tear us apart. Ignoring their perspectives only breeds resentment. Similarly, wives should listen to their husbands. As a husband expresses his needs, hurts, fears, and frustrations, a truly attentive wife can understand and respond sensitively.

Dear Father, I know You always hear me. Help me to hear others. Holy Spirit, show me how I should listen to my spouse. In Jesus' name, Amen.

How would you rate yourself as a listener? What can you do to be a better listener to your spouse?

I WILL stop repeating negative family patterns of communication.

People learn how to talk from their parents and other family members.

May the words of my mouth
and the meditation of my heart
be pleasing to you,
O LORD, my rock and my redeemer (Psalm 19:14).

Your communication patterns are influenced by your upbringing and particularly by your parents and close family members. If your parents were effective communicators who demonstrated praise, kindness, and healthy patterns of communication, they are worthy of admiration and emulation. Their positive influence shaped your own communication style. However, you may have experienced negative communication patterns, such as criticism or constant negativity. If you realize that your parents' communication methods were flawed, it's important to take the necessary steps toward healing and growth. Start by forgiving your parents, breaking off any negative patterns or vows, and redirecting your focus toward Jesus. Pray for His guidance and ask Him to teach you how to communicate according to His Word. Remember, it's never too late to learn and grow in your communication skills.

Dear Father, thank You for my family and for the people who did their best to raise me. Holy Spirit, show me which patterns are healthy and which patterns need to stop. In Jesus' name, Amen.

What negative family patterns do you need to stop repeating?

Day 246

I WILL close the door on past.

God will take the failures of your past and transform them into the successes of your future

He has removed our sins as far from us
as the east is from the west (Psalm 103:12).

One of the greatest traps the devil uses to keep us in bondage is to anchor us to the past. Dwelling on the past will affect your marriage and every other relationship. Consider three tactics the devil uses:

1. **Condemnation:** Do you ever feel you can't find forgiveness for past mistakes?
2. **Regret:** You replay the past, pondering the "what-ifs."
3. **Idealization:** You might dwell on a "better" time and long to relive those moments.

It's like driving backward and using the rearview mirror to see. Freedom means driving forward, eyes on the horizon, full of hope. God's grace surpasses your sins. You may remember past wrongs, but they no longer have a hold on you.

Dear Father, You are calling me forward and not backward. I don't want to be held by the past. Holy Spirit, I need Your grace to help me address past sins and wrongs. In Jesus' name, Amen.

Do you find yourself dwelling on the past, both good and bad? Have you asked God to help you deal with it?

I WILL place all I have in joint ownership with my spouse, including myself.

Marriage is a complete union in which all things previously owned and managed individually (separately) are now owned and managed jointly.

And they shall become one flesh (Genesis 2:24 NKJV).

The Law of Partnership is crucial in establishing trust and intimacy within a relationship. Adhering to this law can create a deep sense of unity and bonding in your marriage. However, unintentional violations of this law can cause severe harm to the trust and intimacy in your relationship. Marriage is a complete union where all previously separate possessions and management are now jointly owned and managed. Anything that is not willingly shared with your spouse is held outside of the union, leading to legitimate jealousy. The act of becoming one flesh involves more than just sex, but also merging everything owned and associated with two individuals into one shared mass. Refusing to merge anything violates your spouse's rights and breaks the Law of Partnership.

Dear Father, Help me to understand Your plan for our marriage to be a full partnership. Holy Spirit, show me how to be one with my spouse. In Jesus' name, Amen.

Have you been withholding parts of yourself or any possessions from your spouse? How does that complicate your marriage?

Day 248

I WILL be an honest person.

Don't lie to yourself, and don't let anyone else, including the devil, tell you lies to justify sin in your life.

"And you will know the truth, and the truth will set you free" (John 8:32).

If the truth sets you free, then dishonesty binds you. Have you ever known a person who justified their sins? You might even know "believers" who, when caught in adultery, claim God sanctioned it. Many might blame others or compare sins to justify their actions. Some even twist Scriptures to their advantage. While the concept of an absolute truth is debated by many, God's Word is pure truth. To uphold moral integrity, you need to define its meaning. True moral integrity aligns with Jesus' teachings and His Word. In a world with ever-changing values, God's Word remains the eternal standard. Never deceive yourself or allow others to mislead you. Embrace the truth.

Dear Father, You always deliver the truth to me. Holy Spirit, forgive me for being dishonest with my words or actions. Convict me and help me to be a truth teller and a truth keeper. In Jesus' name, Amen.

Why do you think telling the truth is important? In what ways have you been harmed by dishonesty? In what ways have you harmed others with dishonesty?

I WILL (as a wife) honor my husband by allowing him to fail.

The best way to change your husband is by honor.

Her husband is well known at the city gates,
  where he sits with the other civic leaders (Proverbs 31:23).

You might say, "I am willing to honor a man who never fails" However, such a man doesn't exist. Every husband will fail sometimes, and what sets a mature wife apart is how she responds when this happens. This is the true test of honor. If you dishonor your husband during those moments, he will feel wounded, and he will draw away from you. Progress isn't made by dishonoring or forcing others to change, but by praying for them and treating them better than they deserve. You have the right to express disagreement to your husband, but do it honorably, leaving it with him while diligently praying for him. Honor you husband even when he doesn't deserve it, and trust the Holy Spirit, not yourself, to enforce your words and create change.

Dear Father, I want to honor my husband through the good times and the bad times. Holy Spirit, please guide and direct him as he leads our family. In Jesus' name, Amen.

How can you continue to support your husband even when you disagree with his decisions?

Day 250

I WILL seek God's guidance and my spouse's consent regarding sexual practices in my marriage.

Remember that the most important aspect of sex is not what it does for you personally. It is what it does between you as a couple and also to each partner's conscience before God.

> Give honor to marriage, and remain faithful to one another in marriage. God will surely judge people who are immoral and those who commit adultery (Hebrews 13:4).

No one can dictate to you what's right or wrong if it's not directly addressed in the Bible. When determining intimate practices not specifically outlined in Scripture, consider these questions:

- Does it build closeness and intimacy?
- Is it enjoyable and do both of you agree?
- Is it hygienically and physically safe?
- Does it align with your faith and God's viewpoint? (God isn't embarrassed by intimacy. If you can't approach something with faith, then reconsider it.)
- Would you hope for your children to adopt this in their marriages?

If a practice stays within these guidelines, then you can embrace it in your marriage. If not, reflect on it or opt out.

Dear Father, I need Your guidance regarding sexual intimacy in my marriage. Holy Spirit, help me to communicate openly with my spouse as we explore what is acceptable and comfortable for our sex life. In Jesus' name, Amen.

What sexual practices would you like to include in your sexual intimacy with your spouse? Have you asked your spouse how they feel about them?

I WILL kindle passion in our marriage by treasuring my spouse.

Every couple can have passion in their marriage for their whole lives.

Who can find a virtuous and capable wife?
She is more precious than rubies. (Proverbs 31:10).

The heart is the seat of the emotions and passions. Thus, wherever you place the treasures of your life, your passion will naturally follow. Essentially, you'll be most zealous about the people, activities, and places where you devote the best of yourself. Your passions always align with how you spend your time, energy, and strengths. If you turn your energy away from your spouse, you will end up emotionally drained and "out of love." You can keep the passion in your marriage by choosing to turn your energy to your spouse—regardless of how you feel. Your heart will follow.

Dear Father, help me to keep the passion in our marriage by treasuring my spouse. Even in times when I do not "feel" it, give me the strength to act for my spouse. I believe that the passion will follow. In Jesus' name, Amen.

Do a quick inventory of your activities. Where do you spend the most of your time and energy? What are one or two ways this week that you can increase or protect the energy you devote to your spouse?

Day 252

I WILL (as a husband) provide detailed communication for my wife.

When a husband will not talk sensitively with his wife or listen attentively to her, their relationship deteriorates significantly and often very quickly.

So encourage each other and build each other up, just as you are already doing (1 Thessalonians 5:11).

Your wife has a strong need for detailed communication. She wants to know the specifics of your life and thoughts, not just a brief overview. For her, "Fine" and "Good" are not complete sentences. If you want to strengthen your bond with your wife, you must commit to meeting this need without whining and complaining. Prioritize open and detailed conversations and address past wounds or hindrances with patience and forgiveness. Stonewalling can harm your relationship, so if you need outside help, be willing to talk to a Christian counselor, pastor, or trusted friend. Say goodbye to the "strong, silent" stereotype, because true strength lies in open communication. Ask the Holy Spirit for His guidance and courage to change.

Dear Father, You knew exactly what I needed when You gave me my wife. Holy Spirit, remind me that detailed communication is a way I can show my love to her. In Jesus' name, Amen.

How have you previously responded when your wife tried to communicate with you? How will you respond going forward?

I WILL make prayer part of our conflict resolution process.

Praying together creates a bond
between us that is greater than us.

Devote yourselves to prayer with an alert mind and a thankful heart
(Colossians 4:2).

As you face challenges within your marriage and family, it's crucial to seek resolution and bring them to a conclusion. Achieving agreement and ending conversations with kindness and resolve are important. Restating the final resolution until both parties agree can be helpful, along with repenting and forgiving if mistakes were made. Repentance shows accountability and seriousness, while forgiveness is crucial for true resolution. Prayer has proven to be a powerful tool in resolving serious marriage problems, as couples who pray together regularly experience healing, strength for change, and reignited passion. The saying "The family that prays together, stays together" holds true, as prayer creates a bond that transcends us, inviting God to intervene and bring healing to hurt feelings.

Dear Father, I believe You care about our concerns and conflicts. I always want to remember that You listen to our every word. Holy Spirit, I want us to always go to You for answers about our deepest problems. In Jesus' name, Amen.

How do you think prayer could change most conflicts? How will you make prayer a part of your conflict resolution process?

Day 254

I WILL teach my children that God has a special purpose for their lives.

Even when children are young, they need to be taught that God has a special purpose for their lives.

But the LORD's plans stand firm forever;
  his intentions can never be shaken (Psalm 33:11).

When your child is young, begin teaching them that they're special and unique, created by God with a specific purpose to be revealed over time. Meeting your child's basic need for purpose involves assigning responsibilities suitable for their age. A balance between responsibilities and free time for fun and friends is crucial. Encourage them to serve in your church and community and educate them about their spiritual gifts. Pray for them to find and fulfill their divine purpose. Remember, fulfillment comes from following God's will. If a child grows without learning responsibility or understanding God's plan, they may feel unfulfilled and unhappy. So assign age-appropriate tasks to instill responsibility from a young age.

Dear Father, I know You have a special purpose for my child. Holy Spirit, help me to guide my child as they grow and discover God's plan for their life. In Jesus' name, Amen.

How can you encourage your child to develop responsibility as they learn about God and His unique purpose for them?

I WILL seek deliverance from any compulsive or destructive behavior.

When you have an addiction or a compulsion in your life, it's not always demonic, but there's a demonic element to it.

"The thief does not come except to steal, and to kill, and to destroy. I have come that they may have life, and that they may have *it* more abundantly" (John 10:10 NKJV).

Many don't believe in demons, but they exist. You can't change, befriend, or train them. The only action against them is to cast them out. When you grapple with harmful actions or thoughts, consider that a demonic spirit might be influencing you. Examples are compulsive gambling, drinking, violence, self-harm, and many more. All these behaviors can destroy your marriage. While not always demonic, uncontrollable compulsions may hint at their presence. The devil tries to control minds, keeping people captive. Believe nothing is impossible with faith in God. You must be close to God to wield authority over evil. Staying away from sinful behaviors increases your spiritual strength. Whenever there's a compulsion, consider the demonic element and take authority over it.

Dear Father, I don't want any habit or substance to control my life. Holy Spirit, deliver me from all addictions. In Jesus' name, Amen.

How has compulsive behavior or addiction affected you in the past or present?

Day 256

I WILL trust God for my security.

If you're going to have security,
then it must begin with God.

He sent His word and healed them,
And delivered *them* from their destructions (Psalm 107:20 NKJV).

Feelings of insecurity can hurt your relationships. To conquer insecurity, first recognize that your true security lies in God. Seeking validation from others or self will leave you disappointed. People can be fickle, but God remains steadfast. If your security isn't rooted in Him, you'll be unstable. Realize that others' opinions shift, but God's love is unwavering. God designed you perfectly and has a unique plan for your life. Even when you stray, He finds ways to guide you back. While people may judge by appearances, God cherishes your heart. True love isn't based on looks or achievements but on genuine understanding and acceptance. People may let you down, but God's love remains constant.

Dear Father, You provide for all my needs. I know when I think I am secure on my own that I am really in danger. Holy Spirit, reassure me that You are watching over me and meeting my needs. In Jesus' name, Amen.

Why is it so difficult for people to believe that God will supply their needs? When did God meet your needs even when you were doubtful or afraid?

I WILL (as a wife) cover my husband's faults and reflect his strengths.

Do not expose his weaknesses.

Above all, love each other deeply, because love covers over a multitude of sins (1 Peter 4:8 NIV).

Although you must be able to privately communicate your concerns, hurts, and needs to your husband in an honoring way, you should cover his faults in other areas. This doesn't mean you live in denial but rather that you avoid exposing his weaknesses to your children, parents, friends, or work associates. Let your husband know that he can trust you completely to honor and protect him. And be trustworthy! If there are serious concerns like abuse that you need to discuss, then seek guidance from your pastor or a trusted Christian counselor. Avoid discussing any marriage problems the two of you have with friends or parents, as it may create further issues unless they are mature and discreet individuals. Keeping matters within a safe and supportive environment will help maintain a healthier relationship.

Dear Father, I am so grateful that You have forgiven me for my many faults and failures. Holy Spirit, help me to be a trusted, loving cover for my husband. In Jesus' name, Amen.

Why is it important to maintain confidentiality with your spouse, especially regarding sensitive issues?

Day 258

I WILL (as a husband) provide leadership.

We lead because it is God's design, and it meets a deep need in our wives as long as we treat them with equality and respect.

> For a husband is the head of his wife as Christ is the head of the church. He is the Savior of his body, the church (Ephesians 5:23).

When a man fails to be a leader in his marriage, his wife feels insecure and frustrated. The lack of leadership is a common complaint among women in counseling. Women are not looking to be dominated and controlled, but they do want a caring, righteous husband who offers guidance and support. Women want their husbands to be involved with the children, finances, spirituality, and more. Interestingly, men who resist leadership often resent their wives stepping up to lead in their absence. Choose today to take the authority given to you by God and lead your family. Listen to your wife, seek her advice, and make decisions together. Your wife will appreciate and support your leadership, and God will reward you for fulfilling your role in the home.

Dear Father, I want to follow Your example of leadership. Holy Spirit, lead me as I lead my family. In Jesus' name, Amen.

Why do you think many husbands and wives struggle over the concept of leadership?

I WILL invest in spiritual intimacy with my spouse.

Spiritual intimacy is a sense of unity and mutual commitment to God's purpose for our lives and marriage.

A person standing alone can be attacked and defeated, but two can stand back-to-back and conquer. Three are even better, for a triple-braided cord is not easily broken (Ecclesiastes 4:12).

Spiritual intimacy is a profound bond, rooted in a mutual commitment to God's purpose and respect for each other's goals and dreams. Consider the acronym **INVEST: Intimacy Necessitates Value, Energy, Sacrifice, and Trust. Value** means cherishing God's plan for your spouse. A balanced marriage values both spouses equally, each aiding the other in fulfilling God's purpose. **Energy** involves actively seeking God, both individually and as a couple. **Sacrifice** demands selflessness. True intimacy flourishes when you prioritize your spouse's needs over your own. Imagine a partnership of two devoted servants. **Trust** creates an environment in which you both comfortably share your deepest aspirations, since the most intense disagreements often relate to unfulfilled dreams. Commit to the investment of spiritual intimacy.

Dear Father, I believe You have invested in me. Holy Spirit, show me how to invest in spiritual intimacy with my spouse. In Jesus' name, Amen.

How would you describe your intimacy with your spouse? Would you say you have spiritual intimacy?

Day 260

I WILL create an atmosphere of praise in my home.

When you praise your spouse, they are drawn to you and want to be around you.

LORD, you are my God;
  I will exalt you and praise your name, ·
for in perfect faithfulness
  you have done wonderful things,
    things planned long ago (Isaiah 25:1 NIV).

Praising your spouse is crucial for a thriving marriage. It creates a space for God's presence to dwell and develops an atmosphere of love and affirmation. As your spouse's biggest supporter, it's important to highlight their admirable qualities and affirm their worth. By focusing on their blessings and strengths, you deepen your connection, draw them closer to you, and open their heart. Just as you enter God's presence with thanksgiving and praise, adopt the same approach with your spouse. Show appreciation, express gratitude, and uplift them with your words. Let your praise become a powerful force that strengthens your relationship and brings joy to your marriage. Together, create a culture of encouragement and affirmation that reflects God's love and grace.

Dear Father, thank You for allowing me to enter Your presence with praise every day. Holy Spirit, help me to create an atmosphere of praise in my home. In Jesus' name, Amen.

What are two things you admire about your spouse? How can you share that with them today?

I WILL take responsibility for my own sins and failures.

The way children learn to take responsibility for their own behavior is, first of all, by watching the examples their parents set for them.

Yes, each of us will give a personal account to God (Romans 14:12).

Regardless of what others do, you are responsible for own your actions. When you stand before God, you won't be able to shift blame onto others. It will be a moment between you and God alone. If you have lived a life of personal responsibility, owning your mistakes without blaming others, then that day will bring blessings and rewards. However, if you've spent your life blaming others for your failures and sins, Judgment Day will be a shocking experience. Blaming others not only affects your relationship with God but also paralyzes you in life. By shifting blame, you wait for others to act, and your own actions become stagnant. Embrace personal responsibility in your marriage, teaching your children through your own example.

Dear Father, I want to take responsibility for my own sins and failures. Holy Spirit, convict me of sin and lead me to repentance. In Jesus' name, Amen.

Have you ever known someone who constantly blamed others for their own failures? How would you describe that person?

Day 262

I WILL make good communication a solid foundation for my marriage.

If you've become lazy in communicating, get to work and realize the importance of this issue.

Everyone enjoys a fitting reply;
it is wonderful to say the right thing at the right time! (Proverbs 15:23).

Communication was the initial bridge that helped you first connect with your spouse, and it will continue to deepen your bond over time. Just as a building can't stand tall on a weak foundation, your marriage won't thrive without solid communication, no matter how long you've been together. When a building has foundation issues, wall cracks or misaligned doors will show up, but those are merely symptoms. The real problem lies beneath. When communication falters in a marriage, tensions will show up in other areas. Regardless of your other commitments, prioritize talking together. If you've been neglecting this aspect of your relationship, acknowledge its significance and commit to improving. Strengthening communication will elevate your marriage.

Dear Father, I want to be an excellent communicator. Holy Spirit, show me the words to use in order to help my spouse truly understand what I am saying, and help me to be a good listener, too. In Jesus' name, Amen.

How much time do you spend talking with your spouse without any distractions? How would more time improve your marriage?

I WILL close the door on pain from the past.

The devil is a professional counselor,
but not a helpful one.

And "don't sin by letting anger control you." Don't let the sun go down while you are still angry, for anger gives a foothold to the devil (Ephesians 4:26–27).

The devil subtly plants harmful thoughts in our minds, which leads to inner bondage. Many of those thoughts are centered around unresolved anger and conflict. The apostle Paul warns against letting the devil gain a foothold in our minds, especially through harbored bitterness and unforgiveness. Such negative emotions not only harm our marriages but also imprison us in past pain. Remember, unresolved anger acts as a chain, binding us to past hurts. The devil thrives on perpetuating these feelings, aiming to destroy marriages. To break free, it's vital to forgive—not just your spouse, but also yourself. In forgiveness, we sever the chains to past pain and shut the door against the devil's deceptions.

Dear Father, I don't want to relive pain and trauma. Holy Spirit, I need You to heal my heart from past hurts. In Jesus' name, Amen.

Who has hurt you in the past that you still have not forgiven? Ask God to reveal anyone like that in your life. Begin the process of forgiveness and freedom today.

Day 264

I WILL choose daily to allow God to transform my mind.

Every day you walk with the Lord, you know more what He wills, and He transforms you by the Holy Spirit more into His image.

Don't copy the behavior and customs of this world, but let God transform you into a new person by changing the way you think. Then you will learn to know God's will for you, which is good and pleasing and perfect (Romans 12:2).

How does God want you to change? Paul says God seeks to transform your thinking. When you embraced Jesus as your Lord and Savior, a profound shift began within you. Perhaps others noticed this transformation. While you might not have had an instantaneous transformation, you changed gradually yet distinctly. God reshapes your mind, which drives behaviors like good deeds. It will definitely change the way you treat your spouse. But remember, your emotions and environment still influence you. You were created to fulfill God's purpose. As your mind transforms, you gain clarity about His intentions. As you journey with God daily, you grasp His desires more deeply, changing more into His image.

Dear Father, You are the Lord of my mind. Holy Spirit, change me into the image of Jesus. In Jesus' name, Amen.

How has God already transformed your mind?

I WILL practice basic manners with my spouse.

Manners are indicators of the kind of people we are.

Your kindness will reward you,
 but your cruelty will destroy you (Proverbs 11:17).

E ver considered the role of manners in your life? Manners are essential for preserving relationships. In marriages, once the honeymoon phase fades, emotions can decline if partners neglect basic courtesy toward each other. Recall the early days of dating: frequent expressions of gratitude, sensitivity, and acts like opening doors were common. As relationships evolve, couples might start to overlook these gestures, signaling that they're taking each other for granted. Your manners reflect your character. Demonstrating good manners indicates you're generous, considerate, and value others. A lack of them can suggest selfishness. If you want a marriage that continually flourishes, never underestimate the power of simple courtesies. Remember, manners can be essential to a thriving relationship.

Dear Father, I know that You are a God of order and You want Your people to have orderly lives. Holy Spirit, help me to be mindful of the things I say and do so I may not cause embarrassment or offense for my spouse. In Jesus' name, Amen.

Are there any areas of your behavior that your spouse has brought to your attention? What are they? Are you willing to change them?

Day 266

I WILL prioritize my marriage so we can raise great children.

Raising great children is much more likely if you have also built a healthy marriage.

Point your kids in the right direction—
when they're old they won't be lost (Proverbs 22:6 MSG).

If you don't succeed, how can you expect your children to? Prioritize your marriage for your children's wellbeing. Here are three guidelines to help you:

1. **Prioritize Correctly:** Put God first. Next, focus on your marriage. Children observe everything. Their wellbeing is linked to the stability of your relationship.
2. **Unified Parenting:** You and your partner must be on the same page. Avoid contradicting each other in front of the kids. If parenting disputes arise, consider seeking external help.
3. **Parent with Faith:** Make sure your children remain on the path toward faith. Don't just talk about it. Lead by example.

Maintain a strong marriage, be a united team, and lead by example. These choices will guide your children toward success.

Dear Father, You care about how we raise our children. Holy Spirit, show us how to be the kind of parents You want us to be. In Jesus' name, Amen.

How do you think marriage affects children? What can you and your spouse do through your marriage to lay the best foundation for your children's marriages?

I WILL follow God's vision of success.

Don't fall for the world's view of success. It will cause you to think you are a success when you're really a failure and a failure when you are truly a success.

"Store your treasures in heaven, where moths and rust cannot destroy, and thieves do not break in and steal" (Matthew 6:20).

How do you perceive success? For some, it's measured in wealth, popularity, or in counting social media likes and followers. Others view power, influence, or achieving a high rank as success. Some base it on relationships, even those outside biblical morals. Some gauge success by intellect, education, special talents, or simply living in peace. But Jesus taught that true success lies with the heavenly Father. Though these measures aren't inherently wrong, they might not align with God's vision of success. Remember, Jesus, by worldly standards, wasn't conventionally successful, yet He was profoundly impactful. Beware of worldly definitions, as they might mislead. Emphasize spiritual growth over materialistic achievements.

Dear Father, Your definition of success is the only one I need. Holy Spirit, help me to succeed by Kingdom standards. In Jesus' name, Amen.

Have you ever known someone who was successful by society's standards but a failure in every other way? How do you think God views that kind of success?

Day 268

I WILL win the war for my words.

*The person who understands the power of words
and commits themselves to positive speech will
reap an abundant harvest as a result.*

The tongue has the power of life and death,
and those who love it will eat its fruit (Proverbs 18:21 NIV).

The future of your marriage depends on who wins the battle for your words. The enemy tries to twist and poison your communication, but God wants to transform your words into sources of life. Every word you speak to your spouse can build them up or tear them down, encourage them or discourage them. Words are never neutral; they carry deep attitudes, emotions, and values. Pleasant words are like a honeycomb, bringing sweetness and health to your relationship. Wise words promote healing, but harsh words hurt like a sword. Gentle words nurture life, while deceitful words crush the spirit. You have the power to use your words for life or death. Every word you say matters, so decide today to speak words of praise, kindness, truth, and love.

Dear Father, I want to bless my spouse with my words. Holy Spirit, show me how to win the war for my words on a daily basis. In Jesus' name, Amen.

What words can you say that will bless your spouse today?

I WILL combat feelings of inadequacy with gratitude.

We can all get everything that God wants us to have, and all be okay.

For you formed my inward parts;
you knitted me together in my mother's womb (Psalm 139:13 ESV).

Have you ever felt like you're just not that special or that you don't measure up? The enemy wants you to feel inadequate and depressed, but it's essential to believe that God created you fearfully and wonderfully in your mother's womb. You are unique in His eyes. When the devil tries to make you feel bad about yourself, you can choose to wake up every morning and thank God for who He made you to be and for the purpose He has for you. When insecurity creeps in, start praising the Lord. Focus on becoming the person God created you to be. When you trust the Lord for favor and opportunity, you won't resort to competition, jealousy, envy, or covetousness. You will be joyful and content, and you will be the best spouse you can be.

Dear Father, I praise You for Your goodness and faithfulness. Holy Spirit, may Your fruit of joy and peace be evident in my daily life. In Jesus' name, Amen.

What are your favorite ways to praise the Lord by yourself and with your spouse?

Day 270

I WILL (as a husband) not confuse servanthood with being passive.

Your naturally gentle personality gives you a solid foundation to become a good leader, but you must learn to act lovingly and lead with decisiveness.

Know the state of your flocks,
  and put your heart into caring for your herds,
for riches don't last forever,
  and the crown might not be passed to the next generation
  (Proverbs 27:23–24).

Passive men avoid doing the "dirty work." They have the power to stand up and be righteous leaders, but they shirk that responsibility. At first, a passive husband may seem sweet and sensitive to his wife, but eventually, his lack of leadership becomes maddening. Whether it's in finances, spirituality, parenting, romance, or any other aspect, a passive man erodes the sense of security and respect his wife once had. Destruction continues as long as the problem persists. The first step for a passive husband is to understand his wife's need for leadership. To initiate healing, he must recognize that remaining passive cannot truly fulfill any of his wife's basic needs.

Dear Father, I want to fulfill my responsibilities as a husband. Holy Spirit, help me to be a servant but not to avoid leadership. In Jesus' name, Amen.

Why do you think some men avoid taking responsibility and leadership?

I WILL proclaim with my spouse that God is the owner of everything we have.

God directs us to test Him with our finances and let Him reveal His power and faithfulness.

The earth is the Lord's, and everything in it.
The world and all its people belong to him (Psalm 24:1).

The first step to financial freedom and security starts with acknowledging God's ownership over everything in our lives. You must repent for not recognizing His authority over your finances and possessions and fully surrender everything you have to Him. Often, people make financial decisions without seeking God's guidance because they presume that they are the owners of their lives. But this only leads to instability at best or disaster at worst. Instead, give all to God. If you handle everything as He directs, then you need not fear. But if you haven't committed everything to Him, your concerns are warranted, because security and blessings only come from total submission to God. In committing everything to Him and being a responsible steward, God promises abundant blessings and rewards.

Dear Father, You are the owner of everything I have and everything I am. Holy Spirit, I submit my life to You, holding nothing back. In Jesus' name, Amen.

What do you need to submit to God's ownership today?

Day 272

I WILL break any cycles of repetitive sin.

Not one of us is immune from sin.

We destroy every proud obstacle that keeps people from knowing God.
We capture their rebellious thoughts and teach them to obey Christ
(2 Corinthians 10:5).

You're not alone in facing temptations, be it worldliness, independence, or the allure of leisure. Repetitive sin will impact your marriage. Just like everyone else, you grapple with lust and fear. So, how should you respond to these temptations? Certainly not like David, who faltered in his moment of weakness, ending up in the wrong place and making choices that cost him dearly. Today's challenges aren't much different. In our culture, many succumb to the temptation of sexual sin, with easy and anonymous access to pornography online. If you're watching it, you're not where you should be spiritually. While you might put on a facade, God sees the truth. No one's exempt. If you're trapped in repetitive sin, real change only begins when you gain control over your thoughts.

Dear Father, I never want to cause You sorrow. I want my life to be a testimony to Your power and glory. Holy Spirit, empower me to deal with stubborn sin. In Jesus' name, Amen.

Where is your greatest struggle with ongoing sin? How long has it been a problem?

I WILL complain without criticizing.

Complaining gets everything out on the table without demeaning your spouse or putting them on the defensive.

An open rebuke
is better than hidden love! (Proverbs 27:5).

For a marriage to be healthy, both spouses must have the freedom to express their true feelings. That's right—it's okay to complain! Just remember that complaining is about sharing your emotions with the goal of mutual understanding and resolution, not attacking your spouse. Complaining allows both of you to discuss issues openly and constructively without putting each other on the defensive. Criticizing, on the other hand, creates hostility and tension as you accuse each other and put each other down. As you approach confrontations, be sure to affirm and respect your spouse. Keep your emotions in check and allow your spouse the freedom to express their concerns. By doing this, difficult discussions will become more pleasant, productive, and nurturing for your marriage. Embrace healthy communication, and you'll see your bond grow stronger day by day.

Dear Father, I want to be able to have healthy, constructive conversations with my spouse. Holy Spirit, please teach me how to complain without criticizing in order to grow in my marriage. In Jesus' name, Amen.

What practical guidelines will help you complain without criticizing?

Day 274

I WILL allow God to shape my attitude.

You choose your attitudes.

Humble yourselves before the Lord, and he will lift you up in honor (James 4:10).

Your attitude, a reflection of your feelings and thoughts, manifests in your behavior. It's shaped by family, education, emotions, and experiences. To shift any mindset, your attitude must first evolve. Nothing, aside from salvation, impacts your life and marriage as much as attitude. Your posture reveals your attitude. People's company shapes attitudes. Every establishment or group emits a certain vibe. The Bible cautions against worldly attitudes; align yourself with God's will. Reflect: have you been gracious or negative? Your present attitude dictates your future. Your attitude isn't a product of circumstance; it's a choice. The apostle Paul encouraged believers to choose joy despite adversity. Influenced by God's Word, choose gratitude, humility, and faith,

Dear Father, You have shown me the attitudes You want me to have. You promise that You will heal and transform me if I submit to Your will and direction. Holy Spirit, forgive me for holding attitudes that are contrary to Your will. I choose to have the right attitude. Help me to keep that commitment. In Jesus' name, Amen.

How would you describe your attitude? How would your spouse describe it? What about your friends and coworkers?

I WILL continue to kindle the spark of love in our marriage.

Remember your first love, and rekindle the fire by doing what you did in the early days.

"But I have this against you, that you have abandoned the love you had at first" (Revelation 2:4 ESV).

There's something about witnessing an exceptional marriage that makes you want to be a better spouse. When you see two people deeply in love, it fills you with hope. You think that if they can have that, so can you. Great marriages aren't just for a lucky few. You too can have an enduring, exciting love story. It's not about fate, luck, or genetics; it's about making the choice to put in the effort. Marriages struggle when they're neglected. Remember the spark that initially brought you together and reignite that courtship. Begin to romance each other anew

Dear Father, I am reminded how I should kindle the flame of romance in our marriage. Help me have creativity and strength of will to keep renewing the passion with regular acts of love. In Jesus' name, Amen.

When was a time that you saw the spark of joy in your spouse's eyes because of something you said or did? When was the last time you kindled that spark? What would cause your spouse's eyes to light up with joy today?

Day 276

I WILL avoid extreme reactions
to my spouse's behavior.

*When one spouse moves to an unhealthy or extreme position,
the other spouse will almost always adjust to the other
extreme to protect themselves and the relationship.*

Be completely humble and gentle; be patient, bearing with one another in love
(Ephesians 4:2 NIV).

I magine sitting on a teeter-totter with your spouse. The balance is perfect
when you sit face-to-face in the middle, but when one of you moves to an
end, the other instinctively moves to the opposite end to restore the balance.
This "teeter-totter syndrome" works on the playground, but it is unhealthy in
relationships. If your spouse is a reckless spender, you might respond by being
very strict with finances. Or if your spouse is a harsh disciplinarian, then you
might try to be the "fun parent." To break free from the emotional teeter-totter,
you must lovingly share your feelings while also humbly taking responsibility
for your actions. Seek outside help if needed, and don't give up until you are
sitting face-to-face again.

*Dear Father, the desire of my heart is to be pleasing to You. Holy Spirit, show
me any extreme behavior that needs to change in my life. In Jesus' name, Amen.*

How do you usually respond to your spouse's behavior? What would be a
better way to respond?

I WILL (as a husband) be a righteous steward of those in my care.

Whether men like it or not, they must realize they have been entrusted by God with the leadership of their families, churches, and society as a whole.

For husbands, this means love your wives, just as Christ loved the church. He gave up his life for her (Ephesians 5:25).

As a man, when you take on the responsibility of being a righteous steward and provide for and protect those in your care, your spouse and children will reflect appreciation and contentment. When you demonstrate godly character and sacrificial love, your spouse will generally be content. However, if you become lazy and ungodly, your spouse may mirror those negative qualities. The lack of righteous male leadership is a root problem in unstable homes. Guidance from God's Word is the source of hope to address this issue. A woman falls in love with a man who sacrificially meets her needs. Sacrificial love is what truly endears a man to a woman.

Dear Father, as a husband, I want to sacrificially meet my wife's needs. Holy Spirit, teach us how to give and receive love from each other. In Jesus' name, Amen.

Do you agree that many problems in society stem from men who will not assume their role as sacrificial leaders? Why or why not?

Day 278

I WILL recognize that only God can meet my deepest needs.

When God created humans in His image, He built in a "Jesus-sized" hole from which all our deepest needs stem.

Jesus replied, "I am the bread of life. Whoever comes to me will never be hungry again. Whoever believes in me will never be thirsty" (John 6:35).

Many people fail to turn to Jesus to fulfill their deepest needs, resulting in a perpetual search for satisfaction in life and marriage. Jesus holds the power to quench our spiritual thirst and hunger. He promises complete fulfillment for those who come to Him. No person or possession can fully satisfy these inner needs. While your spouse may offer love and support, even the most spiritually grounded person has limitations. Relying too heavily on someone else will lead to disappointment and potential disaster. Only God can fully meet your deepest needs. Seek Him first, allowing His perfect love to be your ultimate source of satisfaction.

Dear Father, You created me, so You know my deepest needs. Holy Spirit, help me to keep my eyes and heart on Jesus. I know only He can truly satisfy me. In Jesus' name, Amen.

What have you substituted for God to meet your deepest needs? How did you come to recognize you needed to put God first?

I WILL allow God's vision for our marriage to motivate me.

Having God's vision brings clarity and excitement to our lives and marriages.

Then the LORD said to me,
"Write my answer plainly on tablets,
    so that a runner can carry the correct message to others" (Habakkuk 2:2).

Have you ever felt the excitement and motivation that comes with having a clear vision? Write down your vision so that others can see it and run with it. Having a vision gives us direction and purpose in our lives so we can pursue it with energy. God has a custom-made vision for each of us according to our gifts, circumstances, dreams, and desires. It's not a one-size-fits-all plan, but a personalized one. Don't be like a carpenter without a plan. Get together with your spouse and the Lord so you know what you are trying to achieve, and then excitement and energy will follow like you have never felt before.

Dear Father, give us vision, and we will write it down. Holy Spirit, give us energy and excitement as we follow Your vision. In Jesus' name, Amen.

If you have taken time to seek God's vision for your marriage, have you written it down? Take time to do that as soon as you hear God together.

Day 280

I WILL keep stubbornness in check.

*Pride justifies dominance because it truly believes
it is superior and worthy of control.*

For rebellion *is as* the sin of witchcraft,
and stubbornness *is as* iniquity and idolatry (1 Samuel 15:23 NKJV).

Have you ever wondered why the Bible considers stubbornness as equal to the sin of idolatry? The reason is that it amounts to the worship of your own opinion. When you are stubborn, you become difficult to deal with because you are full of pride and refuse to consider any other viewpoint apart from your own. To overcome this, you need to repent of your pride and stop seeing yourself as superior to your spouse or others. Pride often leads to dominance, and it justifies control because it believes it is superior. However, humility should take the place of pride by lowering yourself and elevating your spouse until there is a level playing field. When humility reigns, great marriages happen.

Dear Father, I know the only way to deal with pride and stubbornness is to repent and turn away from it. Holy Spirit, I need You to speak to me often about pride. In Jesus' name, Amen.

How has pride or stubbornness harmed your relationships? What were the results? How was it resolved?

I WILL strive to be selfless in our sexual relationship.

Sex is a sacrificial act between a husband and wife.

The husband should fulfill his wife's sexual needs, and the wife should fulfill her husband's needs (1 Corinthians 7:3).

Entering marriage, you likely thought of sex as a great marital feature. Why? First, you can't satisfy your own sexual needs alone, and in marriage, you rely on your partner for that. Second, sex in marriage is about mutual giving. It is intended to be a selfless act, relying on a servant spirit. What is the key to sexual success in marriage? Prioritize serving over mere physical attraction. Physical attraction fluctuates; commitment doesn't. If you're committed to serving your spouse, external factors fade in significance. Fear might deter you from a selfless approach. Remember, Jesus served without losing authority. Serving your partner is about mutual fulfillment, not losing yourself. Prioritize mutual sensitivity and never weaponize intimacy. True intimacy arises from selflessness.

Dear Father, You gave Your Son and our Savior as our example. Help me to be more like Him. Holy Spirit, show me how to love my spouse in the best way I can, Amen.

Have you been selfish in your sexual relationship? Take responsibility for any failures and ask your spouse for forgiveness. Ask your spouse to be honest about your sexual relationship.

Day 282

I WILL anchor my relationship in truth, not feelings.

Satan uses rejection to introduce lies that change the way we make decisions and the way we treat people.

This hope is a strong and trustworthy anchor for our souls (Hebrews 6:19).

The desire to be close to your spouse is natural and healthy. Love sparks your will to thrive, but what happens when you feel unloved? Chronic rejection can lead to illness, emotional turmoil, and even higher mortality rates. During moments of hurt, the enemy seizes the opportunity to sow lies that distort your decisions and obstruct God's purpose for your life. In Genesis chapter 3, Satan's deceitful whispers led to humanity's fall. Even today, his lies persist, as he plants seeds of doubt about your worth and lovability. But remember: God's truth always prevails. You can break free from the chains of rejection by seeking God's love and truth. Through His love, discover healing and strength to challenge the lies of the enemy. By nurturing a marital bond anchored in acceptance and grace, you can overcome rejection and embrace the flourishing love God intends for both of you.

Dear Father, thank You that Your love always prevails. Holy Spirit, You are the anchor in the midst of every storm. In Jesus' name, Amen.

Why do you think God's truth always prevails?

I WILL stay on the battlefield for my faith.

No one is truly great who doesn't serve Jesus Christ.

So, my dear brothers and sisters, be strong and immovable. Always work enthusiastically for the Lord, for you know that nothing you do for the Lord is ever useless (1 Corinthians 15:58).

O ur culture often glorifies those who seem to live "the American Dream" and champions figures in business, entertainment, or sports. True greatness isn't about fame or wealth. It's about serving Jesus Christ, both in public and private. When you're surrounded by tempting or distressing images, the truly great individual, the person of God, will stand firm and say, "I belong on the battlefield." If you find yourself amid people who indulge in wrongdoing and hide it, move away. Surround yourself with fellow warriors on the battlefield, those committed to living honorably. When you connect with someone dedicated to winning their inner battles, you've found a true friend. They may have flaws, but they're on the path to genuine greatness.

Dear Father, You fight all my battles. You only ask me to be available to fight through me. Holy Spirit, give me courage to stay in the fight. When I am weary, be my strength. In Jesus' name, Amen.

Where is the greatest spiritual battle in your personal life and marriage?

Day 284

I WILL love my spouse as my closest neighbor.

*We protect each other and rally around
the person who needs us.*

"Love your neighbor as yourself" (Mark 12:31).

In successful marriages, spouses cultivate a sense of mutual concern for one another. You prioritize looking out for each other, adopting the mindset of "If you're not okay, then I'm not okay." From your home, you develop an attitude that protects and supports those in need, extending it outside to your neighborhood, church, city, and beyond. The foundation of a strong society lies in the attitude of mutual concern for our fellow human beings, and that begins in the family. Jesus emphasized the importance of loving others. When questioned about who qualifies as a neighbor, Jesus broadened the definition of "neighbor" to encompass anyone who is in need (Luke 10:30–36). God holds us accountable for helping others, and it starts in our own homes.

Dear Father, I want to love others the way You love me. Holy Spirit, show us how to take the love You have given to us and extend it to others. In Jesus' name, Amen.

Do you and your spouse have a vision for ministering to people outside your home? If so, what is it?

I WILL turn to my spouse and not pornography to meet my sexual needs.

*The sex industry has learned that
sin is what sells their product best.*

I will refuse to look at
  anything vile and vulgar.
I hate all who deal crookedly;
  I will have nothing to do with them (Psalm 101:3).

While it's okay to communicate your intimate desires to your partner, don't let these desires be influenced by pornography or exaggerated tales. Today's explicit content often pushes individuals to prioritize their own desires over their partner's needs. Simply put, a lot of what you see online or in magazines doesn't belong in a loving relationship. If you're dabbling in pornography, step away. It can harm both you and your relationship. Are you trying to make your spouse emulate scenes or act out unreal fantasies? Pause and reflect. Turn to a deeper understanding and share genuine desires with your partner. Aim to please them by respecting their comfort level and prioritizing their needs. This approach ensures mutual satisfaction and a bond that brings joy, not distress.

Dear Father, I never want to put my own desires above my spouse's needs. Holy Spirit, strengthen me as I resist the temptation of pornography. In Jesus' name, Amen.

How can you protect your eyes and heart from the lure of pornography?

I WILL nurture a servant spirit toward my spouse.

The worst marriage is two selfish people in love.

And further, submit to one another out of reverence for Christ (Ephesians 5:21).

A fulfilling marriage requires both spouses to have a servant spirit. Successful marriages are built on love and commitment to serving each other, whereas those that suffer the most are driven by selfishness. In marriage, we become dependent on our spouses to fulfill our needs, and we vow to remain faithful and trust them to fulfill our emotional, physical, and spiritual needs. Imagine your marriage as a store accessible only to you and your spouse; shopping elsewhere is strictly prohibited. However, many couples experience frustration when their needs aren't met. The truth is that every husband has what his wife needs, and every wife has what her husband needs. It's the absence of a mutually submissive servant attitude that causes relationships to go stale. Choose to be a servant to your spouse and watch your marriage thrive!

Dear Father, teach us as a couple to mutually submit to and serve each other as we serve You. Holy Spirit, place within us the hearts of servants. In Jesus' name, Amen.

What do you do to avoid selfishness in your marriage relationship? What do you do to serve your spouse?

I WILL protect my spouse, even from my parents.

In marriage, both spouses must be committed to protect their mates from their parents.

Therefore a man shall leave his father and mother and hold fast to his wife, and the two shall become one flesh (Ephesians 5:31 ESV).

You and your partner must defend each other, even from parental criticisms. Don't complain about your partner to your parents, and don't let them criticize your spouse to you. If your parents overstep, then approach them lovingly and set boundaries. When you both shield each other from outside interference, trust and safety can flourish in your relationship. However, if either of you fails to defend your spouse from family criticisms, it can harm the relationship. Commit now to respecting your spouse, and expect the same from your family. Show your parents love but make it clear there are boundaries. If a parent continues to disrespect these boundaries, then defend your marriage, even if it means distancing yourself from them.

Dear Father, I accept my responsibility to love and protect my spouse. Holy Spirit, guard my mouth against criticism and help me direct my family to respect my spouse in the same way. In Jesus' name, Amen.

What subtle or overt forms of criticism do you need to address with your family?

Day 288

I WILL be intimate with my spouse on every level.

God created marriage to be a place where you could totally expose yourselves to each other—mentally, emotionally, spiritually, sexually, and physically—without shame.

Now the man and his wife were both naked, but they felt no shame (Genesis 2:25).

When God created Adam and Eve in the Garden of Eden, He designed them without clothes and no shame. The term "naked" in Genesis 2:25 implies complete exposure. Thus, God intended marriage as a sanctuary where you can fully reveal yourself without embarrassment. When you embrace this vulnerability, you truly connect. You talk freely, celebrate your sexuality, and confide your deepest fears and dreams without apprehension. However, this ideal depends upon maintaining purity. Remember, Adam and Eve's trust was shattered by sin, disrupting their bond. Thankfully, you can rekindle this paradise in your own marriage. By acknowledging mistakes, seeking forgiveness, and ensuring respect and care in your interactions, you can cultivate a marriage of purity and intimacy, reflecting God's original vision.

Dear Father, my heart's desire is to truly connect with my spouse on every level. Holy Spirit, show me anything I need to repent for as I strive for a marriage based on purity and intimacy. In Jesus' name, Amen.

What do you need to do in order to feel more comfortable fully revealing yourself to your spouse?

I WILL build spiritual intimacy by praying with my spouse.

After the Lord saved our marriage, we began praying together regularly

Don't worry about anything; instead, pray about everything. Tell God what you need, and thank him for all he has done (Philippians 4:6).

By choosing prayer over worry, you are promised a profound peace that acts as a protective shield for your hearts and minds. Praying together is a "guard" that signifies a defense against enemy invasion. So when you and your spouse pray together, God rewards your faith by enveloping you in a supernatural cocoon of peace that the devil cannot penetrate. This spiritual bond unites your spirits and minds, strengthening your connection. Additionally, it's important to recognize that spiritual intimacy enhances your sexual lives. Women have a deep desire for their husbands to be the spiritual leaders in their homes and to pray together. Inviting God into your relationship through prayer revitalizes intimacy and allows true sexual fulfillment to thrive as a result.

Dear Father, help us to be a couple who always wants to talk with You. Holy Spirit, teach us to make prayer a daily part of our marriage. In Jesus' name, Amen.

Do you pray together as a couple? How do you think praying together will help your marriage? Why not start today?

Day 290

I WILL be a friend to my spouse.

Husbands and wives who have fun together
develop a bond that's not easily broken.

The heartfelt counsel of a friend
is as sweet as perfume and incense (Proverbs 27:9).

Friendship acts as the adhesive for lasting relationships. Women typically connect through deep conversations, while men bond over shared activities. A thriving marriage encompasses both open conversations and mutual hobbies. Men forge friendships by doing things together. Whether it's golfing, skiing, or camping, recreational activities are avenues for men to connect. Many men even regard their wives as their "best friends." Fun and intimacy are central for men. If you neglect these elements, your marriage might seem more like you are just roommates. Many husbands feel distant unless shared activities bridge the gap. When wives show disinterest in their husband's passions, men often interpret it as a lack of interest in them. Friendship and fun reinforce the foundation of your relationship.

Dear Father, You are the greatest friend to me. It is joy to serve You. Holy Spirit, help me to create a joyful friendship with my spouse. In Jesus' name, Amen.

What can you do today to restore or grow your friendship with your spouse? Ask your spouse how to be a better friend to them. Commit to doing one thing to demonstrate your friendship.

I WILL not fail with God on my side.

*Satan's worst fear is that you will wake up
to who you are in Christ.*

"The things which are impossible with men are possible with God"
(Luke 18:27 NKJV).

S atan's worst fear is your awakening to your identity in Christ. His greatest
terror occurs when you realize you and your spouse are designed for battle,
equipped with potent weapons to enforce his defeat. He strives to convince you
that you lack what it takes to succeed. However, the devil's efforts are in vain.
You've learned that the real challenge isn't your potential failures or limitations
but the impossibility of failing in God. No situation is insurmountable for Him:
There are no boundaries to your accomplishments when you act in faith upon
God's promises. Choose to commit yourself to God, trusting Him through thick
and thin. You will achieve remarkable feats by keeping your focus on God and
continuously seeking Him.

*Dear Father, I can only know who I am when I know You, because You made
me. Holy Spirit, reassure me of God's presence and power. In Jesus' name, Amen.*

How would you say that God gives you strength to succeed? Have you ever
felt you were in an impossible situation, then God showed up in power? How
did that change your perception of God?

Day 292

I WILL (as a husband) recognize that my attitudes and actions affect my wife.

Men are the reflection of the character of the God they choose, and women are the reflection of the character of the husband they choose.

A man should not wear anything on his head when worshiping, for man is made in God's image and reflects God's glory. And woman reflects man's glory (1 Corinthians 11:7).

Paul reveals an important spiritual truth: men reflect the character of the God they choose, while women reflect the character of the husband they choose. Thus a wife's behavior often mirrors her husband's negative behavior and character. Does this mean women lack independent thinking and only react to their husbands? Absolutely not! Women were created by God as equals to men in every aspect. However, God designed women for a special purpose. Often, pastors and counselors only hear about husbands from their wives without actually meeting the men. Yet these professionals witness the destructive impact of the husband's behavior. The overall suffering caused by destructive husbands can be overwhelming.

Dear Father, I want to reflect You in every area of my life. Holy Spirit, make me aware of the way my attitudes and actions affect my spouse. In Jesus' name, Amen.

As a husband, how have you seen both your positive and negative attitudes reflected in your spouse's reactions?

I WILL forgive myself for past relationship failures just as I forgive others.

No matter how loving and gracious God may be, His forgiveness does not affect your life unless you are willing to receive it.

"And forgive us our debts,
   as we forgive our debtors" (Matthew 6:12 NKJV).

Holding onto unforgiveness harms you more than anyone. Truly, forgiving is a profound act of self-love. It means erasing the emotional debt someone owes you, much like how God forgives you. When you forgive, you release all thoughts of revenge. Jesus taught us to bless those who wrong us, which is key to genuine healing. Praying for those who have hurt you invites God's healing touch. Even more, once you've forgiven others, there's someone else to forgive—yourself. Acknowledge your past mistakes, genuinely repent, and show commitment to change. God's heart is not for you to live in perpetual anguish. Embrace His forgiveness. His grace will flow out from you and touch others. Remember, forgiveness keeps love flowing and your heart pure.

Dear Father, Your forgiveness is an amazing gift that I am blessed to receive every day. Holy Spirit, I want to be free, so I choose to forgive myself and others for past failures. In Jesus' name, Amen.

What failures do you need to forgive and release, both from yourself and from others?

Day 294

I WILL approach all debt with caution.

Although I don't believe it is a sin to borrow money, too much debt is bondage.

Don't agree to guarantee another person's debt
or put up security for someone else (Proverbs 22:26).

You should carefully consider two issues for financial freedom: debt and co-signing debt. Although borrowing isn't sinful, it can lead to bondage if it's excessive. Aim to pay cash, especially for depreciating items, and if you are already in debt, develop a plan to pay it off so you can be debt-free. Consider downsizing your lifestyle to save money and reduce expenses. Remember not to compare yourself with anyone else; you are responsible only for your own financial situation. Co-signing is another concern because it makes you liable for someone else's debt. The Bible advises against it, suggesting you either gift money or let a bank handle it, barring exceptions like aiding your children to establish credit. Even so, make sure you guide them to prevent excessive debt.

Dear Father, I need Your wisdom regarding finances. Holy Spirit, guide me to make the right decisions and help me to be courageous if I need to undo any poor choices. In Jesus' name, Amen.

What has been your approach to debt in the past? Will you do anything different in the future?

I WILL make my home a safe place for everyone to share their hearts.

The home should be a sanctuary where any member can come and open their heart.

"My people will live in peaceful dwelling places,
in secure homes,
in undisturbed places of rest" (Isaiah 32:18 NIV).

S uccessful marriages create a safe place for everyone in the home to share their hearts. Love is consistently expressed, and sincere concern is shown. It is an environment where trust can flourish. Make your home a sanctuary where any member feels comfortable opening up. Children need a reliable place to seek answers rather than going to their friends or social media. God gave parents the responsibility of guiding their children. Openness must also exist between you and your spouse. Dysfunctional families rarely allow such an atmosphere. Certain subjects are off-limits, and discussing them comes at a heavy price. Healthy families address anger, pain, questions, and needs. You can express yourself without fear of judgment, attack, or condemnation.

Dear Father, You have made me feel safe and secure. Holy Spirit, help me to give the people in my home assurance of safety. In Jesus' name, Amen.

Have you ever been in a place where it did not feel safe to share your thoughts and feelings? How can you make sure your spouse never feels unsafe in your relationship?

Day 296

I WILL have victory over the devil in my marriage.

Wake up to what the devil already knows—we have been given the authority and power to take back everything he has stolen from us.

"These things I have spoken to you, that in Me you may have peace. In the world you will have tribulation; but be of good cheer, I have overcome the world" (John 16:33 NKJV).

U nderstand this: what God gives to you is yours. If He bestows it upon you, and the devil attempts to snatch it away, a fight awaits. But it's a fight you will win if you stand your ground. Armed with God's authority, the name and blood of Jesus, and the Word of God, you wield formidable power. Every hellish demon fears you, anticipating the day you awaken to your authority in the anointing of Jesus Christ. Demons oppose your marriage for a reason. You pose a genuine threat to them. You are part of the force that is capable of halting their advance. The enemy tries to convince you that your marriage is destined for defeat or endless battles. Don't believe him.

Dear Father, You defeated the devil. Holy Spirit, arm me with all the weapons I need for spiritual warfare. In Jesus' name, Amen.

Do you see demonic forces at work trying to destroy your marriage?

I WILL constantly renew my friendship with my spouse.

The best marriages are built upon a foundation of good friendship.

Just as lotions and fragrance give sensual delight,
a sweet friendship refreshes the soul (Proverbs 27:9 MSG).

In the journey of marriage, building a strong friendship is vital. Here are seven ways to renew your friendship daily:

1. **Be Loyal:** Stick together, especially during tough times. A friend is consistent even during the storms.
2. **Believe in Each Other:** Support your spouse's dreams and aspirations.
3. **Appreciate Differences:** Embrace and celebrate the uniqueness of your spouse.
4. **Be Genuine:** Honesty builds trust.
5. **Offer Sanctuary:** Be the safe space for your spouse.
6. **Inject Fun:** Introduce joy, laughter, and creativity through shared experiences.
7. **Share Burdens:** Help each other during difficult times.

Cultivating friendship will transform your marriage. If you're not there yet, start today and watch your relationship flourish.

Dear Father, You have shown me that You want to be my friend. I want my spouse to think of me as their best friend. Holy Spirit, help me to do what is necessary to be a worthy friend. In Jesus' name, Amen.

Which of the ways to renew your friendship is most appealing to you? Which gives you the greatest struggle? Ask your spouse how you can be a better friend.

Day 298

I WILL be a worshipper of God.

Every great person is a worshipper of God and pays a price to be so.

"No, I insist on buying it, for I will not present burnt offerings to the LORD my God that have cost me nothing" (2 Samuel 24:24).

I f you aim for greatness, then you must understand the importance of worship. Worship is more than rituals—it's about a sincere connection with God. The Christian faith is not about winning God's favor, but recognizing His immense love in the person of Jesus. How deep your worship goes shows you how real your relationship with God is. Like genuine care in human ties, God wants your attention and affection. Being physically present isn't enough; full engagement on all levels is required. Mere formality doesn't work; it is a daily experience of God's power. Regular moments become worshipful with gratitude toward God. True worship means genuine connection and sacrifice. Pay the price to be a worshipper, and move toward greatness.

Dear Father, You are worthy of all my worship and praise. You are the Author of all that is good. Holy Spirit, fill my heart with joy and awe for Your great deeds. In Jesus' name, Amen.

What is the best way for you to express worship? What about your spouse?

I WILL accept the risk of being hurt.

*We cannot live like Jesus if all we do is seek to
eliminate risk from our relationships.*

You are coming to Christ, who is the living cornerstone of God's temple. He
was rejected by people, but he was chosen by God for great honor (1 Peter 2:4).

H ave you ever let the fear of being hurt stop you from trying something
new? It's a common response to past pain. Now, you should never be
careless in relationships, but it's also possible to be too cautious. To grow in
your marriage, you must be vulnerable, and vulnerability includes the risk of
being hurt. Jesus, our ultimate example, didn't shy away from relationships even
though He knew that some would betray Him. Jesus never closed His heart, and
His openness reminds us that to love deeply, we must embrace the possibility
of hurt. Don't make the mistake of preemptively rejecting your spouse because
you fear they will reject you. By mirroring Jesus' fearless love, you can build a
marriage grounded in genuine connection and acceptance.

*Dear Father, I want to love like Jesus. Holy Spirit, show me how to keep my
heart open toward my spouse. In Jesus' name, Amen.*

What would fearless love look like in your relationship?

Day 300

I WILL turn away from all previous romantic relationships.

The enemy wants to use these unresolved feelings for two purposes in your marriage: to pervert and poison.

No, dear brothers and sisters, I have not achieved [perfection], but I focus on this one thing: Forgetting the past and looking forward to what lies ahead (Philippians 3:13–14).

Many people, even after remarriage, still yearn for an ex-partner, whether they were actually married or not. The Bible teaches that intimacy binds souls (see 1 Corinthians 6:12–20). When separated, remnants remain, and these feelings can disrupt your marriage. The devil also uses past resentments to taint memories, making your new partner bear unresolved emotions. To shield against these deceptions:

1. Express gratitude to God for past growth.
2. Focus on the present, not past misgivings.
3. Embrace forgiveness; it's freeing, not absolving.

No matter what your past romantic history may be, with God you have potential for a wonderful marriage.

Dear Father, I believe Your intent is for us to only have one intimate relationship. Holy Spirit, help me as I break any ties with past romantic relationships. In Jesus' name, Amen.

You may not be ready to discuss a past relationship with your spouse, but be honest with God and ask for His help in breaking past ties.

I WILL express appreciation for my spouse's uniqueness.

Romance is for one person only.

You are altogether beautiful, my darling,
beautiful in every way (Song of Songs 4:7).

Prioritize and isolate your marriage relationship from all others. Without it, there is little difference between your relationship with your spouse and anyone else, except that the two of you share the same house and bed. Women feel romanced when their husbands consistently show them unique and meaningful gestures, such as loving words, creative expressions of affection, gifts, planning special experiences, helping around the house, and assisting with the children. Men feel romanced when their wives show exclusive devotion and appreciation that meets their needs and desires. Consider what you say and do on a consistent basis to communicate your spouse's unique value. Make a list and find creative ways to expand your romantic expressions. This will strengthen your relationship and keep the romance alive.

Dear Father, You recognize and love us individually. Show me how to love my spouse's uniqueness. Holy Spirit, remind me to tell my spouse often how special they are. In Jesus' name, Amen.

How do you express your appreciation for your spouse's uniqueness? Today tell them how you appreciate their unique qualities.

Day 302

I WILL be the first one to do the right thing.

The best person does the right thing first.

The LORD is more pleased when we do what is right and just
than when we offer him sacrifices (Proverbs 21:3).

Destructive conflicts happen in marriages when both spouses are locked in a standoff, each justifying their actions based on the wrongs they perceive in the other. Each person believes their stance is noble and right, and they wait for the other to change first. The problem is that both have the same attitude, leading to a collision of wills and the potential breakdown of the marriage. Pride will be the downfall of any person. Instead of justifying wrongdoing and responding with immaturity, choose humility. Respond with a different spirit and a higher standard. One person doing the right thing can turn things around. When you choose to do the right thing in your marriage, God can use your humility and godly character as a conduit to infuse His love and power into your relationship.

Dear Father, I want You to use me to accomplish Your will. Holy Spirit, help do what I know is right, especially when I don't feel like it. In Jesus' name, Amen.

What "right thing" have you been waiting for your spouse to do first? Will you do it today?

I WILL share my innermost thoughts with my spouse.

The climax of all communication in marriage is the special time we share in intimate discussion.

The fig tree ripens its figs,
    and the vines are in blossom;
    they give forth fragrance.
Arise, my love, my beautiful one,
    and come away (Song of Songs 2:13 ESV).

While many conversations are important for your marriage, deeply personal, intimate discussions are its highlights. As you create and protect a safe environment that encourages open conversation, set aside those special moments where you can both share your deepest thoughts, feelings, and dreams. Use these intimate occasions to express your deep love for your spouse. Whether during a quiet, secluded moment or in the intimacy following sex, never take these moments for granted. Don't hide your inner self; the more honest and vulnerable you become, the better you'll understand each other and deepen your love and intimacy. The pinnacle of communication in your marriage lies in those cherished moments of intimate discussion.

Dear Father, I want my marriage to be a heart-to-heart connection. Holy Spirit, help me to be brave as I open up and share my innermost thoughts with my spouse. In Jesus' name, Amen.

What thoughts have you never shared with your spouse? Are you willing to take a leap of faith and share those thoughts?

Day 304

I WILL (as a wife) strive to understand the importance of sex in my husband's life.

Both spouses should be totally committed to meeting one another's needs.

The husband should fulfill his wife's sexual needs, and the wife should fulfill her husband's needs (1 Corinthians 7:3).

As you work to understand and accept your husband's need for sex, it's essential to communicate your commitment to fulfilling it. Avoid making him beg or feel guilty. Instead, reassure him by saying, "Honey, I know you need sex, and I'm committed to meeting that need. Just tell me what you want, and I'll do my best to fulfill your desire." This approach creates a powerful bond of love and trust. Remember, around 30 percent of women may be more sexual than their husbands, so both partners should prioritize meeting each other's needs. However, if your husband asks something sinful or against your conscience, gently refuse, saying, "I'm sorry, but I can't do that. Is there something else I can do instead?" Open communication is vital for a successful marriage.

Dear Father, I want to understand how important sex is to my husband. Holy Spirit, help me to be thoughtful and supportive as we enjoy our sex life together. In Jesus' name, Amen.

What is the best way for you and your husband to communicate about your sexual desires?

I WILL have faith-focused thinking.

There is a greater reward for doing what is right than there is for doing what is wrong

"Who is this pagan Philistine anyway, that he is allowed to defy the armies of the living God?" (1 Samuel 17:26).

Great lives are shaped by faith-driven thoughts. To connect with God, you must believe in His presence, love, and characteristics right now. Think of David as he was facing Goliath. David knew that he and God were an army. Faith-driven thinking focuses on the unseen over the visible. Challenges will test you. Think of those risks that intimidate you, casting shadows over your God-given destiny. But, with faith, declare, "God is with me!" Focus on God's rewards over earthly fears. David thought about the rewards, not the risks. In life's battles, the turning point is keeping God at the center, trusting His rewards, and seeking His kingdom above all else. (Matthew 6:33). Like David, focus on God's promises and His unchanging love.

Dear Father, You have been with me all my life. I know You are present and working in my life right now. Holy Spirit, drive away doubt and replace it with the fires of faith. In Jesus' name, Amen.

How can you express your trust of God in the most difficult circumstances?

Day 306

I WILL grow in my relationship with the Lord and my local church.

*To run the marathon of marriage
we must have social support.*

Let us think of ways to motivate one another to acts of love and good works. And let us not neglect our meeting together, as some people do, but encourage one another (Hebrews 10:24–25).

Without the Holy Spirit, our emotions are like an engine without oil. We quickly heat up and shut down. His power makes what is impossible for us to become effortless. Many forces in our world can tear at our marriages and test our commitment to each other. But the Holy Spirit's power can overcome anything we face and hold us together. We need social support for our marriages. We need to belong to an army, not isolated on our own. That's why it's important to commit to a Bible-believing local church. Our fellow believers will encourage us to love each other and do the right things. Serving the Lord in our local church will keep us growing together.

Dear Father, I want to be one with my spouse to follow Your purpose. Holy Spirit, let Your love bring us to unity. In Jesus' name, Amen.

How are you serving in your church right now? What is the next step you will take to increase your involvement?

I WILL be in agreement with my spouse about how to discipline our children.

Neither parent should be the sole disciplinarian.
Both should be involved.

May God, who gives this patience and encouragement, help you live in complete harmony with each other, as is fitting for followers of Christ Jesus (Romans 15:5).

When parents disagree on discipline or don't support each other, it can harm both their children and their marriage. Instead of one partner taking on all the discipline, both should be actively involved. Begin by sharing your feelings and beliefs about discipline, always respecting each other's perspectives even if they are different. After discussing, find common ground and stay consistent with the decisions made. Don't let one be the disciplinarian while the other only offers love. Always address concerns privately, away from the kids. It's detrimental for children to see parental disagreement on discipline. Strive for a balance, where both partners love and discipline equally. Trust in God's Word and seek guidance from Him and those who walk with Him.

Dear Father, I realize that discipline is necessary and important for my child to grow into a healthy adult. Holy Spirit, show me how to find common ground with my spouse so that we can be united in our discipline decisions. In Jesus' name, Amen.

Have you and your spouse ever discussed your perspectives on discipline? If not, what is keeping you from doing so today?

Day 308

I WILL recognize the power of my words.

To be able to communicate effectively, you must understand the disproportionate power of words.

> The tongue can bring death or life;
> those who love to talk will reap the consequences (Proverbs 18:21).

Communication is your marriage's lifeline, crucial for understanding, resolving conflicts, and expressing affection. Your words have power. In thriving relationships, kind words are abundant. In strained relationships, words are either scarce or mostly negative. The destiny of your relationship is quite literally on the tip of your tongue. You have the potential to uplift or tear down, to be truthful or deceptive. Reflect on how your upbringing and the society around you influence the way you talk. Many people make a habit of belittling and dismissing their spouse. If you come from a verbally negative background, then break that cycle. If you're unhappy with the current state of your relationship, then change your words and watch the transformation happen.

Dear Father, You designed my words to have power, and I commit to using that power to bless my spouse. Holy Spirit, I ask You to convict me of using any words that bring death to my relationship. In Jesus' name, Amen.

What words can you use to uplift your spouse today?

I WILL maintain an open and teachable spirit.

Everything we need for success in life and marriage is waiting for us, if we only will seek God first

"Seek the Kingdom of God above all else, and live righteously, and he will give you everything you need" (Matthew 6:33).

Everything you need for success in life and marriage is within your reach if you will only prioritize seeking God first. It's easy for pastors and counselors to help a couple willing to study, learn, and make a real effort. However, a significant factor contributing to issues in some marriages happens because one or both spouses are too proud or lazy to learn. Either spouse may harbor a hardened heart. In His parable of the sower, Jesus highlighted the necessity of keeping an open, teachable spirit. Not only should you follow what God's Word advises before your marriage, but you should also strive to maintain an open heart toward Him throughout your life. Don't settle for less than a complete understanding of everything God's Word tells you.

Dear Father, I want to have an open, teachable spirit. Holy Spirit, I surrender myself to Your guidance. In Jesus' name, Amen.

How do you think your relationship with your spouse will grow if you remain open-hearted?

Day 310

I WILL remove divorce from my vocabulary.

You were married for life, so take divorce off the table.

"I hate divorce," says the GOD of Israel. GOD-of-the-Angel-Armies says, "I hate the violent dismembering of the 'one flesh' of marriage." So watch yourselves. Don't let your guard down. Don't cheat (Malachi 2:16 MSG).

O ne vital trait of a thriving marriage is making decisions without being swayed by emotions. Emotions can be fickle and unreliable; they may feel real, yet they can mislead you and cause you to make some disastrous decisions. Recognize that you're human, and inherently emotional. So how can you prevent emotions from affecting your marriage's health? The key is to decide in advance. You committed to a lifelong partnership, so remove divorce from your options. Erase it from your vocabulary. Don't even joke about it. It's not funny. Avoid using divorce threats to influence your spouse. In fact, erase that term from your conversations completely. Address your challenges without resorting to that ultimatum.

Dear Father, I know divorce causes You great sorrow. Holy Spirit, guard my heart and tongue so that divorce will never be an option for me to even consider. In Jesus' name, Amen.

Have you ever threatened divorce or even joked about it? If so, apologize to your spouse and commit to removing divorce consideration or humor.

I WILL not allow fear to invade my life.

The devil knows where God wants to take you, and he wants to scare you away from that place.

Don't be afraid, for I am with you.
> Don't be discouraged, for I am your God.
I will strengthen you and help you.
> I will hold you up with my victorious right hand (Isaiah 41:10).

Jesus came to conquer Satan and death. Since Eden, Satan used the fear of death to chain and imprison people. Jesus broke that chain, freeing us from death's dread. Many so-called phobias stem from a core fear of death. Fear of heights is not about elevation but about a deadly fall. Fear of bugs is based on the potential harm they bring. Satan exploits fear, binding us and restricting our full life experience. When fear gets into a marriage, it shows itself in controlling behaviors or through paralyzing anxiety. Satan's ploy is to instill fear in you, blocking you from God's purpose. But knowing the truth, that in Jesus we're eternally alive and free, empowers us to defy and reject fear.

Dear Father, I know You are not the author of fear. Holy Spirit, guard me from the enemy's voice. In Jesus' name, Amen.

How has being afraid interrupted your life and harmed you? Are you ready to reject fear's voice?

Day 312

I WILL practice selflessness in financial matters.

Selfishness poses a dangerous threat to the wellbeing of any marriage.

For where jealousy and selfish ambition exist, there will be disorder and every vile practice (James 3:16 ESV).

Selfishness can pose a serious risk to your marriage's stability and prosperity. If you or your spouse unfairly control the family finances to satisfy personal wants without being concerned for others, then it can lead to bitterness, resentment, financial instability, or outright chaos. True financial stability and prosperity stem from a shared attitude of selflessness. This may mean voluntarily forgoing your personal wants for the overall good of your marriage and family. Such an attitude mirrors Christ's teachings and is thus blessed by God. He rewards those who are willing to sacrifice for their loved ones and His cause. In your pursuit of financial stability and success, selflessness will not only strengthen your bond but also open up the channel for God's blessings.

Dear Father, I don't want to do anything to block Your blessings from my life. Holy Spirit, convict me of any selfishness in my heart and help me to practice selflessness instead. In Jesus' name, Amen.

What are three ways you can practice selflessness in your financial decisions?

I WILL submit to the authority God places over me.

Until you understand submission to authority, the Bible will remain a clouded book to you.

Let everyone be subject to the governing authorities, for there is no authority except that which God has established. The authorities that exist have been established by God (Romans 13:1 NIV).

Understanding the value of submission to authority can unlock profound spiritual wisdom in your life. Consider how David respected Saul's authority despite adversity or how Jesus consistently prioritized His Father's desires. This isn't about fear but about recognizing God's design behind authority. Rejecting authority leads not only to social chaos but also personal consequences. In Romans 13, Paul warns against resisting authority. Embracing obedience isn't just about actions but is a reflection of your inner beliefs. By truly submitting, you're on a path to true spiritual greatness. Understanding and respecting authority can lead to unparalleled spiritual revelations and blessings. Your growth in faith hinges on recognizing and respecting God's design.

Dear Father, You are my authority, and You have placed people in authority over me. I will not oppose them, because that would be opposing You. Holy Spirit, I pray for the people in authority over me. I ask for Your blessings on them. In Jesus' name, Amen.

What is your biggest struggle with those in authority?

Day 314

I WILL accept God's blessings of sex within marriage.

God's perfect will is for you to have a pleasurable and exciting sex life with your spouse.

You've captured my heart, dear friend.
You looked at me, and I fell in love.
One look my way and I was hopelessly in love! (Song of Songs 4:9 MSG).

For a flourishing sex life in marriage, open communication about desires and needs is crucial. However, one common barrier often stands in the way: repressive attitudes toward sex. Perhaps you've grown up with negative perceptions about sex, stemming from your parents' comments or attitudes. This can have lasting effects in adulthood and marriage. Remember, sex, as intended by God, is beautiful and meant to be enjoyed within the sanctity of marriage. Don't let cultural stigmas or past mistakes hinder your experience. If you feel guilt from past sexual sins, confess and seek forgiveness. If you're curious about the Bible's perspective on sexual pleasure, explore the Song of Songs. It provides a passionate depiction of intimacy within God's design.

Dear Father, I believe You designed sex for married people at Creation. Holy Spirit, help me to recover and embrace God's design for sex with my spouse. In Jesus' name, Amen.

What can you do to make sex a more joyful experience for you and your spouse?

I WILL help my spouse fulfill their dreams for life and marriage.

When you begin to make the necessary changes to stop violating each other's dreams, you've taken the first steps to making your marriage a dream come true.

The hopes of the godly result in happiness,
but the expectations of the wicked come to nothing (Proverbs 10:28).

Many marital conflicts stem from unfulfilled dreams. These desires, often originating from childhood, reside so deep they might not always surface consciously. Perhaps you've dreamed of a picturesque home or a deeply involved partner. Men might desire a doting wife who manages household chores with care. Entering marriage, these dreams fuel your expectations, especially during the early, romantic stages. However, issues arise when actions don't align with these dreams. For instance, a husband working late might shatter his wife's vision of shared responsibilities. On the other hand, a wife's hostility can dampen a husband's dream of unwavering admiration. Recognizing and understanding each other's dreams is vital. Discuss them openly and work to be supporters of each other's dreams.

Dear Father, I believe You brought me together with my spouse. Holy Spirit, help me not to become cynical or lazy as I help my spouse pursue their dreams. In Jesus' name, Amen.

Have you talked to your spouse lately about each of your dreams?

Day 316

I WILL meet my spouse's needs with a joyful attitude.

When our spouses have an unmet need, we should be there with a good attitude to serve them.

"But among you it will be different. Whoever wants to be a leader among you must be your servant" (Matthew 20:26).

Instead of adopting a begrudging and rejecting attitude toward your partner's requests, it is important to listen and serve them with joy. Ask them how they are doing and show genuine interest in their wellbeing. A joyful attitude can have a positive impact on any relationship and can make each other a priority. You should not see your spouse as a burden to carry but rather a joy to serve. It is essential to be there for your partner when they have unmet needs, and to do so with a good attitude. Serving your spouse with a joyful attitude communicates to them love, acceptance, value, and priority, which transforms the atmosphere of your relationship.

Dear Father, I want to have the right attitude when I serve my spouse. Holy Spirit, give me joy in serving my spouse and help me to express it. In Jesus' name, Amen.

Do you serve your spouse with a joyful attitude? What difference does it make when your spouse does the same?

I WILL speak love in my spouse's language.

The best marriages are two servants in love.

Timely advice is lovely,
  like golden apples in a silver basket (Proverbs 25:11).

Successful relationships often involve catering to needs you might not personally feel. This demands a servant's heart from you. Countless times, your partner will express needs you might not relate to. If you're only inclined to address those needs you also feel, you're essentially dismissing your partner's unique qualities by allowing your desires to monopolize the relationship. Recognizing their distinct needs is a start, but genuine impact only comes if you, with a servant's spirit, willingly meet those needs even if you don't resonate with them in that moment. Your spouse's need is an opportunity to learn the language of their heart. True passion and closeness emerge from when you mutually dedicate yourselves to selflessly serving each other.

Dear Father, You have made my spouse with unique needs. You have also made me with the ability to minister to my spouse's needs. Help me to speak my spouse's language of the heart. In Jesus' name, Amen.

What are your spouse's needs? Ask your spouse, "What makes you feel seen and valued?" What can you do today to put your spouse's needs first, even if you do not feel the same way about those needs that they do?

Day 318

I WILL (as a wife) embrace my husband's need for visual stimulation.

Even if you cannot understand what there is about your body that turns him on, rest assured that it really does.

You are altogether beautiful, my darling,
beautiful in every way (Song of Songs 4:7).

Men tend to be more visually stimulated than women, meaning they get sexually excited through sight and touch. This is why men are drawn to pornography and images of scantily clad women, even though it's damaging to them and their marriages. Many women don't want anyone to look at them because they struggle with comparison, self-rejection, and body image issues. But part of understanding your husband's visual needs is accepting yourself and focusing on being the best you can be as God made you. In the privacy of marriage, wives do not need to be ashamed to be naked as they meet their husband's desire for visual stimulation. Extreme shyness and modesty can harm intimacy, so be open with your husband. Embrace your body's appeal to him, because it truly matters in your relationship.

Dear Father, thank You for this body that You created for me. Holy Spirit, show me any insecurities that I need to work on in order to be completely open with my husband. In Jesus' name, Amen.

What is your husband's favorite thing about your body?

I WILL not mistake God's blessings as a source for pride.

Satan can come against us only when we step out from under God's covering of protection.

All who fear the LORD will hate evil.
  Therefore, I hate pride and arrogance,
  corruption and perverse speech (Proverbs 8:13).

You should always ask yourself, "How much can God bless me before I use it against Him?" When you gaze into a mirror, being naturally attractive, you might become arrogant about your looks. If you're gifted with the talent to amass wealth, you stand at the crossroads of becoming arrogant, independent, and unteachable. If you have a great marriage, it might cause you to think you are simply a wonderful spouse. It's easy to give yourself credit for God's blessings and overlook the true Source. When you allow Satan to stand up against you, you face a larger issue than just the devil. Satan can oppose you only when you move away from being under God's protective covering.

Dear Father, I know that every good gift and every great opportunity comes from You. Holy Spirit, guard me from arrogance and selfishness. In Jesus' name, Amen.

Why do you think people so easily think their success is completely to their credit? How can you combat the temptation to forget God in the middle of success?

Day 320

I WILL allow God to use my scars
to prepare me for His purpose.

Why does God allow pain? It's to prepare us for His purpose.

For when I am weak, then I am strong (2 Corinthians 12:10).

You may have started your marriage with high hopes, but life's challenges threw you off balance. Feelings of loneliness and chaos consumed you, and your actions mirrored your heartbreak. You may feel isolated and think no one could understand. We all experience times of hopelessness and despair. You may be mourning a loss, battling an illness, or facing financial struggles. Our deepest pain often aligns with our strongest gifts. Your wounds might hint at your life's purpose. God uses pains to prepare you for your destiny. It's in vulnerability that you truly recognize your need for God. Your scars might be preparing you for a greater purpose. Embrace healing and discover what God has planned for you.

Dear Father, You know every pain I have suffered and every scar I have received. You have been present with me even in my darkest experiences. Holy Spirit, redeem my scars and show me how to use past painful experiences to further Your Kingdom. In Jesus' name, Amen.

Have you discussed your past painful experiences with your spouse? Where do you still need healing so you can step courageously into the future?

I WILL approach disagreements with a soft start-up.

To successfully resolve conflict, you must begin with words of love and affirmation.

Gentle words are a tree of life;
  a deceitful tongue crushes the spirit (Proverbs 15:4).

Studies show that the initial three minutes of a disagreement can set the tone for the entire conversation. Starting off aggressively, like yelling or name-calling, can doom a conversation from the outset. If you start poorly, consider pausing the discussion and revisiting it later. Apologize if you've said something hurtful. When upset, approach your spouse with love and commitment. Start with, "I'm upset and want to discuss it. But first, know that I love you and am committed to you. We'll work through this." This non-threatening approach creates an environment for open dialogue. Always be thoughtful with your words. Words have enduring power, so let wisdom guide you, especially during conflicts. Begin confrontations with love and affirmation and use your words wisely.

Dear Father, I want to approach my spouse with love, even when we disagree. Holy Spirit, help me to be thoughtful with my words so that my spouse always feels safe and respected. In Jesus' name, Amen.

Do you normally jump into a disagreement with aggressive words, or do you connect with a soft start-up? How do the outcomes differ with each approach?

Day 322

I WILL be a safe space for my spouse to communicate honestly.

Promote healing through honest non-judgmental communication.

When you say they are wicked and should be punished, you are condemning yourself, for you who judge others do these very same things (Romans 2:1).

The inability to communicate hampers the healing that could happen with honest conversation. Understand that complaining isn't the same as criticizing. While criticizing attacks the other, complaining simply shares how you feel. Even if your feelings aren't right, they're real, and you need to express them without attacking or judging your partner. Learning how to complain without being harsh is essential, as is starting confrontations positively. Perhaps the most vital step to healing is inviting your spouse to open up, assuring them that honesty won't be punished, even when facing negative emotions and challenging issues. Let them know that you are a safe space where they can express their needs to you. Sharing and hearing these things can be difficult, but they are part of the healing process.

Dear Father, You desire that we speak the truth in love to one another. Help us to share and to hear our deepest feelings, even if they are difficult. Then help us to practice forgiveness and change so that we can be healed. In Jesus' name, Amen.

Are there topics that you are afraid to bring up? Are there issues that you don't want your spouse to mention? How can you begin to make yourself a safe space to hear your spouse?

I WILL (as a wife) be creative and proactive in our sex life together.

Just as a man should aggressively romance his wife, a woman should aggressively pursue her husband sexually.

Kiss me and kiss me again,
   for your love is sweeter than wine (Song of Songs 1:2).

To fulfill your husband's sexual desires, it's essential to be creative and proactive without constantly feeling like you have to learn new tricks. While regular sex is enjoyable, there are times when he craves unrestricted romance and prolonged, creative intimacy. Planning ahead and reserving enough time for these special moments will enhance your pleasure, whether at home or away. Just as your husband should actively pursue you romantically, you should aggressively pursue him sexually. Don't be afraid to be the initiator. When your husband knows exciting moments await the two of you, he'll begin to be more romantic. So be attentive to his needs, and don't make him beg for sex. Be sensitive and available to nurture a fulfilling connection, building a deeper and more passionate bond with each other.

Dear Father, You designed sex to be something both my husband and I enjoy. Holy Spirit, give me creative ideas and help me not to be afraid to try them. In Jesus' name, Amen.

How would your husband respond if you suggested something new and fun for your sex life?

Day 324

I WILL encourage myself every day by trusting God.

God always has an answer for victory,
even in the middle of defeat.

"My sheep listen to my voice; I know them, and they follow me" (John 10:27).

Consciously trust God and listen to His voice. God is always speaking words of encouragement to you. Jesus said, "My sheep listen to my voice." In challenges, seek direction from your Creator and Friend. He will always respond, "Move forward; triumph awaits." Amid defeat, God offers victory. Stay encouraged by relying solely on Him, not on people or situations. He remains in control, providing the right solutions and breathing life into your spirit. Stripped of all, you might feel anger instead of faith, but you can choose trust over resentment. Nurture an unbreakable bond with God, seeking His comfort instead of turning to anger. That is the way to live in a fallen world while trusting in the living Lord.

Dear Father, Your voice is the most important one I can hear. I know You are always speaking and You always hear me. Holy Spirit, I am coming to You with trust and humility, asking for Your guidance. In Jesus' name, Amen.

What do you think is the biggest barrier to trusting God? How do you shut out other voices as You listen to the Lord?

I WILL turn off "autopilot" in my marriage.

The truth about the flight of marriage is that no marriage can fly itself; it requires the input of two engaged human beings.

Guard your heart above all else,
for it determines the course of your life (Proverbs 4:23).

Navigating marriage, avoid the trap of "autopilot." When we get comfortable, we might shift focus away, risking our marriages. Three pitfalls of relationship autopilot are:

1. **Losing Vital Skills:** Over-reliance can lead to diminished sensitivity and empathy. Prioritize understanding and acting on your partner's feelings.
2. **Growing Distractions:** Early days of a marriage often have intense focus. As time progresses, external pursuits might overshadow connection with your spouse. Stay attentive.
3. **Endangering Loved Ones:** Like pilots leaving a cockpit, neglecting your marriage will affect your children's emotional wellbeing. Safeguard them by prioritizing your relationship with your spouse.

Disengage from autopilot in your relationship. Ensure active participation and consistent focus on your spouse to keep your marriage airborne.

Dear Father, You are always active and working in my life. Holy Spirit, convict me of apathy or laziness in my relationships. In Jesus' name, Amen.

Has anyone ever gone on "autopilot" in a relationship with you? How did it make you feel? Commit today never to let your spouse experience those kinds of feelings.

I WILL romance my spouse by paying attention to their needs.

Romance is the language of desire.

Let all that you do be done in love (1 Corinthians 16:14 ESV).

Romance is a daily essential for your marriage, and it's as vital for you as it is for your spouse. Romance means understanding the unspoken needs or desires of your partner. It's not that they never voice it. Instead, it means that you are taking the initiative to notice and address their needs and desires. When you are romantic, you are saying: "I notice you. You're always on my mind. Even when we're apart, my thoughts are with you, willingly. I act out of love because you are my heart's desire. You're not a burden. You're my joy, and it brings me happiness to serve and please you." Embracing romance maintains the positive spirit of your relationship, reinforcing the foundational bonds of your marriage.

Dear Father, You acted to meet our deepest needs before we asked. Help me to follow Your lead and study my spouse to meet their needs before being asked. In Jesus' name, Amen.

How does this description of romance compare with what you have imagined romance is? What can you do today that is "romantic" for your spouse?

I WILL humble myself and do the right thing even when I feel my spouse is in the wrong.

One person doing the right thing can turn a situation around.

And he gives grace generously. As the Scriptures say,
"God opposes the proud
but gives grace to the humble" (James 4:6).

C onsider this: "The best person does the right thing first." In many marital conflicts, both partners can become entrenched, justifying their actions based on the perceived wrongs of their spouse. Typically, each believes they are in the right and waits for the other to make amends. This standoff mirrors the clash between an "irresistible force" and an "immovable object." Pride will almost always tear apart relationships. Choose to embody humility rather than responding with pride. The humblest individuals often take that first step toward reconciliation. Even if not always successful, the success rate is notably higher. By choosing righteousness and humility, God's love can revitalize your relationship.

Dear Father, I do not want pride to tear apart my relationship. Holy Spirit, help me choose to do the right thing in a spirit of humility, even when it feels like I am the only one. In Jesus' name, Amen.

What does "doing the right thing" look like in your relationship with your spouse?

Day 328

I WILL allow my children to be around family members who respect our values.

As a parent, you must not be intimidated, for your children are God's precious and valuable gifts.

Behold, children are a heritage from the LORD,
the fruit of the womb a reward (Psalm 127:3 ESV).

The principle of protection is vital, especially when considering your family's interactions with your children. Remember, the time your extended family members spend with your children is more of a privilege than an inherent right. If, at any point, they expose your child to influences or behaviors you find concerning or disapprove of, it's essential to confront them about it. If they continue to disregard your wishes or boundaries, then make sure your children are only around them when you can directly supervise. As a parent, you must stand strong, even if it feels challenging. Your children are precious, invaluable gifts entrusted to you. It's your responsibility to ensure they're surrounded by those who genuinely respect and support your values.

Dear Father, You have given me the incredible responsibility of protecting my children. Holy Spirit, open my eyes and ears to any negative influences and give me the grace to deal with them in a firm but loving way. In Jesus' name, Amen.

What family members give you concern when they interact with your child? How will you address the issue?

I WILL (as a wife) take an interest in the things my husband enjoys.

Become interested and involved as much as you can in the things he enjoys.

Tell me, my love, where are you leading your flock today?
Where will you rest your sheep at noon? (Song of Songs 1:7).

Become interested and involved in the things your husband enjoys, even if you don't necessarily like every activity he does. Simply being together during the activity will strengthen your friendship, increase your intimacy, and add more fun to your relationship. Without fun and intimacy, a marriage can feel like a business arrangement, which can be quite boring. People thrive when they're having fun, while losing joy can be detrimental to a relationship. Remember how you both worked to have fun together in the early days of your courtship. This isn't just the secret to falling in love but also the key to staying in love. Prioritize enjoyment and shared activities to keep the love alive and maintain a fulfilling connection with your husband.

Dear Father, my husband is so important to me, and I want him to know it. Holy Spirit, fill me with courage to try new things. In Jesus' name, Amen.

What does your husband enjoy doing in his spare time? How can you get involved?

Day 330

I WILL trust in God's goodness even during trying circumstances.

Even if we find ourselves in the valley of the shadow of death, God will not abandon us.

God is our refuge and strength,
always ready to help in times of trouble (Psalm 46:1).

To cultivate an active, trusting connection with God, prioritize relying on Him over circumstances, especially in tough times. David trusted God even in "the valley of death's shadow." He had that assurance because he believed a good God was with him to comfort and protect him from his enemies. God's trustworthiness endures, never abandoning us. In the middle of adversity, He sets a table, remains close, and continuously cares, even in dire moments (see Psalm 46:1). While hindsight reveals God's past deeds, recognize His ongoing work in trials. As you look back, God was guiding you to the place you are today. He helped you navigate challenges and caused you to grow. He's always been present.

Dear Father, You are good, and You always do good. I will trust You at all times. Holy Spirit, remove all doubt and replace it with audacious faith. In Jesus' name, Amen.

Why do you think some people allow circumstances to overwhelm them to the point that they forget about God and His goodness? What would you say to them?

I WILL be free from the bondage of pornography.

Don't give your spouse up to pornography.

"You know the next commandment pretty well, too: 'Don't go to bed with another's spouse.' But don't think you've preserved your virtue simply by staying out of bed. Your *heart* can be corrupted by lust even quicker than your *body*. Those ogling looks you think nobody notices—they also corrupt"
(Matthew 5:27–28 MSG).

Living in today's digital age, you're just a few clicks away from accessing explicit content. While many associate pornography with men, an increasing number of women are drawn to it. Pornography can negatively reshape how men perceive women, leading to objectification. Introducing pornography into a relationship invites comparison, making your spouse feel they aren't enough. The insatiable nature of porn often leads to seeking more explicit content. Overcoming pornography involves repentance, accountability, and renewing your mindset. If affected, seek support from your church or organizations that address this issue. For wives whose husbands struggle with pornography, pray persistently and combat this challenge with understanding, emotional support, and spiritual warfare.

Dear Father, I believe You are always faithful to me. Holy Spirit, convict me of any ways I have been unfaithful to my spouse. In Jesus' name, Amen.

If pornography is a struggle for you, what are you doing to confront this issue?

Day 332

I WILL (as a husband) strive to understand my wife's physical and sexual needs.

A man should care for his wife and love her
in nonsexual ways all day long.

> Live happily with the woman you love through all the meaningless days of life that God has given you under the sun. The wife God gives you is your reward for all your earthly toil (Ecclesiastes 9:9).

I t's important to recognize that men and women often respond differently to intimacy. Just because you're instantly in the mood doesn't mean she will be. A simple way to put it is this: while men might be quick to heat up, like microwaves, women often take time, like slow cookers. Every event in your wife's day can influence her mood in the evening. Expecting your wife to always have intense experiences with every intimate encounter is unrealistic. To truly connect, prioritize understanding and respecting these differences. Be attentive and considerate all day, not just during intimate moments. Keep up your personal hygiene, be patient, and compliment genuinely, and you'll likely find a more receptive and fulfilled partner.

Dear Father, I want to be an understanding husband. Holy Spirit, help me show love to my wife by responding to her needs even when they are different from my own. In Jesus' name, Amen.

How does understanding that women often respond differently to intimacy than men help you understand your wife's needs?

I WILL win the battle for my mind with God's Word.

To understand sexual freedom or any other kind of freedom, we must realize that the battlefield of victory is the mind.

Then Jesus turned to the Jews who had claimed to believe in him. "If you stick with this, living out what I tell you, you are my disciples for sure. Then you will experience for yourselves the truth, and the truth will free you" (John 8:31–32 MSG).

When Jesus was crucified at a place named Golgotha, which means "the place of a skull," there was a symbolic significance. If you've ever seen Golgotha, you'd notice its eerie resemblance to a human skull. This wasn't a mere coincidence. The location of Jesus' crucifixion on a skull-shaped hill emphasizes the importance of the mind in our spiritual battles and our quest for freedom. Many perceive sexual temptation as mainly biological, trying to combat it with sheer willpower. But, as history shows, even the strongest can fall prey to it. The root issue isn't primarily physical or hormonal, but rather, it's how you think.

Dear Father, You have already won the battle for my mind. Holy Spirit, fill me so that all my mind can hear is Your voice. In Jesus' name, Amen.

Where does your mind face its greatest battles?

I WILL take responsibility rather than play "the blame game."

To have a functional and successful marriage and family, we must be willing to be honest and humble people who take responsibility for our own issues.

So humble yourselves under the mighty power of God, and at the right time he will lift you up in honor (1 Peter 5:6).

Do you often find yourself avoiding responsibility in your relationship? Many married people believe that if only their spouse would change, then everything would be perfect. How can you escape this cycle of blame?

- Shift your focus away from your spouse's flaws. Remember, you can't change them, but transforming yourself can reshape the relationship.
- Make it about your connection with God. Address your issues sincerely with Him and find grace and strength.
- Embrace humility. God supports the humble and challenges the proud.

To build a thriving marriage, embrace honesty and humility. Accept responsibility for your actions, and rather than feeling trapped by others' mistakes, recognize your power to prevail by addressing your own faults as you place your trust in God.

Dear Father, thank You that I can always bring my problems to You. Holy Spirit, draw my focus to what I need to do to become a better spouse. In Jesus' name, Amen.

Why is it often easier to blame your spouse than to take responsibility for your own issues?

I WILL have realistic expectations of my marriage.

The best marriages are between two people who go through hell together and come out on the other side having fought for their marriage.

"But you, be strong and do not let your hands be weak, for your work shall be rewarded!" (2 Chronicles 15:7 NKJV).

In the battle for your marriage, you must have realistic expectations. Divorce's leading cause isn't communication gaps, sexual issues, finances, or parenting problems. It's disappointment. Marriage starts with visions of a perfect, trouble-free life, but reality brings challenges. When perfection isn't met, hearts break due to unrealistic hopes. The devil then whispers, "You married the wrong person. Seek your soulmate online." Counter this with realistic, not lowered, expectations. Successful marriages merge high expectations with a strong work ethic. Face the devil's challenges head-on. The best marriages come from adversity, united through battles, emerging with victories in hand, having fought for their family, embracing the victory promised by the One who conquered the world.

Dear Father, I want to have high expectations for my marriage, but I never want my spouse to think I expect perfection. Holy Spirit, help me to express my thoughts in a way that is tender to my spouse's feelings. In Jesus' name, Amen.

What would be an unrealistic expectation for marriage?

Day 336

I WILL believe in the faithfulness of God.

God is willing to pick you up where you are right now and turn you toward your destiny.

We can rejoice, too, when we run into problems and trials, for we know that they help us develop endurance (Romans 5:3).

In your and your spouse's darkest hours, find encouragement through an active, trusting connection with God. Despite appearances, declare blessings to the Lord, acknowledging His goodness. Even in death's shadow, He remains beside you. Amid conflicting voices, trust His Word. Remember His past faithfulness and unseen current work. There's always more than meets the eye. This doesn't mean you have to enjoy hardship, but believe God is faithful and working. Learn from adversity, Through it, you will step into your destiny. Recall God's constant faithfulness, rest in His hidden work, and lift up your head in the darkest times. Nurture an active, trusting relationship with God. It will give you encouragement on the path ahead and keep you from straying.

Dear Father, You never change. You are always light and never darkness. Holy Spirit, help me to trust You more. You are my only hope. In Jesus' name, Amen.

When was a time God showed His faithfulness to you and your spouse? Did this experience change the way you experienced God?

I WILL (as a wife) strive to understand my husband's physical and sexual needs.

The more you know and understand, the more you will be able to meet your husband's needs.

Do not deprive each other of sexual relations, unless you both agree to refrain from sexual intimacy for a limited time so you can give yourselves more completely to prayer (1 Corinthians 7:5).

Many women don't fully grasp how men are wired sexually. While you might lean more toward romance and emotion, men are often driven by visual and physical cues. Just as your husband should respond to your need for love and romance, you can respond to his visual and physical inclinations. By understanding and embracing the significance of intimacy in his life, it becomes easier to connect on this level. Your proactive and imaginative approach in this area can strengthen your relationship immensely. If you're unsure about his needs and how he responds, consider diving into reputable resources on the topic. The more insight you gain, the better equipped you'll be to nurture your bond.

Dear Father, I want to be an understanding wife. Holy Spirit, help me to show love to my husband by responding to his needs, even when they are different from my own. In Jesus' name, Amen.

What are some ways you can demonstrate to your husband that you understand how important intimacy is in his life?

Day 338

I WILL share control in our marriage.

By seeing your spouse as your equal and sharing control, you are sharing life.

And over all these virtues put on love, which binds them all together in perfect unity (Colossians 3:14 NIV).

Research shows that sharing control is one of the most important elements of success in a marriage. For your strengths to be dynamic and not dangerous, you must maintain total equality. In your marriage, both of you should submit to God, turning to Him for decisions. Then you move from being two stubborn individuals clashing over decisions to becoming two humble souls seeking the best for your marriage. If you are the dominant one, respect and treat your spouse as an equal. If you are dominated, then assert yourself and lovingly require respect. When you respect your partner and make decisions jointly, your intimacy and happiness will soar. By sharing control, you are truly sharing life.

Dear Father, thank You for giving me a spouse so that I do not have to make important decisions alone. Help me to see my spouse as my equal and share control in the decisions of our home. In Jesus' name, Amen.

Do you tend to take control and make decisions or do you tend to let your spouse take control and make decisions?

I WILL fight for the souls of my children.

*To have children who are good, accept the
fact you are going to have to battle.*

"All your children *shall be* taught by the L ORD,
And great *shall be* the peace of your children" (Isaiah 54:13 NKJV).

A s parents, we must fight for our children. Tough times are inevitable, and just when you think you've figured things out, new challenges arise as they grow older. Notice the pattern? You conquer the "terrible twos," only for them to turn three. Suddenly, puberty arrives, followed by the teenage years. Someone has said that parenting success truly shows when your children reach 30. Mothers, especially, feel vulnerable to discouragement from child-related struggles. The devil seizes disappointing moments, magnifying them to make you doubt your parenting. Even the best parent faces challenges. No child arrives perfect; there's no such thing. To raise good children, embrace the reality that battles are part of the journey.

Dear Father, You gave my children to me to steward and train. Holy Spirit, guide me as I try to show the love of Jesus to them. In Jesus' name, Amen.

What is the greatest challenge facing children today? How do Christians confront this problem? If you have children, what do you think is the greatest issue facing your own children?

Day 340

I WILL build trust in my communication with my spouse.

Communication is something we do with our hearts.

For you are God, O Sovereign LORD. Your words are truth, and you have promised these good things to your servant (2 Samuel 7:28).

Communication in your marriage doesn't truly occur until you connect on a heartfelt level. It's more than just sharing facts; it's about genuinely relating and caring for one another. For this bond to grow, you need to cultivate a deep-seated trust. Our words and actions can build or diminish trust. Earning trust requires you to be a sanctuary where your spouse can bare their soul. Being judgmental or absent erodes that trust. Likewise, attentiveness and compassion earn trust, whereas distractions and indifference diminish it. Acknowledging your mistakes and seeking forgiveness builds trust, while pointing fingers and arrogance breaks it. Trust is nurtured with consistent commitment and loyalty in fulfilling your partner's needs and remaining faithful. However, inconsistencies or prioritizing other things or people can destroy it. Heartfelt communication is essential to healthy marriages and hinges on trust.

Dear Father, You have called us to build trust with one another. Help us to do that through communication that prioritizes each other. In Jesus' name, Amen.

Reflect on your most recent conversation with your spouse. Did your tone and words and body language invite trust? How can you build trust in your next conversation?

Day 341

I WILL confront the pain of my past.

All emotional and spiritual pain ends in Jesus.

But if we confess our sins to him, he is faithful and just to forgive us our sins and to cleanse us from all wickedness (1 John 1:9).

You've faced pain in your life, like everyone does. Sometimes this pain, if left untreated, will hold you back from achieving your true potential. For a fulfilled life aligned with God's vision, you must address and heal these wounds. First, confront your past. Acknowledge the emotions, but don't let them imprison you. Second, understand that God wants to free you from shame and offer unconditional love. Learn to distinguish between guilt and shame, and embrace God's forgiveness. Finally, let Jesus guide you away from the pain. Remember, all emotional and spiritual turmoil finds resolution in Him. By allowing Jesus into every corner of your life, He will heal your pain.

Dear Father, You are my Healer and Defender. Holy Spirit, I hand You my pain because it is too much for me to bear on my own. In Jesus' name, Amen.

Whether your pain is from past sin or you were a victim of evil, tell God you are giving Him those past experiences to heal and deliver you from bondage to them.

Day 342

I WILL refuse to accept physical curses or ailments that come through my DNA or bloodline.

You must say, I'm not going to live my life in the bondage of sickness and disease any longer.

But he was pierced for our rebellion,
    crushed for our sins.
He was beaten so we could be whole.
    He was whipped so we could be healed (Isaiah 53:5).

Some chronic illness isn't merely physical—it's demonic. I believe in doctors and medical science. But there are certain places doctors and medicine cannot go, and there are illnesses they cannot touch. Some sicknesses have a spiritual origin. Refuse to let negativity, illness, or any curse take hold due to past influences or inherited vulnerabilities. Don't just stand by, fearing repercussions from a history that no longer defines you. Remember, you are part of a new lineage now—the lineage of Abraham. Through the sacrifices of Jesus, you've been granted complete healing. This legacy of wellness and prosperity is not just for you, but also for your children and their children.

Dear Father, You knit together every part of me. I am Yours, which means I am blessed and never cursed. Holy Spirit, by faith I stand under Your healing power. In Jesus' name, Amen.

Has a genetic test caused you alarm? How can God's reassurance that He is your Healer give you strength and hope?

I WILL (as a wife) be a cheerleader in our marriage.

The key to your husband's heart is praise.

Let us think of ways to motivate one another to acts of love and good works (Hebrews 10:24).

Praise can turn struggling teams into victors. Nothing is more attractive to a man than a woman who cheers him on, even when things are going badly. Your praise is a powerful motivator for your husband—even more than sex. He needs to know that you admire him in good times and bad. In fact, the bad times might be when he needs it most. When you are your husband's biggest cheerleader, you become the most irresistible woman to him. More than that, your praise spurs him on to be a better man. Remember the power of your words and unleash that encouragement on your husband.

Dear Father, You have called me to speak words that honor and lift up my husband. In good times and bad times, help me to see his heart and positive qualities. Give me the strength and wisdom to praise him. In Jesus' name, Amen.

What are the top three qualities you admire most about your husband? When was the last time you praised him for those qualities? Watch your husband closely today to see specific ways you can cheer him on.

Day 344

I WILL maintain a Word-based view of reality.

We will never rise above our circumstances as long as we are dependent upon the circumstances to tell us what is real.

"See, God has come to save me.
I will trust in him and not be afraid.
The LORD GOD is my strength and my song;
he has given me victory" (Isaiah 12:2).

Many times, you link your encouragement to situations. During discouragement, you wait for conditions to shift—finances, family, challenges—hoping for encouragement. However, you don't have to wait for change to lift your head and change your mind. View reality through the lens of God's Word. This means believing the Bible over the whispers of circumstances. This secret is important because that is how you and your spouse will stay encouraged, even when change is delayed. Remain determined to find encouragement through hearing from God and relying on His Word. Believing His promises will empower you and your spouse. Depending on circumstances alone to define your reality will keep you from rising above them.

Dear Father, I love Your Word. It is sweet to me. I trust it for my nourishment every day. Holy Spirit, shine Your light on God's Word. In Jesus' name, Amen.

How would you tell someone what the Bible means to you?

I WILL show appreciation for my spouse every day.

Show your spouse how much you appreciate them.
Then tell your spouse how thankful you are for them.

You're so beautiful, my darling,
    so beautiful, and your dove eyes are veiled
By your hair as it flows and shimmers,
    like a flock of goats in the distance
    streaming down a hillside in the sunshine (Song of Songs 4:1–5 MSG).

Your actions resonate deeply with your spouse, reflecting your appreciation and how much you value them. But gratitude isn't expressed only through behavior. Consider your words: How do you address your spouse? Are you critical or grateful? Is your tone encouraging or accusing? Do you uplift them with compliments or undermine them with harshness? Jesus set an example by sacrificing for his bride, the Church, demonstrating our immeasurable worth to Him. He declared love with words and confirmed it with deeds. Enhance your marriage by emulating Jesus' example. Express appreciation to your spouse both in word and deed. Voice your gratitude. Expressing appreciation isn't merely about your own self-growth; it's about strengthening your marriage.

Dear Father, You have shown me how to love. Holy Spirit, guide me to express genuine appreciation for my spouse. In Jesus' name, Amen.

Think of one way to express appreciation for your spouse today through words or actions.

Day 346

I WILL (as a husband) express affection to my wife and children.

*The way we worship God is often indicative of
how we relate to the people we love.*

God knows how much I love you and long for you with the tender compassion
of Christ Jesus (Philippians 1:8).

T he way you connect with loved ones may be related to the way you worship
God. Being expressive toward God often makes it easier to show affection in your closest relationships. However, if pride or fear holds you back, it
may hinder your connections with others. This is especially pivotal for men, as
women generally express themselves more instinctively. Women crave nonsexual affection and open communication, while many men sometimes struggle to
communicate their feelings. Children, too, need their fathers' affirmation; boys
seek encouragement, and girls need validation of their worth. There's always
room for growth in expressing love, both toward God and those close to you.
While women naturally lean toward relational connections, they can also grow
in this area.

*Dear Father, You speak love and affection to me every day. I want to follow
Your example. Holy Spirit, show me how to love my spouse with depth and purity.
In Jesus' name, Amen.*

Ask your spouse how they would like to receive affection from you. Choose
to express affection to them today.

I WILL seek peace in my marriage.

God created marriage to be a paradise, and the most important ingredient in a paradise is peace.

"You're blessed when you can show people how to cooperate instead of compete or fight. That's when you discover who you really are, and your place in God's family" (Matthew 5:9 MSG).

God designed marriage to be a haven of peace. Here are four cornerstones to help you cultivate peace:

1. **Prior Agreement:** If you and your spouse are heading in opposite directions, it will breed conflict. Address the big questions and try to be on the same page before disagreement occurs.
2. **Purpose:** Recognize your bigger story. Understand the purpose for which God brought you two together.
3. **Partnership:** Marriage thrives on equality. If one dominates, it threatens harmony. Prioritize shared decisions.
4. **Prayer:** Hand your anxieties to God. Trade your worries for prayers, allowing His peace to replace your stress.

A marriage will flourish in peace when it is grounded in agreement, purpose, partnership, and prayer.

Dear Father, You have given me peace that passes human understanding. Holy Spirit, make me an instrument of peace in my marriage. In Jesus' name, Amen.

What can you do to create more peace in your home and marriage? What would more peace mean to you?

Day 348

I WILL approach my spouse with compassion and grace.

The problem is that everyone—yes, everyone—has pain.

If one part suffers, all the parts suffer with it, and if one part is honored, all the parts are glad (1 Corinthians 12:26).

People often dream of achieving positions of great influence, wealth, and authority. They want to be famous like Billy Graham or the president. It's easy to reduce successful people to surface-level judgments and find their flaws and faults. However, hidden behind the burden of fake smiles and tired eyes is the weight of stress. Stress has a way of dampening the joy in even the most exciting accomplishment. You might envy other couples, believing their relationships to be smoother or their lives easier. But remember, everyone has pain. Many people try to keep their pain hidden, but it's still there, and it hurts deeply. As a husband or wife, don't jump to the conclusion that "Everything is fine" with your spouse. Instead, you should approach them with the compassion and grace that Jesus has showered upon you.

Dear Father, You are the Great Physician. Holy Spirit, help me to be a safe place for my spouse to share their pain. In Jesus' name, Amen.

How would you like someone to approach you when you're dealing with pain?

I WILL join with my spouse to have a vision for our marriage.

If God has a purpose for your marriage then vision is letting God reveal to you what that purpose is.

Be joyful. Grow to maturity. Encourage each other. Live in harmony and peace. Then the God of love and peace will be with you (2 Corinthians 13:11).

If you believe God has a purpose for your marriage, then it's crucial to let Him show you that purpose. Consider why a vision for your marriage is so crucial.

1. **Clarity:** God aims to offer clarity, dispelling confusion, and illuminating your path.
2. **Energy and Passion:** Once you grasp your shared vision, you'll chase it with fervor.
3. **Purity:.** Without a vision you are subject to negative guidance. With a purpose, you stay on God's path together.
4. **Unity:** Disagreements arise when visions diverge. A unified vision ensures you're both aligned.
5. **Victory:** Without vision, you're a racer without a finish line.

Seek God's vision, and let it transform your marriage.

Dear Father, I believe You give vision to Your children. Holy Spirit, fill us with hope and vision. In Jesus' name, Amen.

Why do you think your marriage needs vision? What are you going to do to pursue understanding and claim that vision? Have you taken a vision retreat? If not, plan one today.

I WILL not limit what God can do.

Nothing is incurable with God.

"For with God nothing will be impossible" (Luke 1:37 NKJV).

You can find assurance from the Bible that God's creation is good. Observing the physical world, you can see the beauty of nature. But sometimes physical reality contradicts spiritual or scriptural truth. Ailing bodies, for instance, are a physical reality. But what about a doctor's report declaring something incurable? While it might align with natural knowledge and physical laws, it doesn't align with higher truth. Nothing is impossible with God. And with God, nothing is incurable. When someone declares something "impossible" or "incurable" without qualifiers, they overlook a higher reality. You may think your marriage is unfixable, but don't impose limits on God. Every piece of physical evidence might challenge everything God's told you, but believe God first.

Dear Father, there is no beginning or end to You. If I have ever thought about You in another way, I confess that I was wrong. You are beyond my mind and words. Holy Spirit, give me a glimpse of God's majesty and magnificence. In Jesus' name, Amen.

Have you seen God do miracles? What happened, and how did it change you? What would you say to someone who believes God is not alive and active in our world?

I WILL (as a wife) renounce prideful independence.

God's design for marriage avoids chaos
and maintains harmony.

True humility and fear of the LORD
lead to riches, honor, and long life (Proverbs 22:4).

When Eve sinned, she did so through prideful independence. She made a radical, life-altering decision without asking God about it or consulting with Adam. In fact, she wanted to know as much as God, which would also mean knowing more than Adam. Every wife faces the temptation to take the reins and be in charge. Instead, God's design is for the wife to be an equal partner in the marriage and helper to her husband. As a wife, you are gifted with unique insight and wisdom that your husband needs. God's design is that you work together.

Dear Father, I am sorry for times when I have tried to seize control and run things my own way. I renounce the sin of prideful independence. Help me to embrace my partnership with my husband with humility and respect. In Jesus' name, Amen.

When is it difficult for you to step back and work with your husband? What has been the result of the times that you have seized the reins to be in control? What happened when you turned to your husband as your partner?

Day 352

I WILL agree with God's standards for sexual purity.

Satan's temptations always begin with a thought that is contrary to the standard of God's Word.

Put on salvation as your helmet, and take the sword of the Spirit, which is the word of God (Ephesians 6:17).

If you're truly honest with yourself, do you agree with the Bible's teachings on sex? With so much immorality around, it might not be a stretch for you to deviate from these standards. Have you genuinely thought about it? Do you think sex outside of marriage is wrong? Did God put boundaries on sex for your benefit, or for harm? How about Jesus' words equating a lustful glance to adultery—fair or not? Does "being in love" validate sexual misconduct for you? Can one truly live in sexual purity? Does violating these guidelines lead to repercussions as the Bible suggests? Your beliefs are vital. Why? Because the Bible, your primary tool for sexual integrity, is effective only if you trust it.

Dear Father, I believe You set boundaries around sex to protect and not to harm me. Holy Spirit, I never want to hurt my spouse or my relationship with You. In Jesus' name, Amen.

Where has been your greatest struggle with sexual purity? What do you believe God would say about the challenges you have faced?

I WILL be a helper to my spouse.

The best way to improve yourself or to repair your relationship is to follow the example of Jesus.

Never walk away from someone who deserves help;
your hand is *God's* hand for that person (Proverbs 3:27 MSG).

In a thriving marriage, you don't just watch your spouse struggle; you step in and offer what they need. It could be simple support or even a comforting embrace. As a helper, you fill in the gaps. God paired you with complementary strengths. One might be the thinker, the other, the doer. Together, you bolster each other in various ways. Imagine if Jesus withdrew during your struggles. He doesn't. He aids and nurtures us to resemble Him more. Your marriage thrives when you grasp the significance of mutual support. Desiring a stronger relationship? Feel distant from your spouse? To grow and mend ties, behave like Jesus. For a stronger union, follow His example.

Dear Father, I never want my spouse to feel alone or abandoned. Holy Spirit, You are my Helper. Show me how to be a better helper to my spouse. In Jesus' name, Amen.

Discuss with your spouse ways you can be a better helper to them? Be open about areas where you need help. Avoid accusation as you approach each other with sincere humility.

Day 354

I WILL (as a husband) lead with love and purpose.

Husbands are called by God to lead with love and purpose.

When the godly are in authority, the people rejoice.
But when the wicked are in power, they groan (Proverbs 29:2).

God entrusted Adam with the naming of creatures and subduing creation. He was called to be a leader, representing God's name and Word upon the earth. When Eve was tempted, Adam did nothing to refute the serpent or help Eve. Adam's sin was passivity. This remains the temptation for every man: to relinquish responsibility. God has called you as a husband to assert God's authority, to provide, protect, and initiate. God does not mean for you to dominate, but you are called to guide your family into holiness and godly living. This means you are called to nurture your wife, shepherd your children, and tend to the physical and spiritual security of your home.

Dear Father, I am sorry for the times when I have stood by passively in our marriage. I ask that You show me how to be an active husband who fulfills his responsibilities with joy. Grant me Your strength. In Jesus' name, Amen.

Take a brief inventory: Where have you taken the initiative to fulfill your responsibilities? In what ways do you realize you have been passive?

I WILL enter God's presence every day.

The more we walk by faith, the more we please God and the more we experience His victory in our lives.

Bless the LORD, O my soul;
And all that is within me, *bless* His holy name!
Bless the LORD, O my soul,
And forget not all His benefits (Psalm 103:1–2 NKJV).

God is ever-present, even when you don't engage in worship or prayer. However, not actively praising and worshipping Him causes you to lose the sense of His presence, making you react as if He's absent. This is when the devil seizes an opportunity to drown you in discouragement. Why should you bless God? Because less praise and acknowledgment of His blessings leads to forgetting His presence and power, breeding discouragement. On the other hand, talking about God's deeds and rehearsing His faithfulness and promises bring encouragement and strengthen your faith, As you keep God's unchanging faithfulness in view, you remember that "Jesus Christ *is* the same yesterday, today, and forever" (Hebrews 13:8 NKJV).

Dear Father, Your presence gives me peace and security. I love the time I spend with You. Holy Spirit, give me spiritual eyes to see God at work all around me. In Jesus' name, Amen.

What is the best way for you to experience God's presence?

Day 356

I WILL stop comparison from wreaking havoc on my marriage.

Comparison is a curse on our lives.

> Those who are dominated by the sinful nature think about sinful things, but those who are controlled by the Holy Spirit think about things that please the Spirit. (Romans 8:5).

Comparison brings havoc into your life, breeding bitterness, competition, and gossip. It distorts your perception and leads to harmful thoughts and feelings. Comparison is a destructive force that sows negativity and reaps both arrogance and insecurity. It can tempt you to feel superior and prideful or inferior and full of self-doubt. Comparing yourself or your marriage with others is a relentlessly destructive cycle. It chips away at your self-worth and leaves you feeling beaten down. Remember, God created you as a unique individual, with your own special strengths and qualities. Embrace your uniqueness and focus on your journey and your relationship with your spouse rather than constantly sizing yourself up against others. Let go of comparison and embrace the freedom to be who God made you to be.

Dear Father, I believe Your design for my life and marriage is just right. Holy Spirit, help me to recognize and uproot any seeds of comparison in my heart. In Jesus' name, Amen.

What effect has comparison had on your marriage up to this point?

I WILL recognize that both my spouse and I need intimacy.

Many people believe romance is mainly for women. But it's not true.

Beloved, let us love one another, for love is from God, and whoever loves has been born of God and knows God (1 John 4:7 ESV).

G od created you to love and be loved. That is your deepest need. It is a universal desire that applies to both men and women, as well as children. Marriage exists to provide an opportunity for you to love another person on the deepest and most fulfilling level possible. In other words, intimate love is something everyone yearns for. Contrary to common belief, romance is not solely for women. Men also have a need for romance, and they require it consistently, every day. However, they may express or receive it differently than women do. We all have a daily need for intimacy; men and women, not just a select few.

Dear Father, I believe I am created in Your image to love and be loved. Holy Spirit, help me to be honest about my needs and help me to show my love to my spouse. In Jesus' name, Amen.

How comfortable are you with showing love? How comfortable are you with receiving it? Commit to being more aware of your need to give and receive intimacy.

Day 358

I WILL respect my spouse's perspective on finances.

Be your spouse's dream maker.

All the believers were one in heart and mind. No one claimed that any of their possessions was their own, but they shared everything they had (Acts 4:32 NIV).

Financial psychologists have observed that people tend to have a variety of perspectives on finances. One perspective is to use money to show love by demonstrating how it has improved their lives. Another is to see money as a means to ward off problems and plan for future eventualities. Still others use money to share with others and create opportunities to enhance relationships. Finally, some may use money to gain respect and admiration. There are strengths and weaknesses inherent to each of these perspectives. A key to your marriage is to understand your spouse's perspective and respect it.

Dear Father, help me to remember that my spouse's perspective on finances is important and worthy of respect. Help me to share my perspective in a loving way. Help us both to work to fulfill each other's dreams. In Jesus' name, Amen.

Which of these perspectives do you think best fits you and your spouse? How does your perspective complement that of your spouse? Or do you share the same perspective? Can you imagine ways to put those perspectives together to achieve a common dream?

I WILL take my marriage struggles to Jesus.

The most important issue in your marriage is your personal relationship with Jesus Christ.

Jesus said, "Everyone who drinks this water will get thirsty again and again. Anyone who drinks the water I give will never thirst—not ever. The water I give will be an artesian spring within, gushing fountains of endless life" (John 4:13–14 MSG).

In facing challenges in your marriage, where do you go for help? A friend, family, or social media? Or do you present your problems to Jesus? Consider the Samaritan woman in John 4. Despite cultural norms, Jesus spoke to her, a woman with many past relationships. She was pushed aside by society. But Jesus showed her kindness. He introduced Himself as the Living Water, letting her know she'd never feel emptiness again. You probably did not anticipate all the challenges in marriage. Every day, you seek acceptance, purpose, identity, and security, but God is the only real source for these. Are your relationship challenges because you've been looking in the wrong places? Turn to Jesus, and everything else will follow.

Dear Father, I believe You hear me. Holy Spirit, be my Helper and Comforter as I confront marriage struggles. In Jesus' name, Amen.

Have you genuinely asked God to help your with your marriage struggles?

Day 360

I WILL rejoice in God's vision for our marriage.

There is no greater joy in marriage than living out God's vision for you as a couple.

You can make many plans,
but the LORD's purpose will prevail (Proverbs 19:21).

There's nothing more exhilarating than uncovering the purpose God has in store for you. Joy comes from living out God's vision for both of you together. God's purpose for marriage is universal. He has a singular plan for every marriage: to honor one another with love, respect, and dignity. It's about crafting your union as a reflection of God's covenant with humanity. However, God's vision for each marriage is unique. His vision for your marriage is how that universal purpose works out and differs from that of others. Begin to pray and dream about the unique way God's purpose can be fulfilled in your marriage.

Dear Father, thank You that You have a unique vision for our marriage. Help me to begin to imagine what that vision is. Help us to be open to hearing Your voice as we live out Your purpose for our marriage. In Jesus' name, Amen.

What is unique about your marriage and life situation? What would it look like for your unique qualities to be used in fulfilling God's divine purpose?

I WILL embrace the freedom of forgiveness.

Practice daily forgiveness to keep love alive and bitterness at bay in your marriage.

Do not judge others, and you will not be judged. Do not condemn others, or it will all come back against you. Forgive others, and you will be forgiven (Luke 6:37).

Forgiveness isn't something you do once to put the past behind you. It's something you must do daily, especially for those closest to you, like your spouse. If you hold grudges and keep score, you will grow bitter over time. Bitterness is a bondage that changes you. The more bitter you become, the more hard-hearted you become toward your spouse and others, growing cynical, cold, sarcastic, and mean-spirited. You might even fall out of love, questioning why you ever married. Be willing to forgive each other, even if there isn't an apology. A vital practice in your marriage is to never go to bed angry. This discipline keeps your heart tender, helping you live and love freely. Put grievances in God's hands and trust Him.

Dear Father, I thank You for forgiving all of my sins. Holy Spirit, me to recognize that Your power is at work in my life as I forgive my spouse in the same way. In Jesus' name, Amen.

Are you holding grudges and keeping score? Can you envision how you would feel and how your marriage would be if you let those go?

Day 362

I WILL take a stand for my home and community.

You can kick the devil out the front door, or you can let him in; it's totally in your power.

"And I will give you the keys of the Kingdom of Heaven. Whatever you forbid on earth will be forbidden in heaven, and whatever you permit on earth will be permitted in heaven" (Matthew 16:19).

You may be observing the devastation in many homes across our nation caused by silent husbands, wives, and parents. It is crucial for you to stand up against the forces wreaking havoc in your homes and neighborhoods. You hold the responsibility to resist and subdue the darkness seeking to destroy you and your family. God has granted you authority, not just as a blessing or gift, but as a duty. Remember the words of Jesus to His Church: "I give you the keys …" You possess the power to stop evil in your home and cast out the devil. It is within your hands, not his. Take action now because the devil is already working hard to capture your home. Use your greater authority to protect your family, marriage, city, and church.

Dear Father, I believe You have given Your children authority. Holy Spirit, train me to defeat the devil through Your power. In Jesus' name, Amen.

In what area do you need to take authority over the devil right now?

I WILL listen to my spouse even when it makes me feel uncomfortable.

Not to listen is to build resentment, but careful,
honest listening brings healing.

Post this at all the intersections, dear friends: Lead with your ears, follow up
with your tongue, and let anger straggle along in the rear (James 1:19 MSG).

Both partners should feel free to voice concerns and share when they've been
hurt by the other's actions. When these moments arise, it's essential for you
to listen without immediately getting defensive. Men, have you ever asked your
partner about any behaviors they wish you'd adjust? Most women possess a keen
sense of intuition, and their insights are valuable. It's crucial to truly hear them
out. Similarly, women need to attentively listen to their partners. As he shares his
worries and feelings, your understanding and timely response can make all the
difference. By genuinely listening to each other, you address potential problems
before they escalate. Ignoring or avoiding can lead to resentment, but attentive,
sincere listening promotes healing.

Dear Father, You are always listening and always ready to hear me. Even
when my mind and heart are not in the right place, I have Your ear. Holy Spirit,
help me to listen to my spouse. In Jesus' name, Amen.

Ask your spouse how you can be a better listener and supporter.

Day 364

I WILL take responsibility for my mistakes.

Taking responsibility is what makes the
difference between failure and success.

Therefore, confess your sins to one another and pray for one another, that you may be healed. The prayer of a righteous person has great power as it is working (James 5:16 ESV).

You might have made grave mistakes, maybe violating your own moral standards. It could range from betraying a loved one, succumbing to addiction, to dishonesty in your job. Understand this: Everyone makes mistakes. Your past wrongs won't hinder the greatness God envisions for you. What truly matters is how you handle these missteps. Owning up and taking responsibility sets you apart. True greatness emerges when you confront, rather than deny, your mistakes. This age-old habit of avoiding responsibility has persisted. However, Jesus exemplified taking responsibility, even for the sins of others. His selflessness, even ensuring his mother's care as He was crucified, displays the kind of greatness we should pursue.

Dear Father, I know You want my honesty. I know I can hide nothing from You. Holy Spirit, You bring everything into the light. Help me to take responsibility for my actions. In Jesus' name, Amen.

Why is admitting mistakes so difficult for us? What area of your life needs God's work the most right now?

I WILL maintain optimism and hope for my marriage.

The attitude of hope is where healing begins.

May the God of hope fill you with all joy and peace in believing, so that by the power of the Holy Spirit you may abound in hope (Romans 15:13 ESV).

Paul was straightforward about the challenges of marriage. At XO Marriage, we receive many messages from struggling couples. Their issues often revolve around common themes like infidelity, pornography, abuse, and stress. Although some reports suggest a declining divorce rate, could it be because fewer people are choosing marriage? Many now prefer cohabitation or single-hood, likely due to the anxieties surrounding commitment. A concerning statistic: the divorce rate for those over 50 has doubled in recent decades. Reaching decades into a marriage doesn't guarantee success anymore. Yet, there's hope. Marriage, based on God's design, can be fulfilling, vibrant, and joyful. Your marriage can thrive and be resilient against external pressures. No union is irreparable. Do you approach your marriage with hope?

Dear Father, with You, I will never run out of hope. Holy Spirit, reinvigorate me with new hope and optimism for my marriage. In Jesus' name, Amen.

Have you felt hopeless about your marriage? Reach out today to someone who will walk with you on the path to health and healing for your relationship.

Bonus

I WILL be a warrior who fights for all marriages, not just my own.

You have an anointing straight from God to deliver people whom the devil is oppressing.

Do not neglect to do good and to share what you have, for such sacrifices are pleasing to God (Hebrews 13:16 ESV).

At your core, you're a warrior. God shaped you with this spirit, destined to combat darkness. God is calling you to share the message of salvation and bring hope to others. You bear a unique anointing to liberate those who are oppressed. God wants you to learn how to be successful in marriage, not just for your own marriage but also to help others. He is not calling you to amass wealth or worldly comforts. He wants you to be successful serving and aiding others under His guidance. True greatness stems from confronting the enemy and resisting temptations and fears. Stand firm, embracing your warrior spirit. God has given you the power to face the challenges ahead.

Dear Father, You love marriage and have called me to love it too. Holy Spirit, we are facing a war against marriage. I know that You will equip me in every way possible as long as I am willing to fight for the things that You love. In Jesus' name, Amen.

How will you fight for marriage going forward?